T0077352

The Guardians

Escape across Tirgonia

F. Thomas Jones

Abbott Press books may be ordered through booksellers or by contacting:

Abbott Press
1663 Liberty Drive
Bloomington, IN 47403
www.abbottpress.com
Phone: 1-866-697-5310

ISBN: 978-1-4582-1156-9 (sc)
ISBN: 978-1-4582-1155-2 (e)

Library of Congress Control Number: 2013916593

Printed in the United States of America.

Abbott Press rev. date: 04/01/2014

IN LOVING MEMORY OF

MY LATE WIFE

ANN

THE BEGINNING

Since the beginning of time, war and conflict have been a constant plague on a planet called Terra Firma. The people who inhabit this violent place in the universe commonly referred to this planet as Earth. Cultural, political, and religious differences are the usual causes for the bloodshed, which never seems to end. By the end of their twentieth century, the people of two vastly different political regions began to explore the vast emptiness of space surrounding their world. This exploration finally leads to a unified peace for the inhabitants of this once brutal planet.

The twenty-first century began with the continuing exploration of the dark void of space and, maintaining the fragile peace. However, the bloodshed and carnage returns during the last half of the century, consuming several regions with completely different religious and political philosophies. Exploration of the unknown area surrounding Earth comes to a virtual halt as the killing and destruction extended outward into the vastness of the dark void. Finally, during the twenty-second century, Earth becomes a world without political borders to separate one person from another. The costly wars revealed that differences, no matter how great, could be resolved through words of understanding, instead of weapons of destruction. The exploration of space, as history would prove to be an unnecessary long and costly delay, is continued.

No longer separated, the people of Earth realized that above all else they have to protect their new peace and understanding. The Guardians, as they now call themselves, soon learned to live by a simple creed of non-confrontation. A new ruling body, called the Council of Elders, is established. With the formation of this new world government, the Council of Elders had the authority to mediate all disputes, without any violence or bloodshed. Any decision made by the Council, whether locally, regionally, or globally, becomes final. Total will peace will continue for the next two hundred years.

With the continuation of space exploration, the Guardians soon find other planets with the similar characteristics as their own home world. One planet, located almost three hundred light years from Earth, possessed intelligent life. At first, the Guardians are welcomed as honored guests. However, this new race of beings is vastly different in their political and philosophical beliefs for existence. The Tirgonians believe that peace and tranquility is only for the meek and timid. The Guardians quickly realized they must return to the bloodbath of war if they are to survive as a free and unconquered race.

The fighting between the Guardians and Tirgonians continues for nearly half a century, without either side being able to achieve a decisive victory over the other. Near the end of the twenty-sixth century, the Guardian Council of Elders and the Supreme Senate of the Tirgonian Empire agree to end the hostilities. The leaders of these two vastly different societies decide that a boundary should separate their individual territories. No one could to enter, or cross, the Agreed Zone without the expressed permission from the other.

The leading force behind this effort for peace is a young Captain of the Guardian Space Defense Fleet by the name of Gandle Hoppinzorinski, and an equally young Sub-Culmit of the Tirgonian Space Defense Forces called Serligh Teka. Each, piloting their worlds most advanced space fighter of the time, become engaged in a hotly contested battle that closely resembles an old Earth style of aerial battle that once filled the lower atmosphere of Earth during the many previous conflicts. These two enemies, after forcing each other to make an emergency landing on a remote planet, soon learn that if they were to survive, they must first learn to learn to trust the other. Through this small and seemingly insignificant event, these two unimportant individuals became the primary forces behind the future the Agreement of Centrarius.

With the treaty is signed, and the Agreed Zone established, Hoppinzorinski and Teka believed that their paths will never again cross. However, their paths do indeed cross again. Each will have to remember what they learned so long ago as war between the Guardians and Tirgonians is once again becomes a reality. Only one question remains, will these two individuals be able to survive a second time?

CHAPTER ONE

The fighting begins as an urgent distress call from a Guardian outpost, called Capricorn Seven, monitors several sectors along the Agreed Zone. One of the long-range patrols, referred to as a Probe, receives a disturbing message as it reaches the outer limits of its assigned sector.

"What the . . ." comes the calm voice of the Probe Leader. "That can't be right. The Tirgs would have had to go through our entire defensive grid to hit Seven."

"It sounded real to me," replies Major Jo-Ich, the Probe Leaders wingman.

"I don't know. Lamminta ordered new alert drills the other day. Routine Probes aren't supposed to respond. Something just doesn't sound right," cautiously replies Lieutenant Commander Hoppinzorinski as he contacts the outpost, "Cap Seven, this is Red One, over."

"Red," screams a voice over the vehi-com! "Get back here fast! We are under attack! The Tirgs have crossed the Agreed Zone! This is not a drill! Alpha Whisky Five! Acknowledge!"

"Roger, Cap Seven," answers an unbelieving Probe Leader. "We're on our way and should be there in about forty-two minutes."

"Get back here as fast as you can! They are all over us! We can't hold them off much longer," calls the frightened voice over the small fighters' communication system!

"Red! Hit it," rapidly orders Hops, as he prefers to be called, "and don't spare the horses! We've got a fight to go to!"

Instantly, five Guardian Mark Two Space Fighters, nicknamed Dragons, accelerate to three-quarters light speed.

"Listen up, Red," calls Hops as the Probe speeds towards the embattled outpost, "Let's keep it tight until we get there. I'll tell you when to break. Regardless of what we see, or what we hear, we're going in as close as we can before we split. It we break too soon we're going to end up being the main course on their supper table. If we break too late, we're not going to be doing anyone any good. We're going to have to do this one by the book." No urgency shows in his voice, or his orders, as he leads his Probe back towards Capricorn Seven and into an unknown and, potentially dangerous, situation. Maintaining his composure, Hops continues giving orders. "One more thing, don't think, and just fly the way you know how. If things start to get a little shaky, you're not going to have to have time to do anything except to go on instinct. Don't get stupid on me and keep track of your wingman. Keep an eye on your weapons energy and fuel reserves. We don't have any filling stations out here, so don't run out of anything."

"Roger," replies Captain Hoblick. "Hey George, don't lose me. I might need your help getting my butt out of a sling."

"Don't worry about me, Hobby," answers Lieutenant George. "I've gotten used to keeping your butt covered. I just wish you'd start paying me for all the trouble I have to get you out of."

"I'll start paying just as . . ."

"Save you're squawking for the Tirgs. You'll have plenty of time to figure out who pays whom later." interrupts Hops. "Tigh, are you still with us?"

"Right where I'm supposed to be," answers the newest member of the team. "I know what I'm supposed to do, sir."

"Loosen up," says Hops as he tries to ease the tension he hears in the young Ensigns' voice. "When we break it's going to be a two-one-two. I want you to go with Jo. I still think this is one of the old man's drills, regardless of what we just heard. If it isn't, just remember we're faster, better armed, and can fly rings around their best drivers on their best day when we're having one of our worse. Just relax. Besides, you'll probably be the first one of us who ropes a Horse. Just do what you know how and don't worry about anything except covering Jo. Understood?"

"Yes, sir. You can count on me. I won't screw up."

Twenty thousand kilometers from the outpost, Probe Red begins to encounter an unusual amount of debris and wreckage. There is so much debris that it doesn't take an expert to understand what has happened.

"Holy shit," breaks the eerie silence!

"This can't be right," exclaims Hoblick.

"Where in the hell are our Dragons," yells Jo-Ich!

"Hold up you guys. We ain't going any further until we find out what's going on," orders Hops as he contacts the outpost. "Cap Seven, this is Red One, over."

The vehi-com remains silent, too silent.

"Capricorn Seven, this is Red One," again calls Hops.

Still no answer, no sound is heard, not even the normal subtle space static, just an all too clear silence.

"Red, this is Red One. Foxtrot Echo Uniform, over."

The pilots of Probe Red realize something is drastically wrong. Beside the fact of not being able to get an answer from the com-link on their home station, they are hearing proper vehi-com procedures from a man who only uses the Flight Regulations Manual as an occasional paperweight.

"Red Two," answers Major Jo-Ich.

"Red Three," cautiously replied Captain Hoblick.

"Red Four," acknowledges Lieutenant George.

"Red Five," says Ensign Tigh nervously.

"Red, this is Red One. Staggered minimum thrust on my lead. Try to stay behind as much of this junk as possible."

Again, almost proper orders from a man who, whenever possible, would thumb his nose at regulation and procedure. The orders come straight from the Flight Operation and Communication Training Manual that every Cadet is required to memorize before entering a launch bay, or an actual Dragon.

Each pilot automatically maneuvers to a tentative position based on the position of the Probe Leader. It is a slow procedure to use this safer, and more protective, formation, to traverse the last fifteen thousand kilometers. Finally, they are able to scan ahead effectively, hoping to find out what exactly was happening around Capricorn Seven before flying blindly into a fight.

As the scanners analyze the debris, the members of Probe Red keep a watchful eye for any indication they are not the only living beings remaining in the immediate vicinity. Capricorn Seven has a stable population of nearly two hundred and fifty thousand people. Someone had to have survived, and these survivors will be able to explain what happened.

"Red, this is Red One. Maintain position," orders Hops as the Probe reaches effective scanner range of the outpost. "Secure Beta One Alpha. Deploy Charlie Papa Whiskey. Alpha Three Zero Mike. Confirm."

"This is Red Two. Roger on Beta One Alpha. Deploy Charlie Papa Whiskey. Romeo Three Zero Mike. Alpha Three Zero Mike confirmed. Watch your six," answers Jo-Ich as he assumes temporary command of the Probe. "Okay Red, you heard the orders. Let's do it."

Hope leaves his Probe as the four Dragons maneuver into an extremely tight defensive formation, facing inward at various angles. Though unusual in appearance, this defensive protective posture is very effective against a sudden attack by a larger force. He has also informed Jo-Ich to assume full command of the Probe in the event he does not return within thirty minutes.

The closer he moves towards the outpost, the slower he proceeds. If detected, he hoped that a lone Dragon would not be worth the attention of an entire Tirg patrol. After ten minutes of careful maneuvering, trying to use as much of the floating debris as possible to hide behind, Hops is finally close enough to the outpost to see what he hoped he would not find. Capricorn Seven is no longer an effective Guardian outpost.

"How," mutters Hops silently? "How could so many Tirg Fighting Stars get so far on this side of the Agreed Zone without being detected?"

Almost two and a half years ago, Fleet Research and Development had successfully countered the latest type of concealment device used by the Tirgs. Since then, the Guardians improved their technology and could now detect and pinpoint any ship the Tirgs could deploy from a Fighting Star down to their Hunters, a small three-man class of scout ships, with uncanny accuracy. In addition, for the number of warships the Tirgs would have needed to destroy an outpost, the assault force would have required to have the support of at least four Fighting Stars, two complete Tirgonian Battle Groups. How could four Fighting Stars, a small Armada of man-made ships, shaped like its name-sake, with defensive energy cannon batteries located every hundred meters along its surface, in addition to four horizontal launch arms that are over a hundred and fifty meters square at the junction with the main structure and more than a five hundred meters long, go unnoticed?

Lieutenant Commander Hoppinzorinski cautiously moves forward as questions continually race through his mind. "What do I do to keep us alive? Can we make it to another outpost? How much more . . ."

"Capricorn Seven, this is Probe Orange, over," explodes over the vehi-com! "Capricorn Seven, this is Probe Orange. Do you read me? Over!"

"A trap," races through Hops mind as he snaps back to reality! "I've never heard of Orange."

"Capricorn Seven, this is Probe Orange! Over," calls the voice with urgency and frustration! "Capricorn Seven! This is Probe Orange! Theta Twelve Hotel Delta November! Come in! Over!"

"They have to be ours. They have the proper code, but who in the hell are they," mutters Hops as he presses the vehi-com sensor and whispers into the voice-meter in his flight helmet? "Probe Orange. Zulu Four Terra."

"This is Orange One," replies a relieved voice "Five Nil Theta Dagger Three.

"Roger, Orange One. Scanner vector six two seven by three four two, over," instructs Hops.

"Understand scanner vector six two seven by three four two, out."

Hops maneuvers his small fighter towards the coordinates he has just instructed Probe Orange to meet him at. His weapons are armed and ready just in case this indeed turns out to be a Tirgonian trap. Moving slowly, he cautiously moves closer. Suddenly twelve of the most beautiful scanner images he has seen since returning to Capricorn Seven appear on the small screen.

"Guardian Dragon, I have you on scanner," calls Orange One. "What happened? How in the hell . . ."

"Take it easy, Orange One. This is Red One, and I wish I could answer your questions, but I can't. Right now, I want you to keep you're britches on and you're peepers peeled until I get the rest of my people over here. Then maybe we can do something together. Just hang loose for a little while longer."

"If that means to stay where I am then that's what I'll do because this is your station," says Orange One, "However, you do understand that I can see you Dragon, not what's occupying the pilots' seat. If you turn out not to be whom you say you are, you just might be in for a little more trouble than you bargained for. If this is a trap by some son-of-a bitch of a motherless Tirg, one of us . . ."

"Stop you're squawking, Orange One," interrupts Hops. "I'd like to remind you of the same thing. Only I think I'm in a slightly better position to be the one who makes it out of here with a whole skin. Just keep your eyes open for any stray mustangs. Those damned wranglers just might want to round up a few strays, and I for one don't feel like getting hog-tied and branded just yet."

"Do what you need to Red One, just make it quick," answers Orange One. "I don't know how much longer we're going to be able to stay out here."

"I'll do best I can, just make sure you don't get stupid on me," says Hops as he contacts Jo-Ich "Red Two, this is Red One. Get a lock onto me beam and come on in. There still might be a couple of stray Horses round here so don't get a case of the dumb-ass just yet."

"Roger, boss," answers Jo-Ich. "What did you find out about Seven?"

"You'll find out when you get here," says Hops.

"Roger, we're on our way."

"Orange One, this is Red One."

"Go," answers the Probe Leader.

"I just put the welcome mat out for me people. I don't want any of your folks to get too trigger-happy. I'm heading down for a look-see. My people are going to meet me there. I want you to get you're Dragons behind some of this debris to give us a little protection until I can call you done."

"Roger, Red One, we're not going anywhere," answers Orange One. "Just make it fast. We've been on reserve power for almost the past hour. We're flying on fumes and can't stay out here much longer."

Probe Red has been on what is left of Capricorn Seven for a little more than half of an hour before Hops believes that it's safe enough for the newcomers to join them. The main Com-link suffered heavy damage during the Tirg attack so the only way Hops is able to communicate with Orange One is with his Dragons' vehi-com. It takes all of the strength he can muster to climb up to the cockpit and reach for his flight helmet.

"Orange One, this is Red One."

"Go."

"You can come on down but you're going to have to be real careful. Come in one at a time. This place is in a real mess down here."

"Roger, Red One," acknowledges Orange One. "I'll see shortly."

It takes more than twenty minutes for an operation that, under normal circumstances, required less than five minutes. Finally, the leader of Probe Orange lands on the once highly sophisticated outpost.

"Glad to see you," says Hops as Orange One climbs out of his battle scared Dragon "I'm Lieutenant Commander Hoppinzorinski, but just call me Hops, it's less of a mouthful."

"Major Orin Williams," says the leader of Orange One as he accepts Hops outstretched hand. "I guess I'm in charge of what's left of the Probes from Status Duo."

"Sudden call for help from your com-link," asks Hops?

"Yeah," says Williams. "We were on long-range Probe a few hours ago when all of a sudden Duo just blew up. We tried to make it back but ran into at least three full squadrons of Horseheads. I don't have any idea of where they came from, but one minute we were on normal patrol, and the next we're fighting for our lives. We managed to make it out of there with what you see here. I don't know how we did it or for that matter, how we made it this far. For the last hour, we've all been flying on reserve energy. I don't know how much longer we could have stayed out there if you hadn't been here."

"Duo had over fifty Probes, and you're telling me, you're at all that's left?"

"Exactly," answers Williams. "We didn't have anything to land so we headed here, and just barely made it."

"We're you able to get a message out to fleet?"

"From the way things happened so fast, I don't think Fleet has any idea of what's happened. I'm not even sure there's a Fleet left, and from what I was able to get from their communication frequencies, they hit everything we had at the same time. How in the hell they managed to pull that off is beyond me."

"I don't think we got anything out either. From the looks of things here I think the cowboys won this one," says Hops as he begins walking towards what's left of the main operations center, surveying at the devastation and destruction that surrounds them. Approaching the group of pilots standing idly around the once operational monitoring stations Hops begins giving his orders, "Let's see if we can get this place cleaned up a little. How about getting you're people started on that. George, you can take a couple of Major Williams's people and start on getting the Dragons serviced. Hobby and Tigh, go see if there's anything left in the commissary and storerooms. Jo, check what's left in the hanger bays that we might be able to use?"

After crew introductions, they move the Dragons to a more secure area so as not be detected by any Tirg patrols that might still be in the area. The survivors of the two devastated outposts did not want any indication these surviving Guardians, though few in number were on what remained of Capricorn Seven. A short while later a cry rings out.

"Hey! Over here," calls Jo-Ich excitedly as he manages to pry the hanger bay door open! "You're not going to believe this!"

Everyone in the main maintenance bay drops what he is doing and rushes to the now open Hanger Bay door. The hanger contains an unbelievable sight for an outpost that only a few hours before had been savagely attacked. Two complete Probes, ten virtually untouched Dragon are in line, waiting to move to the launch bay, but there is also death. Crews lay crumpled on the deck, lifeless pilots slumped over in their cockpits, all dead.

"There isn't anything we can do for them now except to get them down to the burial chapel, if it is still accessible," says Hops solemnly as he surveys the scene before him.

It takes almost five hours to remove the bodies of the pilots and crewmembers. It is hard for the members of Probe Red to do what they needed to do without showing their emotions. Finally, they gently lay the last body in a burial pod and move it to the chapel.

The survivors have now been on the destroyed outpost a little more than seven hours without a single Dragon launched. Hops and Williams though it would not be wise to advertise their presence, but now it was different, they needed rest.

"Everyone over here and listen up," calls Hops as he and Williams crawl from under the main com-link terminal. "It looks like we can put out contacting Fleet, if there's a Fleet left, for the time being. We can talk with any Dragons we send outside, but the range will be limited to about thirty-five thousand kilometers, which isn't far. It looks like most of the other essential equipment is partially operational."

"What I can't figure out is why the Dragons in the hanger bay weren't destroyed," say Jo-Ich. "This place is in shambles, yet we have two complete Probes virtually unharmed."

"Neither do I," agrees Hops as he looks about the almost debris strewn bay in front of him. "What do we have that we can still use?"

"Primary power is almost gone, but we should have emergency power back on line in about another fifteen to twenty minutes. The secondary life support system is on line," reports Williams. "I still have a couple of my guys working on the back-up system."

"Okay," say Hops. "What about the . . ."

"Commissary hasn't been touched," calls Tigh as the last two pilots return to the Maintenance Bay. "We could use a hand getting the rest of what we need down here."

Major Williams nods towards three of his pilots who eagerly follow Hoblick and Tigh out of the bay.

"After we finish getting the sleeping quarters squared away, Jo and I are going to need to take a little sight-seeing tour," continues Hops as he watches the men leave. "I want to get a better look at what's left from the outside. I don't want this place to suddenly fall apart on us while we're still here." Returning his gaze to the pilots still in front of him, he begins giving his instructions, "Harris, Toby, and Penicutt are to be ready to come out like gangbusters if we run into any trouble. Cole, Coff, ah . . . Sims will operate the landing bay batteries. Orin, who do you have that handle that pile of junk you've been working on?"

"Pile of junk," replies from Major Williams as he points to several scribbled symbols and almost unintelligible writing on the bulkhead behind the communications station! "Excuse me, sir, but if you remember right, you did the diagramming and all I did was to try to follow your beautiful artwork, but don't worry, I'll handle the com-link on this end. Just make sure you let me know when you're coming back in. The intruder identification system still has a few bugs in it. I don't want anyone to open fire on anything except some damned Tirg who might want to get too close. I don't think it would be a good idea for my guys to try to shoot at you and Major Jo-Ich."

"I don't think I'd appreciate that either," replies Hops. "Everyone else needs get something to eat and some rest, but don't go too far. We may need some help out there. I think it'd be a good idea for everyone to go over their bird and make sure everything works. I'd hate someone to be late because an ignition relay was stuck. When we get back, Major Williams and I will put together a Probe schedule until we can figure out what we're going to do next. We should have it worked out before breakfast. I hope that by then we'll have a better idea of where we stand and that we'll have a quiet night. Any questions?"

"I have one, sir," says one of the members from Probe Orange. "What's a gangbuster?"

This brings a chuckle from the pilots of Probe Red who are used to the unusual twentieth vocabulary used by Hops.

"Toby, don't worry about the meaning," answers Hops as he nods towards to Jo and begins moving towards his Dragon. "Just get outside and help us as fast as you can."

The two men climb into their tiny ships and strap themselves in. As they begin the pre-flight checks Hops notices Jo-Ich is more nervous than usual. Catching Jo's attention Hops gives him a thumbs-up.

"Probe Red, this is launch control, com-link and anything else you want to call it," says Major Williams as sits in front of an almost unrecognizable bank of switches, sensors, knobs, dials, gages, and a view screen. "You have launch control so you can launch anytime you're ready. Good luck, and try to get back here in one piece."

"Roger Com-link," acknowledges Hops. "Getting back in one piece is exactly what I have in mind. I don't think I'd like being run over by a herd of stampeding horses, unless some damned cowboy gets real lucky."

K-K-K-K-E-E-E-E-E-R-R-R-R-W-W-W-W-O-O-O-O-O-S-S-S-S-S-H-H-H-H-H. In a whisper of sound, the two Dragons launch.

"Whatever you're calling yourself these days, this is Red One," calls Hops as he clears the launch ramp.

"Roger, Red One, everything looks fine on this end. I think I have a lock on you and Red Two but I need you to move around a little so I can make sure I'm not tracking a piece of junk out there," replies Williams. "Okay, that's good and I've got a positive lock. The intruder identification system still isn't working right. It keeps coming in and out."

"Understood," says Hops. "Let's go Jo. We need to see if Seven is going to hold together for a little while longer and we need to do it quick."

"I'm on your wing," calls a much calmer sounding wingman. "By the way, thank you."

CHAPTER TWO

The two-ship patrol is usual in that nothing happened. Hops and Jo-Ich look over the surface of the destroyed outpost, discovering, that though severely damaged, Capricorn Seven was holding together remarkably well.

"Cap Seven, this is Red One, over."

"Go," answers Williams.

"We're coming in. Make sure you're people know the difference between a Dragon and a Horsehead."

"We won't know that until you come around on final. You're cleared to land," says Williams.

The two men land without any trouble. As soon as the engines shut down, several pilots begin moving towards the ships to begin hooking up various lines and hoses required to service the Guardian fighters.

Hops climbing out of his cockpit, reporting, "It's so quiet out there that I almost forgot that we just got . . ."

"Capricorn Seven," explodes over the Com-link! "This is Probe Gold from Alpha Cheris! Over!"

"Johnny! Cole! Coff! Get outside! Now," yells Major Williams from the Command Center!

Instantly the trio race to their ships. In a single motion flight helmets are on, restraining straps tightened, and the launch sequence initiated. The intercept course is loaded into the small fighters' flight computers. The three Dragons are launch through the only launch tube that is still serviceable.

"Capricorn Seven! This is . . ." calls the female voice again, trailing off in shocked amazement. "This can't be true."

"I see it but I don't believe it," says a second female voice.

"Someone had to survive. We're almost out of flight energy. I've got to keep trying," says the first woman. "Capricorn Seven, this is Probe Gold from Alpha Cheris! Theta Twelve Hotel Delta November! Come in! Over!"

Major Williams reaches towards a sensor on the Com-link control panel when Hops grabs his arm.

"Not yet, Orin, it could be a trap. The Tirgs could have picked up our transmissions when I first answered you're call for help. No communications until we get confirmation. Can you get anything on the intruder system yet?"

"No, it's still giving sporadic readings," answers Williams.

Again, the frightened and pleading voice of the first female comes in over the com-link speaker, "Capricorn Seven, this is Probe Gold from Alpha Cheris. Theta Twelve Hotel Delta November! We have two Omegas! Please reply! Over!"

By now, all of the pilots on the crushed outpost have gathered around the Command Center, to wait for the patrol to intercept the incoming ships and identifies them as friend or foe.

"Cap Seven, this is Orange Two, and I confirm six of ours with two Omegas."

"Roger, Orange Two," acknowledges Hops "Probe Gold, this is Cap Seven."

"Thank God you're here," comes a hurried, and much relieved sounding, reply from the apparent Probe Leader, as the com-link becomes jammed with other female voices.

"What happened?"

"Where is everyone?"

"Where's your cover!"

"Why are women always trying to talk at the same time and never seem to be able to say what they mean, or mean what they say," asks Hops as he repositions a spare headset so he can talk to the Probe Leader.

"Put a lid on it. We haven't gotten down in one piece yet so save our celebration for later," says the Probe Leader as she regains control over her excited pilots, "if there is a later. Capricorn Seven, this is Gold One, request instructions, over."

"Okay ladies," says Hops as he again adjusts the headset that won't stay in place, "we're going to bring you down one at a time, and like Gold One said, save you're celebration for later. You need to calm down before you bring the Tirgs back here to finish what they already think they have. Orange Two should have linked up with you by now so just follow his lead when you come in. The two Omegas' will come in on one five four November, landing bay two."

"Roger, Capricorn Seven," acknowledges Gold One. "Confirm Omegas on one five four November, landing bay two."

"Well, Hops," says Williams as he listened quietly to the exchange, "what do you think? Six more pilots, four more Dragons and hopefully two more for spare parts."

"I don't know," say Hops. "Women aren't exactly what I would call top notch Dragon drivers. I've never heard of one of them trying to get out of Tirg trap."

"You might be right, Hops, but why don't we wait until they land before we pass judgment. They did make it this far without help."

Without answering Williams, Hops returns his attention to the incoming Probe.

"Gold One," says Hops as he again adjusts his headset, "which Omega is going to be coming in first?"

"Gold Two," answers the Probe Leader.

"Gold Two, this is Cap Seven. Can you read me?"

"Roger, Capricorn Seven," calls another female voice.

"Approach vector is one five four November, landing bay two," instructs Hops.

"Confirm approach vector is one five four November, landing bay two," acknowledged the female pilot.

"Next you're going to eject on my mark."

"Roger. Eject on your mark."

"Okay Gold Two, here we go. Five, four, three, two, one, mark!"

The only sound heard over the com-link is that of the canopy and emergency escape pod is blown clear of the damaged ship. The crippled Dragon stays on course and continues towards the landing bay. It makes contact and lands safely under control of the automated guidance system.

The second mutilated Guardian fighter receives the same instructions. The pilot ejects on command and the ship stays on course but explodes violently the moment it makes contact with the landing ramp.

"Guess that means we don't have any spare parts," says Hops as he steadies himself against the shaking outpost.

"Yeah," agrees Williams. "It looks like we will just have to make sure we don't get into any fights for a while. We're going to have a hell of a time trying to fix a Dragon without spare parts."

"Let's get them down before they tear up anything else. Make sure we pick up those two girls floating around out there."

It takes almost half an hour to get the remaining four pilots down.

"Welcome aboard, Major," says Hops as the Gold One climbs down from her cockpit. "I'm Lieutenant Commander Hoppinzorinski of what's left of Cap Seven. This is Major Williams from Status Duo."

"I'm Major Carol Quince," begins the female Probe Leader as the remaining pilots gather behind her. "This is Captain Star, Lieutenants Capernia and Ray, and Ensigns Fa and Merthium."

"What happened at Alpha Cheris," asks Hops?

"From the looks of things here, I'd say we got trampled by the same herd," answers the petite Probe Leader. "We were on routine Probe duty when we received a distress call. By the time we got back, we were too late. There wasn't anything to land on so we headed here. If you hadn't been here, I don't know what we would have done. We were almost out of fuel energy and our life support systems were just about gone."

"I guess we're all that's left," observes Jo-Ich.

"Yeah," agrees Hops. "The Tirgs must have had some pretty good intelligence to hit all three outposts just as our long range Probes reach their most distant point."

"Commander, where do we start," asks the five foot-two inch Major. Quietly surveying the shattered Maintenance Bay, she also asks, "What do you need my people to help with?"

"First," begins Hops, "since Jo-Ich said it and it appears that we're the only ones left, I'm assuming full command and martial rule is in effect as of right now. Major Williams, I want you to put together a watch roster until zero-seven hundred. Major Quince, get a couple of your girls to fix something to eat for everyone. The rest of . . ."

"Excuse me, Commander," almost yells a visibly enraged officer, her eyes flashing in anger as she violently turns, directly facing Hops! Her sudden reaction to the words of the senior officer causes her long auburn hair to fly wildly about her face. "Just because my Probe happens to be female, instead of male, does not mean we will be treated any differently from any other pilot! If we are equal in rank, then we are equal in authority and responsibility!"

"Excuse me, Major. You don't need to get you're pantyhose wrapped around your ankles," says Hops with a slight smirk on his face. "Tigh, would you please take one of these lovely ladies to help you fix one of your gourmet entrees? Major Quince, would you be kind enough to help Major Williams with the watch roster, or would you prefer to do something else?"

Major Quince, glaring at Hops, says, "I'll gladly help Major Williams with the roster," before adding a very contemptuous, "Sir!"

"The rest of you need to get the birds that just come in refueled and rearmed," continues Hops as he appears to be unaffected by the words from Major Quince. "Hobby, how about taking the two ladies that need a new set of wings over to the hanger bay and let them pick out a set that they might like?"

"Sure thing, sir," says Captain Hoblick as he motions for the two pilots to follow him.

"I don't think it would be a good idea to send anyone else outside just yet. If the Tirgs do return I don't want any welcome mat set out for them to tell them that they missed a few of us. If they do decide to show up again I want everyone to be ready for an immediate launch. Maybe we can give them a little surprise party of our own. After we get some rest, we'll worry about what we're going to do next. Jo, you and whomever Major Quince wants to help you to set up some sleeping quarters. We just might have gone co-ed on the Probes, but I don't think it'd be a good idea to get too co-ed right now. Anyone got any questions?" Whiskey. Alpha Three Zero Mike.

With the orders given the now larger group of survivors begin going about their tasks. There is very little conversation as they work to get whatever they can ready for whatever may happen next. A short while later Tigh and Capernia return with the food they had prepared. Everyone grabs something to eat and continues working on their individual Dragon. Soon, almost everyone is asleep, either in the cockpit or under the stubby wing of his or her fighter. Everyone except Hops, Williams, and Quince,

"Well," mutters Hops as he surveys the scene in front of him, "if they want to act like men and look like men, then by damned I'll treat them like men."

Quince and Williams finalize the duty roster and hand it to the first name on the list. No one really cares when his or her watch duty is. When their hour of watch duty is over, they call the next name on the list. That pilot gets up, pulls their hour of duty at the com-link, and calls the next name on the list.

The three Probe Leaders also have several other details to take care of. Details such as Probe assignment and rotation schedule, who would operate the com-link and defensive batteries. They also needed to consider such things as eating, sleeping, maintenance, launch and recovery operations. Twenty-three survivors are all that are available to do the work that, under normal circumstances, required the attention of more than one hundred.

"Okay gang," shouts Hops after a few hours of sleep! "Let's go! We have a lot of work to do and not much time to get it done! Come on! Out of the fart sacks! Move it! Everyone get over here. Grab something to eat and listen for your Probe assignment."

The pilots begin to move slowly as they again stare in disbelief at their surroundings as Hops continues, "Everyone's been broken down as evenly as possible. We're going to be at sixty percent at all times unless we get company. We're going to be using the same Probe designation. Red is going to have seven birds. Orange and Gold will fly with eight. Red, with me in Alpha Section will be Ray, Cole, and Coff. With Jo in Bravo are Star and Fa. With Major Williams are Hobby, Tigh, Capernia, Lucas, Johnny, Merthium, and Charlie. The rest of you will be under the superb leadership of Major Quince and Probe Gold." The last name said in a chauvinistic tone. "Red will start with a three-four cover for eight hours. When a section is down, make sure you work on your bird, re-arm, and refuel. Orange will take the first watch at the com-link and operating the defensive cannon batteries. Gold will be off watch for the first eight hours but will help as necessary. At sixteen hundred hours, Gold will replace Red. We'll take care of the com-link and cannon batteries while Orange goes on rest period. At twenty-four hundred, we do the same rotation. Any questions?"

"I have one, Commander," yells a voice from the entrance to the hanger bay! "When are you going to get your butt moving?"

Everyone instantly spins towards the sudden voice with the pilots from the Status Duo and Alpha Cheris drawing their sidearm from an instinctive couching positing.

"I'll be a son of a . . . Hold you're fire," yells Hops! "Put you're weapons down! It's Commander Lamminta! I can't believe . . . How in the hell . . . Commander?"

"I'll explain later," answers the rightful commander of Capricorn Seven. "Right now I think you had better get ready to launch, and take your entire Probe with you. I think I have enough people her to take care of everything on this end, now get moving. You'll be relieved on schedule." Turning his attention towards the two other Probe Leaders, Lamminta continues. "Majors Williams and Quince, I want you to get your pilots ready to fly at a moment's notice and I would like to see both of you in the command center in thirty minutes."

As Lamminta finishes giving his instructions, people begin appearing from every entranceway leading into the maintenance bay. Maintenance personnel quickly move the Dragons to the only serviceable launch ramp and prepare them for launch.

"Probe Red, this is launch control," comes the familiar voice of the com-link operator "Transferring launch control. Launch when ready."

K-K-K-K-E-E-E-E-E-R-R-R-R-W-W-W-W-O-O-O-O-O-S-S-S-S-S-H-H-H-H-H.

"Hey, Jo," calls Hops as soon as Probe Red reached the debris-strewn vastness still surrounding the devastated outpost.

"Yeah, boss?"

"Take your section and check everything from quadrant three through nine. I'll check the other way round. Make sure you look at everything from top to bottom and stay within twenty thousand. We'll let the others go out further if the old man says so."

"Roger on three through nine within twenty," acknowledges Jo-Ich. "Okay guys, you heard the orders so just follow my lead."

"What about us," asks Lieutenant Star? "Or is this one of you male only parties?"

"Forgive me ladies but I think I'm going to need everyone on this flight," replies Jo-Ich who, like Hops, is unaccustomed to having women under his command, or anywhere near him, in a critical situation. "I would like to cordially invite you lovely ladies to help me check out the far side of what we have left."

"Four, this is One," again call Hops.

"Go, One."

"Just want to remind you not to pull any heroic stunts. If you get into something that smells a little fishy you better give me a yell before you do something that we all might regret later. This is just a simple recon mission so don't try to rope a Horse without help."

"You're always taking the fun out of everything I do," says Jo-Ich jokingly. "Why can't I try to have a little fun on my own for once?"

"Listen, Jo," answers Hops jokingly, "it's not that I like looking at your ugly mug every time I turn around. It's just that I might need you to pull my bacon out of the fire if I run into any strays on the other side of Seven. Just keep your peepers peeled and your finger off the ionizer. Understand?"

"Yeah," responds Jo, "I understand even though I don't like it. You're going to buy the first round for all of us when we get out of this mass."

"You got it, but only if we don't jump out of the frying pan and land in the fire. So let's get busy and get back to work."

Majors Williams and Quince, after taking care of their Probes, head for the makeshift command center to meet with the commander of Capricorn Seven.

"Please, come in," greets Lamminta as he sees the two officers approaching. "I'm Commander Lamminta and I think it's time, now that things seem to have gotten back to some semblance of order and to try to answer your obvious questions as to what happened and how we seemed to suddenly appear out of nowhere. Please sit down and make yourself as comfortable as possible."

"Thank you, sir," say both officers in unison.

"First, and as you already know," begins Lamminta, "everything was going on as usual two days ago. All Probes were reporting in and the long-range scans did not indicate anything out of the ordinary. Then all of a sudden, the screens were full of Horses, war hawks, four cruisers, and two destroyers. A full Battle Group, deployed in attack formation, was all that they needed for their sneak attack. Before we could raise the defensive screen, close the absorption shields, and launch the remaining Probes, it was too late. They must have developed a new generation of concealment device to hit us so hard and fast, and before we could put up any kind of fight. They had to have had at least one more Battle Group hidden to hit us with so much firepower at once. We just couldn't hold out against such a devastating force."

"That is the same thing happened at Status Duo, sir," says Williams. "The only question I have is that when I got here and Commander Hoppinzorinski came down to see what was left, we scanned this place for a considerable amount of time and from every possible angle. We didn't pick any indication of any being alive here, Guardian or Tirg. This place was deserted, and then all of a sudden, you and everyone else come out of nowhere. Where was everyone hiding?"

"We have been experimenting with a new concealment device of our own," explains Lamminta. "It was, and technically still is, in the early developmental stage. When I realized the Tirgs were getting ready to board Seven I gave the order to use it."

"Why didn't you turn it off when we got here," asks Major Quince? "You had to know we weren't the Tirgs returning."

"We tried," answers Lamminta, "but somehow it got stuck in the automatic mode. The survivors you have seen are here only as a direct result of that malfunction."

"And what about the Dragons," asks Major Quince? "Why didn't the Tirgs destroy them? In addition, why did they leave Seven in a state of possible use? They never leave a fight without total domination and they never leave anything of use once they finish."

"I wish I could answer your questions, Major, but I can't," answers Lamminta. "I know what they did, or didn't do, goes completely against their doctrine but at the same time. Right now, I'm very satisfied with this minor deviation from their training. If they had followed their policy of total destruction, we would not be here now. So far, they did return once and luckily, we were still under the protection to the malfunctioning concealment device. They went over this place with a not so fine toothcomb. They were more interested in our data banks than completing their destruction. They began to download the main computer core. One of their Culmits began to run readout of our defensive systems. However, they all left before the download was finished. They didn't get any information that they didn't already know. I know it doesn't make any sense and I have no explanation for it."

CHAPTER THREE

After splitting into the two sections and proceeding to their designated sectors, Probe Red begin the inspection of the exterior of Capricorn Seven.

"Four, this is One, any trouble yet?"

"Nope. Nice and quiet out here," answers Jo.

"Let's try to keep it that way," says Hops. "Just take it easy so we can get back in one piece."

"Aw shit," yells Jo-Ich! "I just got a bogie in Sector Six Quadrant Four!"

"I'm on my way," replies Hops hurriedly. "Just remember, you're not allowed to get a case of the dumb-ass on me. Get your people behind a piece of junk until we can get a positive identification. We just may end this little look-see sooner than the old man wants."

"Don't worry about me," say Jo-Ich. "I think I'm going to play it smart on this one. Range forty thousand. Vector eight nine two Oscar by seven nine five Alpha, and by the way that bogie just got a hell of a lot bigger. It's too small to be a cruisers or a destroyer. It has to be a Hunter or a herd of Horses real close together. We're heading for cover."

"Don't do it," yells Hops! "I just got a positive lock on them and it's a small herd of Horses! There's too many of them for us to handle without help. We need to get back inside while we still have a chance. Alpha Section! Stay on my ass so we can link up with Bravo! We're going to burn rubber!"

"We're going to do what," exclaims a confused Lieutenant Fa! "I don't want your ass and I'm not burning anything in my ship!"

"Don't worry about the vernacular, honey," says Jo-Ich. "You'll understand what he means the longer you're around him. Right now he's your only chance of getting out of here with all your parts where they belong."

"Don't call me *Honey,*" snaps an angry pilot as she pushes her Dragon to maximum thrust, catching up with Hops! "And it's not any of your business where my parts are!"

"Jo," calls Hops, "have you been able to get a number yet?"

"Sure have boss, and you're not going to like being right," answers Jo. "I count at least sixteen Horses. If we're going to make it back to inside we're going to need a little help out here."

"Understood," says Hops. "Looks like you're about to get cut-off so find a place to hide. I'll try to get them to follow me. Cap Seven, this is Red One. We have a small problem heading our way and it's going to be like having your mother-in-law show up at last year at Christmas and she's still here."

"Roger, Red One, just stay on station. Orange is launching to give you a hand," replies the calm orders over the com-link. "You mother-in-law may not be staying much longer."

"They'd better make it fast," answers Hops. "I don't like the way Jo hands out invites."

"Red One, this is Orange One," immediate replies from Major Williams. "Is this fast enough for you?"

"If you're out here then where in the hell are you?"

"I don't have time to explain right now because we have a fight to go to," says Williams. "Link up with the rest of your Probe and keep it tight. As long as I can see you, we should be able to win this one."

"I don't think I'm going to like what you're going to tell me," says Hops. "Red! This sounds crazy but link up with Jo! I hope the old man knows what he's doing. Orange One, Red One."

"Go, Red."

"Where in the hell are you? I can't get any kind of fix on you."

"Stop worrying, Red One. We're here and have a firm lock on your Probe," answers Williams. "These orders came straight from Lamminta. When I say break, do a two three two and head straight for Status Duo."

"Damn it! I still can't pick you up," yells Hops! "Where in the hell are you! And what in the hell am I doing heading for Duo!"

"I'm on your six, two thousand high, so get moving," orders Williams. "I'm about ready to have my hands full!"

"If you say so. I'm not sure I like being the setting duck during hunting season," says Hops. "Okay Red, you heard the orders. I'm don't know what we're supposed to be doing, but it looks like we're going to have to do some fancy flying. When we break, head for Duo, scattered formation. Watch you're sixes and grab some gears!"

"Red One, now what in the hell are you talking about," shouts Fa! "I still don't want your ass! I don't understand what burn rubber means and I'll be damned if I know where I supposed to put any extra equipment that you want me to grab!"

"Just stay on my wing, Lieutenant," sharply orders Hops! "And don't get lost!"

"Just lead the way if you know how," angrily shouts Fa! "I can still fly rings around you! Just give orders so I can understand what you're talking about!"

"Damn it, Lieutenant! Just stay with me," yells Hops!" Orange One, this is Red One!"

"Go."

"Just want to make sure you're still out here."

"Same position, six high," answers Williams. "When I give the word to break, don't move out too fast. Give them time to catch up and follow you. Just make you stay ahead of them."

"I just wish I could get a fix on you," replies Hops. "Red, anyone got a fix on anything?"

"Nope."

"Not a thing."

"Negative. Just a clean screen."

"Clear, except for the Tirgs."

"Not a blip."

"Nothing."

"Orange One, Red One," again calls Hops.

"Now what," answers Williams? "Make it short because you're about to get your chance to prove you're still a better pilot than they are! Delta One X-Ray! NOW!"

"Red," shouts Hops! "Now! Break!"

"The Guardians are running for their life," says the Tirg leader as his patrol begins chasing after the seven fleeing Dragons. "They will make mistakes and become easier targets. Divide into three sections and destroy them."

Immediately the Tirg patrol splits and opens fire on the highly maneuverable enemy fighters. The blue-blackness of space suddenly erupts with the reddish-orange bursts of Tirgonian energy cannons. Almost immediately, a tremendous burst of light engulfs one of the Tirgonian Horsehead fighters, annihilating it.

"All ships! Watch you're fire," hotly orders the patrol leader! "Someone just fired on one of our own! Be careful and make sure only the Guardians are targeted!"

Again, a brilliant flash of light disintegrates another Tirgonian Horsehead.

"Whoever is firing will be . . ."

Another burst of light and another Tirgonian fighter is lost. Repeatedly, this strange firing occurs as one by one the Tirgonian Empire loses one fighter after another. Within two minutes, only three remain. Whenever a Dragon from Probe Orange fires, another Type Three Battle Assault Ship, and its two occupants no longer exists. Major Williams fires once more and there is one less Horsehead to worry about. Lieutenant Capernia fires, destroying the one of the remaining Tirgonian fighters.

"Red, this is Orange One. Regroup on your One and head for home," quietly says Williams as Hoblick destroys the lone remaining enemy fighter, ending the one-sided engagement.

"If you say so, we're on our way but I'll be damned if I understand what we just did," answers Hops. "Where in the hell are you?"

"Right where I've always been," replies Williams. "I'm still on your six high. However, right now you have to be low on fuel energy, so get back to Seven before you run out. As soon as you're down you're supposed to report directly to Commander Lamminta."

"Roger, Orange One," acknowledges Hops. "Red, form up on my beam and follow me home. Let's kick it in the ass and get out of here."

"Red One, this is Red Three," calls the calm voice of Fa. "That is one order that I do understand and I'll be more than happy to kick yours."

"I doubt that, Lieutenant," replies Hops. "Just get your butt in gear and follow my beam. Move it!"

As Probe Red reforms on Hops, Commander Lamminta says over the vehi-com, "If you're still with us Orange One, that was some real fancy shooting."

"We're still here, sir. Final score is sixteen to zip. Game two is ours."

"Well done, Major. Seven, out."

"Wait a minute," yells Hops! "What in the hell is going on? I get orders to run from a herd of Horses. Then I watch someone, who I can't even see, blow them out of their socks, and I don't fire a shot! Did my Probe just become a part of a shoot 'em up cartoon?"

"All in due time, Hops, all in due time," answers Lamminta. "The only thing you need to worry about at the moment is getting back here before your fuel reserves are completely expended, or you run into another Tirg patrol. The choice is yours, but if you decide to get back here, then you might be able to explain to me who, or what, a 'shoot 'em up cartoon' is."

"I'm bringing my people home. When I get back I'd like some answers as to what we just did and what in the hell is going on!"

"You will get your answers but you have to make it back here first. The refueling transport is still down so if you don't make it close enough for the catch beam to bring you in you're going to be out there for quite a while longer."

It takes another half of an hour before the last member of Probe Red is safely aboard the devastated outpost. As members of the normal maintenance crew begin servicing the Dragons, the pilots of Probe Red gather around their Probe Leader. They are safe, even though they are unsure of what they just accomplished. In another thirty minutes, Probe Orange completes its landing operation. Hops immediately heads towards the ship of his counterpart, arriving just as Williams's climbs out of his cockpit.

"Hey Orin, what in the hell . . ."

"Commander Hoppinzorinski and Major Williams, report to the Command Center. Commander Hoppinzorinski and Major Williams, report to the Command Center."

"I guess that means he wants to see us right now," call Hops as he ducks under the stubby wing and weapons pod of Major Williams' Dragon. "The old man sounds a little irritated because I didn't report as soon as I landed. He doesn't like to be kept waiting, not even if you're using the john."

"He has got to at least give me a chance to get out of my Dragon. I don't think it will fit in the command center."

Both men depart the landing bay and head for their meeting with Lamminta. They move as fast as possible along the debris-strewn corridors and passageways without speaking. Both men remain silent until the doors of the command center close behind them.

"What in the hell is going on all of a sudden around here," quickly asks Hops as he turns and faces Williams? "You're out there and I couldn't get any kind of lock on you. I get orders to run from a herd of Horses that are blown to hell, and I don't fire a shot. What in the hell . . ."

"Calm down, Hops," says Lamminta from his seat in front of several monitoring screens, which no longer work.

"You don't understand . . ." begins Hops,

"If you will just calm down, I will explain everything," continues the Commander as he stands and moves with a deliberate motion towards the two Probe Leaders. To pass this slight man of medium build anywhere, one would never guess that he is the foremost authority on the Tirgonian Empire and a leading expert on battle tactics used but the Guardian Space Defense Fleet. "First, a P C D, a personal concealment device, has been developed, or is the final stages of development. Once I realized we couldn't stop the Tirgs from boarding Seven, I gave the order to use it. The only problem with the device is that it has yet to be fully tested, and it has not received final approval from Fleet Research and Development. We didn't have any problem staying concealed until we tried to turn it off. Somehow, it stuck in the automatic mode and it took Trilla a while to get it unstuck. That should explain why you couldn't see us when you first returned.

"Trilla was also able to modify the P C D to conceal a Dragon. Major Williams' Probe was just about ready to test it when you decided to run into that Tirg patrol. We didn't really have any choice except to send Probe Orange out and hope everything worked out. And from the results I would say everything worked out just fine."

"I didn't know R and D was working on anything like that," says Hops. "When did they start?"

"I didn't know either and it was almost two years ago," replies Lamminta as he motions towards a few chairs around the command console. "When Trilla told me about the device, he said that he had received very specific instruction from Fleet R and D that the device would be developed under the strict secrecy and security. No one, to include myself, knew anything about what he was doing. Fleet wanted this project hushed up to prevent any unauthorized disclosure of information. We might as well take a seat because this meeting is going to take a little longer than I originally thought.

"Now as far as I have been able to determine," continues Lamminta, "we are the only survivors of the Tirg attack. To the best of my knowledge, our living population numbers no more than five hundred. To the Tirgs we no longer exist."

A thread could have snapped and it would have pierced the silence as loudly as if energy cannon had just fired as a stifled gasp from the doorway breaks the eerie silence.

"Come in, Major Quince, and please be seated," invites Lamminta as he continues his analysis. "I have not been able to contact any of the other outposts, Fleet, or anyone on any channel, which means we have an extremely difficult job ahead of us. As long as any of us continue to survive this atrocity our society must continue will live on.

"As of right now, I have no choice in this matter except to declare a full state of emergency. Let the records of this meeting reflect that I, as the senior officer, am assuming full authority as High Commander and Council General. The three of you are now members of a temporary Council of Elders, in addition to your normal Probe duties. We will select a fifth temporary Council Member until we can organize a proper election to select a permanent Council. We must continue with our normal governing authority, and our due process, as our laws and traditions require. We will remain in this configuration until we are able to select a more permanent Council.

"By now the Tirgs must know that they did not destroy all of their targets as completely as they previously thought. I just hope that our little ruse works. All evidence of their destroyed patrol should indicate a relatively strong force remains on Status Duo, not here on Seven. Any search party they send out should head there instead of here. The trail Major Williams left for them to follow should make that extremely clear. That trail, and their overly strict use of logic, should indicate Duo as their primary target. Hopefully, we should be safe here a little while longer."

"Staying the frying pan to keep out of the fire isn't exactly my idea of being safe," interjects Hops.

"Commander, would you please hold your observations until I'm finished. If I didn't need you in your Dragon right now I'd throw you in the brig for insubordination," says Lamminta, and then jokingly adds, "On second thought, since we no longer have a brig, I just might throw you to the Tirgs and see if they could control you.

"We're still hoping to find other survivors but, as I said before, we haven't had any luck contacting anyone yet. We're also exploring out options as to where we could possible find a safer place to live. In addition, since we can't move Seven, I instructed Trilla to come up with some type of ship that which we could live on and fight from until we can find a more peaceful environment. From what Trilla has told me, I'm still playing catch up. It seems that he has had his section working on a new ship for quite some time. However, this time just about everyone knew about it except me. It was to be my next command and Trilla says that it is almost ready for testing, so, I think I'll have command a little sooner that Fleet had anticipated."

"For being the head cheese around this place you sure was in the dark about what was going on right under your own nose," mumbles Hops.

"That will be enough, Lieutenant Commander," admonishes Lamminta as he stares harshly as Hops as he continues, "I guess that sums everything up for the moment. We will remain on full alert until Trilla informs me that the ship is ready. All Probes, and patrol rotation schedules, will remain as they are. Are there any questions before we all get back to work?"

"I got one, sir," says Hops "I think the Probe assignments should . . ."

"The personnel assignments will remain as they are without any reassignments until further notice," quickly counters Lamminta. "You will continue to be responsible for the two female pilots that you yourself assigned to your Probe. Are there any other questions?" All remained silent. "Good, now let's get back to work."

Major Quince gives Hops a disgusted look as she walks past him on her way out of the command center.

The remainder of the day passes without any further incidents. Williams continues on the intruder identification system and finally reports that it is back in operation but with limited range capabilities. The Tirgs do not send any additional patrols, allowing the work to continue on the new ship. Early the next morning, Commander Lamminta receives the report that the Hope, the name of the new ship, is ready for testing.

"Launch the cover Probes," instructs Lamminta as he patiently awaits the first formal launch of the Hope.

"Probe Red and Gold prepare to launch," orders the com-link operator.

"This is Red One, roger and launching," answers Hops.

"Com-link this is Gold One," replies Major Quince. "Launching."

"Hope, this is com-link, over."

"Roger, com-link. All systems green," answers Major Cherrick as he prepares for permission to launch.

"Roger, Hope. You may launch when ready."

"Wilco," acknowledges Cherrick as he presses the ignition sensor, launching the Hope on its mission.

"Continue with the test maneuvers," instructs Lamminta as he watches the scanner screen in the operations center.

"She handles like a dream," replies Cherrick as he completes a series of gentle maneuvers. "Landing bay crews are standing by to receive the Probes."

"Understand, Hope," answers the com-link operator. "Proceed with the remainder of the test. No need for further reports at this time."

"Roger, Seven. Proceeding as planned," acknowledges Cherrick. "Probe Red, this is the Hope. Prepare for landing sequence. All landing bays are prepared to receive and complete the rearming and refueling simulation. Launch immediately upon simulation completion."

"Understand, Hope. Request permission to come aboard," answers Hops.

"Permission granted, Red One. Just remember that once you land, don't touch anything. Let the automation do what it's designed to."

"Roger, Hope. You got the lead on this one," acknowledges Hops. "Okay, Red Four, let's go. You take Bravo and I'll take Alpha. Gold One, this is Red One. I don't want you to get too lonely out here by yourself, so we'll be back just as quick as we can."

"Just do your job, Red One, and I'll do mine," angrily answers Carol! "Out!"

"Red Bravo," calls Major Jo-Ich. "We're heading for landing lay Bravo. On my lead."

Everyone remains quiet until the first Dragon lands aboard the Hope.

"Wow," exclaims one of the pilots, "would you look at this!"

"I see it but I don't believe it."

"This is great."

The Hope is not like any ship these they had ever seen. The fully automated landing process is a vast improvement over the previous procedure. As soon as a Dragon lands, automation guides it into an empty maintenance stall. There, with only one crewmember standing by, it is completely rearmed and refueled. Each landing bay has the capability of handling up to twenty Dragons at once. This is a vast improvement over the standard operation of any existing operation of this type. Not only is the number of required personnel greatly reduced, the amount of time required to service a Dragon, and return it to the fight, is cut in half. As each Dragon completes the simulation, automation once again takes over, moving each Dragon into the launch bay and positions it on the launch rail without the pilot ever touching any control. The complete rearming and refueling of all the Dragons takes under three minutes, with the entire operation in completed in under five minutes.

As the last Dragon leaves the launch tube, the Hope executes an amazingly sharp, diving turn, first to starboard, then to port. For a ship of this size, the Hope has the agility of a considerably smaller ship. The Hope is capable of outmaneuvering anything the Tirgonian Empire possesses of similar size and could outmaneuver several of the Empires smaller classes of ships as well. Major Trilla, the Chief Engineer responsible for the R and D Section, had created an engineering masterpiece.

CHAPTER FOUR

During the time since the initial attacks against the Guardian outposts, the commander of the Fifth Tirgonian Battle Group had not been idle. His constant use of long-range patrols kept him informed as to the presence of any possible pockets of Guardian resistance. Only one patrol remains unaccounted. Telecoup Mular, commanding the Fighting Stars Landex and Napla, received the last report from his overdue patrol that indicated the Guardians still had the capability and the will to fight.

"All fighters will form on the patrol leader," begins the Tirgonian General as he personally briefs the search team. "Maintain one thousand meters separation at all times. If there are any Guardians remaining, and they are foolish enough to attack a reinforced patrol, each ship will have enough room to maneuver against them. We will find them, and when we do, we will destroy them. Culmit Hescion, you will maintain open communications and immediately report when you find Nisrofs' patrol. You will not leave effective scanner range of the Landex. I want Culmit Nisrofs patrol found."

"Understood, sir," acknowledges Hescion. "We will not fail."

"For your sake, I know you will succeed," replies Mular as he turns and leaves the briefing room.

Mular returns to the bridge of the Landex and keeps a watchful eye on the small view screen next to his command chair.

For the next several hours, Culmit Hescion searches for the overdue patrol. Suddenly, the small scanner screen in his cockpit sounds a warning.

"Landex, this is Miklo One."

"Report," yells Mular as his deep concentration is broken!

"I'm picking up indications of a recent battle. It appears that several of our fighters have been destroyed," reports Culmit Hescion. "Shall I proceed?"

"Of course," orders Mular hotly! "What about the Guardians? What wreckage of theirs have you found? These peace loving dirt scavengers could not have mounted an attack that would have destroyed the entire patrol."

"All wreckage and debris appears to be from our fighters. I am not receiving any indication of any destroyed or damaged Guardian ships."

"Impossible," screams Mular! "There has to be a malfunction in your sensor readings! Maneuvering! Come to full power! I want a complete scanner sweep of the entire area! We will catch these devils and destroy them as we did the others! Culmit Hescion! In what direction were these whoremongers fleeing?"

"They were heading towards Status Duo, sir."

"Follow the same course," bellows Mular in disbelief!

"Excuse me, Telecoup," interrupts Culmit Olderin, Mular's second in command. "This could be a trick to lead us away from their actual location. The outpost called Capricorn Seven in much closer."

"We will follow the trail to Status Duo," angrily orders Mular as he turns and faces Olderin! "Inform me the moment you have located Culmit Nisrofs patrol. The Guardians could not have destroyed his entire patrol. There can only be an insignificant number of their Dragons remaining. They would want the safety of their own home as soon as possible after such an encounter with a superior force. A wounded dog always heads for known safety by the quickest route. Remain on course for Status Duo."

Olderin, equal in rank to a Lieutenant Commander in the Guardian Defense Fleet, can only follow his orders, even though he believes the Guardians would be at the closer outpost of Capricorn Seven, and not Status Duo.

At the same time Telecoup Mular is ordering his forces towards Status Duo, the enemy he seeks discovers the Tirg patrol.

"Bogies entering Sector Seventeen," calls Sub-Culmit Dramek. "I have a positive identification on another herd of Horses."

"Red Alert! Probes Red and Gold prepare for launch," orders Lamminta. "What's their course?"

"They're heading towards Status Duo, Commander," reports Nuk-Ma.

"Keep a fix on them. Let me know if they alter course by even the slightest deviation," orders Lamminta. "Hops, Major Quince, delay your launch for the moment. But if I give the word, I want your Probes outside immediately."

"Understand, sir," acknowledges Hops as he waits in the cramped cockpit of his Dragon. "We're standing by."

"Major Trilla," calls Lamminta over the intercom system.

"Trilla here, sir."

"I want you ready to activate the concealment device on a moment's notice. We may use that instead of the Dragons."

"Will do, Commander," replies Trilla.

"I just hope it doesn't get stuck again," quietly mumbles Lamminta.

"Nor do I," agrees Trilla just as quietly.

"Ensign, where are they now," asks Lamminta as he peers over the shoulder of the scanner operator?

"Right there, sir," points the young officer. "Still following the same course as before. No deviation."

"Don't lose them. Keep their course plotted," softly orders Lamminta. "Red One."

"Still standing by, sir. What's going on? If we are going to launch I wish you would give the order. These things get a little uncomfortable just setting here for a while."

"Relax and just sit tight," says Lamminta. "Use your relief tube if the pressure is getting to you. I want to make sure that if I have to send you and Gold out you don't fly into another trap."

"Understand. Red One, out."

"Hope, this is Seven," calls Lamminta.

"Hope, sir."

"How soon can you be ready to launch?"

"Just waiting for you and the rest of the bridge crew, sir."

"Do you have the Tirgs on scanner?"

"Affirmative. I picked them up about a second before you did."

"Good. Trilla, can you operate the concealment device form the Hope?"

"That's where I've been, sir," calmly answers the Senior R and D officer.

"All personnel, report to the Hope," orders Lamminta as he leads the bridge crew towards the ship that is about to become their new home. "Trilla, launch the cover Probes. Make sure they're using their concealment device. Major Cherrick, launch the Hope as soon as all personnel are aboard. Nuk-Ma, do you still have the Tirgs on screen?"

"Just lost them, sir," answers the scanner operator. "There wasn't any deviation in their course or speed."

"Damn," mutters Lamminta. "Has everyone made it to the Hope yet?"

"All hands on board and accounted for, sir," answers Major Cherrick. "We can launch as soon as you're aboard and the hatch is sealed sir."

"We're on our way," calls Lamminta as he and the remaining bridge personnel reach the launch bay and board the Hope. "Engage the concealment device and launch! Now! Damn it! Launch!"

In a whisper of sound, the Hope silently moves out of the launch bay and begins heading away from Capricorn Seven. Lamminta, and the rest of the bridge crew, after a few wrong turns, finally find the main bridge of their new ship.

"Ensign Nuk-Ma, have you had any further contact with that Tirg patrol," asks Lamminta as he finally enters the bridge?

"Not with the patrol, sir, but I did get a rather large blip just as we launched. I wasn't able to get a complete scan but from the size of it, I would say it had to be a Fighting Star."

"Why did they wait so long before sending out their recon patrols," ponders Lamminta as he moves towards the scanner station? "Everything they have done since the initial attack hasn't made any sense. Where was that blip, Ensign?"

"Right here, sir," answers Ensign Nuk-Ma as he points to the edge of the scanner screen.

"Major Trilla," asks Lamminta as he moves towards the captain's chair, "how fast can this ship move?"

"We tested her up to nine point four before we started to get a slight vibration from horizontal stabilizing coil. I didn't want to push her any further. I'm not sure what her maximum sustaining speed is, but I'd place a safe bet that she could outrun anything the Tirgs have. A Fighting Star might be able to give us a decent run for our money, but I still think we could stay ahead of one if we really had to. I just don't think that would be a good idea right now. We had to rush completion by almost ten weeks. I'm going to need at least that much time to finish what still needs to be done and make sure everything is up to the proper specs."

"I'll try to give you as much time as I can. However, the Tirgs will be the ones who determine exactly how much time you will actually have. You may have to work a little faster than you want to," acknowledges Lamminta. "Launch control, bring our Dragons home. I don't think we're going to need them outside any longer. Nuk-Ma, do you have anything else on that possible Fighting Star?"

"Screen still clear, sir."

"Helm, come to course one seven three by nine six five."

"Course plotted and locked in, sir."

"Launch control," calls Lamminta. "Have the Probes been recovered yet?"

"Major Quince just landed. Landing operations complete and secure."

"Helm, execute new heading at maximum speed. Major Trilla, I want all the power she can handle."

Telecoup Mular, and the Fifth Battle Group, continues towards the Guardian outpost he believes is still capable of fighting.

"Telecoup, we are within full scanner range of Status Duo," reports Olderin. "We have found nothing to indicate there are any Guardians here."

"Establish a standard orbit and begin the attack," orders Mular. "I want nothing of use to remain. They are out here somewhere and I want to know where they are!"

The second attack against Status Duo is as savage as the first. Every fighter and energy cannon aboard the Landex and Napla fire at the already devastated outpost from every conceivable angle. For more than twenty minutes, the assault continues without any Guardian defensive fire returned.

"Cease the attack," orders Mular! "As soon as the last fighter is secured I want a direct course set for Capricorn Seven! Maximum speed!"

"Commander, I've got something moving in on Cap Seven," Nuk-Ma suddenly calls out. "It looks like it could be that Star I picked up just as we launched."

"Put it on my screen, I'd like to see what's going on back there," requests Lamminta. As he looks down at the small screen on the arm of his chair, a worried look crosses his face. "Launch control, I want two Probes on stand-by. Trilla, what's the status of the concealment device?"

"Still operational without any signs of strain, all systems still show green."

"Nuk-Ma, I want to know the instant you pick up the slightest hint of anything trying to follow us."

"Will do, Commander."

"Telecoup, long range sensors are indicating a large unidentified disturbance moving away from Capricorn Seven at an unbelievable speed," reports Culmit Sprahvic, the Landex scanner officer. "I've never seen anything like it. Unable to establish any signature identification."

"What have you picked up from the outpost," quickly questions Mular?

"Nothing sir, no life forms or any sign of activity."

"I want maximum power to all engines! Full power to forward deflectors and shields! Direct a signal towards that disturbance on all frequencies! Concentrate on all known Guardian frequencies first," orders Mular! "Sensing, relay their projected course to the helm. Helm, plot the heading of that disturbance and follow!"

"I no longer have contact with the disturbance, sir. I just lost it," reports Under-Culmit Sprahvic.

"What," screams Mular as he turns sharply towards the scanner operator! "I'm completely surrounded by incompetence and fools! We have an unidentified disturbance in our immediate area and I cannot depend on my own crew to maintain contact!"

"I was surprised to see such unusual readings, or a disturbance of such size in this area," explains Sprahvic.

"Surprised," shouts Mular! "You incompetent son of a scavenging dirt whore! A Tirgonian officer is never surprised! If you cannot properly monitor your station, I will find someone who can! Another mistake and you will no longer be a member of this crew! Is that clear!"

"Yes, sir," answers the embarrassed officer.

The Landex and Napla finally reach the outpost from which the Guardians recently departed. Suddenly a brilliant ball of fire begins to engulf the abandoned station. It grows in size, and intensity, until the entire outpost bursts apart. In an instant, nothing of the outpost remains except space dust and debris. The magnitude of the explosion violently rocks the Fighting Stars, throwing most the crew, and anything else not securely fastened down, to the hard deck plating.

"This disturbance has to have been caused by a concealed, Guardian ship," says Mular as he regains his feet and looks about his bridge. "These fools must have set delayed explosive charges to destroy their outpost and attempt to destroy us in the process. These curs may love peace, but still may be capable of giving us a good fight after all. Sensing! Do you have an educated guess on the course and speed of this Guardian ship when you lost it?"

"Yes, sir. Estimated course and speed being transferred to the helm."

"Fighter command!"

"Sub-Telecoup Zu-Art, sir."

"I want all long-range patrols to our front and flanks doubled until further notice. Notify you crews they are to remain on full alert status until we find and destroy this Guardian ship."

"Understood, Telecoup."

"Communications, have you received any response from this ship?"

"No response, sir."

"Keep repeating the signal. Inform the Napla to follow, standard protocol. Also notify the Supreme Commander that we have an unidentified ship in this sector which I believe to be Guardian and that we are in pursuit."

"Yes, sir."

"Sensing, have you been able to locate that disturbance yet?"

"No sir, not yet but a ship of that size must use a tremendous amount of zithium. I'm attempting to locate their exhaust signature. They cannot easily find fuel, so they must conserve what they have. They cannot maintain such a speed for very long."

"Very well," acknowledges Mular. "Helm, maintain speed and continue on this heading until we find them."

The Guardians continue their escape through the vast emptiness of space at an incredible speed.

"Captain Aflo," calls Lamminta as he activates the Hopes' intercom, "what's our current speed? There seems to be something wrong with the helm reading."

"Current speed is eight point seven nine three, sir."

"Damn, why can't he give me a simple straightforward answer," mumbles Lamminta over the still open intercom?

"Sorry, sir," says Aflo.

"Don't worry about it," says Lamminta. "How long will we be able to maintain this speed?"

"At the present consumption rate we can maintain all systems at full capacity for at least the next three years. We'll probably run out of food before we run out of fuel."

"Three years," exclaims Lamminta! "What's out consumption rate?"

"Point zero three two per daily cycle."

"How much zithium do we have on board? Is it safely contained," asks Lamminta? "A Fighting Star has always had slightly better fuel efficiency, and one of them requires refueling every two and a half years."

"Normal capacity for a ship of this size, sir. It's a new engine design approved by Fleet about four years ago. I can give you a complete run down at your next briefing."

"I'm going to need a complete run down on what you've put together. Lamminta, out. Helm, come to course two one three by seven zero three."

"Aye, sir," acknowledges Cherrick. "Coming to course two one three by seven zero three."

"Com-link, get me the Probe leaders and all Section Chiefs in my ready room for a complete briefing and analysis at thirteen hundred," says Lamminta as he leave the bridge. As the doors silently close behind him, he quietly adds, "If I can find it myself."

The Captains' ready room, located next to the bridge, is impressive. A series of large glass portals line the outside bulkhead, giving the room a much larger appearance. The focus of this place of solitude is the main console area. Within this seemingly small section of the room, all necessary monitors, view screens and other normal duty station components as found on the main bridge, only of a smaller design, are located. Lamminta is able to monitor all ships operations from here just as if he were actually on the bridge. A comfortable high-backed chair completes this important part of the room.

Equally impressive is the long conference table located next to the outside bulkhead. Oval at one end with the same high-backed chair at the opposite, notched end. View screens are positions, not only at the notched end, but also between every other smaller designed padded chair.

After surveying the new surroundings, Lamminta seats himself at the work console and adjusts the lighting to a more comfortable level. Quietly he waits for the arrival of his senior staff. At the appointed time, all personnel enter and begin seating themselves around the conference table.

"Thank you all for coming on such short notice," welcomes Lamminta as he takes his place at the head of the table. "I will try to keep this meeting as short as possible because I know that all of you still have a lot of work to complete."

"No need to worry about that, sir," says Hops with a slight grin. "It seems that all we have right now is time."

"I hope you're right, Commander," says Lamminta. "I guess we need to get started. Since this is the first time some of us have the pleasure of working together I believe full introductions are in order.

"Everyone already knows Lieutenant Commander Hoppinzorinski, Red One. Next to him is Major Williams, joining us from Status Duo and leader of Probe Orange. He brought an additional eleven pilots with him. Next is Major Quince leads Probe Gold. She, and five more pilots, are joining us from Alpha Cheris. Next to Major Quince is Ensign Nuk-Ma, our Senior Communications Officer. He is also our primary Scanning Officer. Major Trilla is in charge of Research and Development. He is directly responsible for the design and construction of our new home. Captain Wicks is the Chief Medical Officer, Captain Aflo is our Ships Propulsion Officer, Lieutenant Novac is responsible for making sure we don't get lost, Major Dunlipee is in charge of Probe Operations, Ensign Gallaski, Ski for short, is in charge of Maintenance and Repair. He is our 'fix-it' man, and is responsible for keeping our Dragons, and the Hope, at operational readiness. Next is Lieutenant Fab, our Weapons Officer. Ensign Tu will be handling Personnel and Security. Next is Ensign Wallop, who is in charge of our Commissary and Supply Section, and last but certainly not least, is Major O'Connell, our Senior Chaplain.

"I'd like for each Section Chief to report on the status of his, or her section, current capabilities, and you need to keep your section operational. Nuk-Ma, we'll begin with Communications and Sensing."

"The scanners and sensors are an upgraded design and far better than what we have been using for the past eight years. The range and sensitivity are double of what we had been using. We are able to see and identify any Tirg ship from a greater distance, which give us a little more time to prepare for whatever needs to be done. We still have the same number of standard and secure communications channels. Each channel has a primary and secondary security mode. I currently have two operators and could use at least three more to handle things properly."

"That is something that Tu can take once she gets a firm handle on what personnel are available," replies Lamminta.

"I have a question for Nuk-Ma, sir," says Trilla.

"Go ahead, Major."

"How did you locate that Fighting Star? I know the capabilities of the scanners have been enhances, but you have me baffled on how you identified it as a Fighting Star. It should still have been too far out to get any kind of positive identification."

"I thought I caught a glimpse of something just as we left Seven, sir. I realigned the sensitivity of the enhanced display circuit on the scanner frequency rely coil.

That increased the sensitivity of the osculation collection unit, which allowed us to penetrate whatever they are now using as a concealment device."

"Damn good idea. I should have thought of that when the Hope was designed," says Trilla.

"I agree," says Lamminta. "As long as we can see them before they can see us, we should be able to remain safe, and hopefully avoid any further contact, for a little while longer. Fab, when we do have to fight, what do we have to fight with?"

"All main defensive batteries are identical in design to what we have been using," begins the Hopes' Senior Weapons Officer. "We have ion batteries at almost every possible location and a few are even located where you wouldn't expect to find one. I would like to have a two more batteries placed over and under each landing bay ramp. I could give the Dragons better protection when they're inbound. It would also make the ramps a little more secure against any attacks in that area of the Hope. As of right now, I can give one hundred and ten degrees of protection with the beuting torpedoes and complete three sixty with the ion cannons. All systems have an increased range of at least twenty-five percent. We shouldn't have any problem defending the Hope, sir."

"Very well, Trilla and Ski, both of you coordinate with Fab and see what can be done to put in the additional batteries," instructs Lamminta. "Next, Dun? What about Flight Operations?"

"Damnedest design I've ever seen, sir. It's a box divided into four quadrants down there. The upper outside quadrant is where the Dragons launched. Directly under them are the launch and landing ramps. As soon as a ship lands, it maneuvers to an empty refit stall for the refit. After the rearming and refueling is completed, it moves in the assembly area located at the opposite end of the bay, is launched back into the fight. If a ship needs maintenance, we have it moved to the maintenance bay. Once it's fixed, the ship it goes to the upper inside quadrant where the hanger bays are located. From the hanger bays, a ship moves to the upper or lower launch ramps, depending on the active situation. Like I said sir, two upper and lower launch and landing ramps, lower maintenance bay, and upper hanger bay. Launch, recovery and maintenance operations all at the same time without any one operation interfering with anything else. With the way things are located down there," continues Dunlipee as he glances sideways towards Hops. "I can launch every available Dragon in less time than it takes you to chew out certain an un-named individual. I don't think I'll have any problems with flight operations, sir."

"Ski, how do we stand on spare parts, maintenance for the Dragons and the rest of the ship," asks Lamminta.

"First, like Dun said, I've got a complete repair shop next to each service bay. In-between the two repair shops is the fabrication shop. Right now, if something breaks, I can get it fixed. Raw stock and spare parts aren't a problem, but the more repairs I make the more stock and spare parts I'll have to use. Eventually I'm going to run out of parts and supplies. Just how fast that happens will depend on how many repairs I have to make to whatever breaks. I have enough of everything right now to handle three or four full-scale attacks with substantial damage. After that I don't know."

"Just do the best you can with what you have," says Lamminta with a slight smile on his face at the comment of his Flight Operations Chief. "Ensign Wallop, how often can we expect to eat?"

"From what I've been able to inventory so far sir, quite often," begins the Commissary and Supply Officer. "I would say that there is enough food, and other necessities aboard, for twice our number to last at least two years or longer. Water may become a problem if both distillation units go out at the same time, which I consider that likely. All processors and duplicators are better designed and more efficient that the ones we used back on Seven. I would like to use one of the spare storage bays and turn it into a hydroponics garden so the crew could have access to fresh fruits and vegetables to supplement the duplicators. Other than that, I don't foresee any major problems except for a few more personnel. I can get with Tu on that later."

"Okay. Aflo, how are the engine power and life support systems holding up?"

"One of the finest engine designs I've ever seen, sir. So far, the only problem I've had to fix has been with the horizontal stabilizer. Other than that, we haven't put any significant strain on the engines whatsoever. We also have a new design for the zithium reaction converters. We are using almost sixty percent less than our normal fuel consumption, which means we can go a heck of a lot further on the same amount of fuel because we're using a lot less zithium to achieve the same speeds as we did before. Moreover, as far as the zithium containment units, sir, they are completely secure. If we do get a rupture due to an amazingly accurate hit from a Tirg energy blast, the unit will engage it emergency containment field instantaneously, stopping any possible leak before it could actually occur. We currently have enough fuel, at the current consumption rate, to last us for at least the next three, maybe four years before we would have to consider any type of refueling option. The life support systems are exactly the same design as we have been using so there shouldn't be any problems with their function or maintenance."

"Very well. Now, how soon before we will have to consider ourselves as being lost, Lieutenant Novac," continues Lamminta?

"Not any time soon, sir. It will depend on where we finally end up heading. We have updated star charts of our space, but the latest charts covering Tirgonian space are about three years old. As far as I can tell, there haven't been any new discoveries on either side of the Agreed Zone in almost five years. We shouldn't get lost unless we end up somewhere we haven't been before. With the integration of the navigational systems with the scanner and sensing systems, as well as the helm control, I don't think we will have any problem with knowing exactly where we are or where we're heading.

"Let's hope not," says Lamminta. "Ensign Tu, have you been able to get any kind of accurate head count yet?"

"As of right now, sir, I have a basic count of four hundred and eighty-seven adults and thirty-six children, most of who are now orphans. Several civilians have begun taking care of them. As far as accurate records, I do have what I need for all surviving Fleet personnel. I need to get records started on all non-Fleet individuals. After I get a complete set of records established, I'll be able to begin filling whatever vacancies I can, according to individual qualifications. Since I don't have accurate any civilian personnel records, I'll just have to take everyone's word as to what they can and can't do.

"As far as security is concerned, I currently have a total of twelve people who are currently assigned to guard all critical, and sensitive, areas. I also have four additional individuals assigned to the Detention Cell that I plan to reassign them as necessary," then glancing at Hops as she adds, "at least until I actually have someone in a detention cell. I would like to assign Ensign Bell to be the Security Officer. I feel that she's quite capable and that would give me more time to concentrate on the current personnel situation."

"That would not be a bad idea Ensign, but she will report directly to my Executive Officer," instructs Lamminta. "Now, how are we doing down in Sickbay, Doc?"

"Everything I could have ever hoped for, sir," begins Captain Wicks. "I can handle just about anything down there. The medical lab has more equipment than I ever received on Seven. The research lab is just as complete. I also need to start records on all non-Fleet personnel and ensure everyone has had the proper inoculations. I should be able to have everything finished within the next week to ten days."

"Very well, coordinate with Tu and make sure no one falls through the cracks," says Lamminta as he calls on the next section leaders to report. "Chaplain, how are we doing in the spiritual area?"

"The main chapel is fully functional for all known faiths and beliefs just as it was on Seven, sir," begins the senior Chaplain. "I currently have four Chaplains. All have their individual capabilities. I believe we should be able to fulfill the needs of anyone onboard seeking our assistance. The main chapel on deck seven is fully functional with all known beliefs represented. If I have any problem assisting anyone with their individual beliefs or ceremonies, I think that particular individual would understand and assist my staff in correcting any deficiencies which might currently exist."

"Thank you, Chaplain. Now, what about the Dragons and our pilots? Hops, we know that everyone can fly, but what is our exact status?"

"Fair to middling, sir. Thirty-one Dragons and twenty-three drivers, without taking into account the birds assigned to the Academy cadets we still have. Counting the cadets, and their birds, which are not exactly battle ready, we will have a total of sixty Dragons and fifty-two drivers, once they graduate. Their birds could be battle ready in about another four to five days. The cadets might be ready in about another two to three months if we cut the bull shi . . . unnecessary classes and just concentrate on the stuff that really matters like battle tactics and flying to stay alive.

"All normal pilots are . . ." pausing slightly, he looks towards Major Quince, ". . . fairly well qualified. With the new concealment device, we should be able to handle whatever those bastards throw at us. Major Williams already proved that. We may need to launch a Probe at any given moment, so I would like everyone to go through a familiarization program just to make sure we're all on the same page and singing the same tune. I don't think it'd be a good idea for me to be playing old time rock and roll while someone else is trying to sing the Tirgonian blues. Realignment of all drivers should be finished by tomorrow morning. I'd also like to continue the cadets training and get them ready for duty as soon as possible. Major Williams, Major Quince, and I should be able to finish their training with minimum difficulty."

"Sounds like a plan to me," accepts Lamminta. "Concentrate on finishing the Corps of Cadets training and make sure you maintain a complete male - female mix when you work on your Probe realignment. It will be good for morale."

Major Quince has a hard time controlling the grin creeping across her face. Several others in the room, knowing about Hops disdain for women in battle, share the same problem, including Lamminta.

"But, sir. I . . ." begins Hops as he tries to continue.

"A male - female mix Lieutenant Commander Hoppinzorinski," interrupts Lamminta as he tries in vain to control his grinning as he continues. "Now that we all know where we stand, it should go without saying, but to make it official as our laws require, I will say what everyone already understands. First, every section will maintain complete and accurate log entries, and these logs are be entered into the ships' memory core. Next, as the senior member of any sort of governing body I am hereby declaring martial law, effective immediately. The Articles of Defense are in full effect, and as senior officer, I'm assuming full authority and responsibility as Council General of the Council of Elders and High Commander of the Space Defense Fleet. Based on their individual qualifications, all civilian personnel are now members of what we have left of the Space Defense Fleet Headquarters. Tu will reassign them based on their qualifications.

"With that out of the way, this is what I am going to need from all of you. Tu, once you finish classifying and assigning, or reassigning, the personnel onboard I want a complete and accurate ship roster given to each section. All qualified personnel are to have an appropriate rating, however; no one will receive a rating higher than that of the personnel currently in this room, which brings me to my next point. As the senior officer of you individual section and the normal rank for senior staff members is that of Lieutenant Commander, all of you now have that rank. Tu, you will make the appropriate entries in the personnel files of everyone here, with the exception of Lieutenant Commander Hoppinzorinski who is my Executive Officer and Probe Squadron Leader." Looking directly at Hops, he says, "You are now a full Commander. Wally will make sure everyone gets the appropriate uniform and insignia changes.

"Now Commander Hoppinzorinski, this is what you're going to do for me. I want all pilots broken down into normal Probes, maintaining a male - female mix. You will not assign yourself to any specific Probe. Continue the cadets training and get them ready to join the Fleet as quickly as possible. Establish a Probe schedule that we can implement at a moments' notice. Don't send anything outside unless necessary. Keep your pilots on ready standby until further notice.

"I want all departments to give Tu, Wally, and Doc a complete roster of current personnel and vacancies. Keep the minimum number of personnel you'll need to get the job done. We'll worry about the extra personnel after Tu can get a full accountability of whom we have to do what job. Each section will begin a normal as possible duty rotation schedule and I don't want just duty time. I want time set aside for everyone to use the Recreation Lounge and Personal Stimulation Facilities which I noticed somewhere on this ship. Wally, you're now the Morale Officer so I want you to organize any type of recreation and relaxation for the crew that you or anyone else can think of. People need something to do in their off duty time besides sitting and thinking about what has happened and the fact that they can't do anything about it. Does anyone have anything else the needs to be addressed at this time?" No one speaks, allowing Lamminta to continue, "Then we all know what we have to do so let's get started on what we need to do and try to get out of here."

Everyone follows the example of Lamminta and depart the ready room for their respective sections and areas to begin the tasks they had just been given.

"I'll be back in the wheelhouse in about an hour sir. I want to talk to Williams and Quince and get them started on the training program for the cadets," calls Hops as he heads away from the bridge.

"In the what," questions Lamminta? "I wish you would remember what you were supposed to have learned, if you actually completed Flight Communications training. I presume you did learn the proper use of our language. I would greatly appreciate you and your talents a lot more if I could ever understand what you saying. And I would also appreciate it if you would stay out of the Historical Information Center so that I could understand you without an interpreter."

CHAPTER FIVE

The Tirgonian Fifth Battle Group continues on what Telecoup Mular believes to be the course of the fleeing Guardians.

"What is the status of the patrols," questions the Tirgonian General as his Senior Flight Officer enters the bridge.

"Maintaining as ordered, sir. I have not received any contact report," replies Sub-Telecoup Zu-Art. "If we are following an accurate course we should have overtaken them by now. The Guardians have nothing that is capable of outrunning a Fighting Star."

"I agree," says Mular thoughtfully. "We will eventually find them and when we do we will once again have them at our mercy."

"Shall I continue the patrols," asks Zu-Art?

"No, discontinue. However, at the first indication that we have found them, I want all fighters launched. Your squadrons will attack and disable their engines. Whatever else has survived I will then destroy. Helm, return to maximum speed and course as soon as all of the fighters have been recovered."

"Bridge, this is Trilla. The concealment device is reacting to a circuit failure. The primary induction frequency is beginning to waiver. If I don't shut it down now we're going to have a much bigger problem later."

"Exactly what's going on and how long for repairs," asks Lamminta as he begins to receive the basic information on his small view screen?

"The reflective enhancement coil is rejecting the primary input command from the inducement imager. If I don't realign the coil, the reflective imaging holodine will over load and take out the entire system. I can take the system off line and have the repairs completed in about four hours. If I don't do it now and the entire system goes out it will take at least a day and a half to get it operational and back on line."

"How long can we stay hid before it goes completely bonkers," asks Hops as he looks over Lammintas' shoulder?

"I'm not exactly of what you mean, Commander, but it you're asking how long it will stay operational, no more than four or five minutes at the most. I have got to shut it down now, sir."

"Fighting Star just entered scanner range," calls out Nuk-Ma!

"How close are they?"

"Close enough to possible cause us a problem, sir."

"Aflo, how much more speed can you get out of the engines," hurriedly calls Lamminta.

"We're pushing light eight. I might be able to get another one and a half out of them. I just don't think it would be a good idea to stay at that speed for very long."

"Do it," orders Lamminta. "Helm, come to course six seven eight by six three zero. Trilla! Shut it down at the last possible second. Give me a five count on your mark."

"Launch control! Get our umbrella ready but keep it closed," orders Hops. "It hasn't started to rain on our parade yet so let's hope it stays that away. Nuk-Ma, anything else on those Fighting Stars?"

"No, sir. If they haven't modified their scanners we should be out of their range."

"Shutting down the concealment device on my mark. Five, four, three, two, one, MARK," reports Trilla! "If we're within their scanner range they can definitely see us now."

"Understood," acknowledges Lamminta. "Launch the covering Probe and keep them close. No greetings unless we have to. Nuk-Ma, have their scanners picked us up yet?"

"Launching covering Probes," acknowledges Hops.

"I don't think so, sir. They're maintaining course and speed."

"Unidentified ship barely within scanner range," calls out Culmit Sprahvic. "It must be traveling at more than nine point two!"

"Helm, increase to maximum emergency speed," immediately orders Mular. "Identify that ship!"

"It's the Guardians, sir! They just launched a five Dragons covering Probe," reports the scanner operator! "Course plotted and transferred to the helm."

"Now I have them," mumbles Mular. "As soon as we are within effective fighter range I want all fighters launched. Even with their Dragon cover I will destroy that ship without any help!"

"I just lost contact with the Dragons," informs Sprahvic.

"This could get interesting," observes Mular. "They've recalled their covering force so they must be weaker than I thought."

"Telecoup, this is Zu-Art. All fighters are launching and moving into attack positions."

"Very well, proceed with the attack," orders Mular quietly as he watches his fighter squadrons moving towards the Guardian ship. "Now they shall finally perish."

"We have a problem, Commander," calls Nuk-Ma. "The lead Fighting Star just opened the barn doors and it looks like it's time to play cowboys and Indians."

"Red Alert," orders Lamminta! "And I wish you would stay away from Hops. I get all the ancient clichés that I need from him. Aflo, I need all the extra power that you can give me and I need it on command. Attack Plan Lima Two. Hops, I'm going to need you to assist Fab on fire control. Close the absorbing shields and get the deflectors on line."

Immediately, Lieutenant Commander Fab begins giving his own orders over the Fire Control Channel to the defensive fire batteries. "Port batteries, fire on confirmed targets only. Do not engage in defensive barrage. It's going to be congested and I don't want to hit one of our Dragons by mistake. I say again, port batteries confirmed targets only. Starboard batteries have weapons free. Fire at anything that moves and use barrage fire as necessary on any target."

Hops immediately gives the information to his Probes. "All Dragons keep to port. No starboard dancing. That dance floor is reserved strictly for the Horses."

"Orange and Gold are on station and ready for a good fight."

"Negative, Orange One," orders Hops. "Don't fight them on their terms. Show yourself, fire, and delay back here. You will get better support if you stay close to the bunkhouse. It isn't a real good idea to try to rope that many Horses with just two of you out there. Turn you're concealment devices off because it's about to get a little crowded out there and I don't want any of you to run into each other in the confusion."

"Roger. Confirm attack and delay. Just make sure those gunners know the difference between a Dragon and a Horsehead. Concealment device disengaged."

"There won't be any problem with identification if you stay to port. Starboard has weapons free and barrage fire. I don't think you want to get caught on the wrong side of the Hope."

"Understood, Hope. Port side of this fight sounds fine to me."

"Confirm port side," acknowledges Lieutenant Commander Quince. "Disengaging concealment device."

The small scanner screens of the Dragons now show the leading of the Tirgonian attack formation.

"Orange, this is Orange One. We're going to need a little breathing room. Break on my lead and as Hops says, I don't need anyone to get a case of the smart-ass on me," instructs Williams.

"Let's do it."

"I'm on you wing."

"Let's show these bastards that's there's still a few of us left and we still know how to fight!"

"I get the first shot!"

"Okay gang, let's got," orders Williams!

"Gold! Dive," yells Quince at the same moment!

The reddish-yellow blasts of the Dragons ion cannons are immediately answered by the blue-white bursts of the Tirgs energy weapons. The Guardians are now engaged in a bitter battle for survival. The vehi-com of the slightly more maneuverable Dragons is jammed with the voices of the embattled pilots.

"Watch it!"

"I got one!"

"Damn it! Missed!"

"Orange Five! How bad are you hit?"

"I'll get that son of a bitch!"

"Star! Where are you?"

"I'm on one!"

"Watch your wing!"

"Cover me! There're three on my six!"

"I'm coming in! Hold on!"

"Aw shit!"

"Got the mother!"

The battle raged with total disregard of the odds. The Tirgs, surprised by the attacking tactic of the outnumbered Guardians are initially unable to take advantage of their superior numbers.

"Bridge! I found the problem," suddenly calls Trilla! "Inter-polarization coupling came loose! Helm should control!"

As the pitched battle reaches a fever pitch never before witnessed by Lamminta, he gives the order everyone has been waiting for.

"Now, Major Cherrick, execute!"

"Landex Command, this is Miklo One! The Guardian ship has turned to an intercept course!"

"Understand, Miklo One." acknowledges the Communications Officer of the Tirgonian Fighting Star. "Telecoup Mular, the Guardian ship has turned and is on an intercept course towards the engagement area."

"The ship is doing what," questions an unbelieving Tirgonian Group Commander? "Full scanner display on my screen! Surely, their commander understands such a move will prove to be nothing less than fatal for his ship. Helm, maintain our current position. There is already enough firepower out there to keep up the attack against their puny Dragons and still attack that mother ship. Fighter Command. Keep the pressure against the Dragons. Once they are destroyed concentrate on their mother ship as soon as it is within effective weapons range."

"All Probes! Delay and return," quickly orders Lamminta. "Fab, get all you batteries ready. It's going to get a little rough out there."

"Aye, sir. All batteries ready and on line."

The Dragon pilots acknowledge the orders and begin to draw the battle closer to the Hope.

"Cherrick, move the Hope between their Horses and that Fighting Star," continues Lamminta. "Let's give our people as much help as possible. Drop the landing bay shields so they can land. Don't let any of those Horses get close enough to do any damage."

"Orange secure. Gold coming in," immediately reports from Dunlipee in the Flight Operations Center.

The Tirgs begin paying a heavy toll. Within minutes of the Hope joining the fight, the Tirgonian Empire lose almost fifteen percent of the battle fighters normally assigned to a Fighting Star without the loss of a single Guardian Dragon, though several did sustain heavy damage. One of the Tirg squadron leaders suddenly realizes that there are fewer and fewer Dragons remaining in the engagement area but he is still losing one ship after another.

"All fighters! Return to the Landex! It's a trap," orders Zu-Art! "Telecoup Mular! They have cut us off! The Guardian vessel is outflanking us!"

"What are your orders, sir," quickly asks the Communications Officer?

"All batteries! Fire on that ship! If I cannot rely on my fighters to accomplish a simple mission, I will personally destroy the enemies of the Empire," orders a frustrated commander.

The Tirg energy cannons have a reputation for being deadly accurate, but theses murderous weapons are now experiencing a very unusual difficulty. The Guardian ship is still out of range as the Landex begins to suffer severe damage.

"Telecoup," calls the Senior Weapons Officer. "Perimeter batteries nine, ten thirteen, fourteen, sixteen and twenty-one are inoperable! Batteries seven, eleven, and fifteen have been reduced to twenty-five effectiveness!"

"Keep firing," orders Mular! "Sensing! Damage report on the Guardians!"

"Negative damage indicated, sir!"

"Give me the damage report excluding the defensive batteries!"

"Port quadrants seven and eight Alpha have severe damage. Repairs are already underway. We have extensive hull damage in quadrants six Alpha, seven, eight, and nine Bravo. The primary fire control system in those quadrants is inoperable. We've lost communications with all damaged areas. Security, sensing and scanning in these areas is . . ."

"Helm! Reverse course," frantically orders Mular! "Engineering! All available power to the engines! Maximum input to maneuvering!"

"But sir," protests Zu-Art! "My fighters! They cannot . . ."

"I will get replacement squadrons," shouts Mular! "Those few fighters have no chance of returning and I will not risk any more damage to the Landex for a few measly fighters! Withdraw! Inform the Napla to provide covering fire!"

"Sir! That Fighting Star is withdrawing," reports Nuk-ma! "Their Horses are trying to go with it but I don't think they are going to make it. It looks this show is over."

"Hops," asks Lammintas, "did all the Dragons make it back?"

"Everybody is as snug as a bug in a rug, but I think Ski's going to be real busy for a while."

"Helm, return to our original course," orders Lamminta. "Commander Bell, maintain Yellow Alert until we know for certain that Fighting Star isn't going to suddenly return. Also continue to maintain full security scans."

"Commander, that course will take us across the Agreed Zone," observes Cherrick.

"That it will," acknowledges Lamminta. "That will be the last place the Tirgs should be looking for us. The most obvious area they should concentrate their search for us should be the place where we would feel most comfortable, on our side of the Agreed Zone. We need to think of the obvious, and then do whatever we normally wouldn't do. Just maintain course, reduce speed to seven point zero, and continue to maintain a full scan. I don't want to be surprised by the sudden appearance of anyone who might be on friendly terms with the Tirgs."

"Fighting Star maintaining course and speed," reports Nuk-Ma. "Distance now one hundred seventy thousand kilometers and steadily increasing."

"Damage report," requests Lamminta.

"I don't know how you did but there's very little damage, sir," says Ski. "That Star didn't put a scratch on us. All of the damage came from their Horseheads and that wasn't much. Repairs should be complete within the hour. The repairs on the Dragons is going take a while longer."

"Nuk-Ma? Were you able to determine the damage sustained by that Fighting Star," asks Lamminta, "and which one was it?"

"It was the Landex, sir. We were able to knock out quite a few of their defensive batteries, including two or three of their torpedo launchers. At least seven quadrants are going to need some fancy repairs before we see that Star again."

"Then it was Mular," softly mutters Lamminta. "If he's here, there has to be another Star around somewhere. Hops, go down to the intelligence section and see if you find out the name of Mulars' sister ship and, who the commander is. If they return, I'm going to need as much information as possible on how they do things."

"On my way, sir."

The Executive Officer of the Guardian Battleship Hope departs the bridge and heads, indirectly, towards the intelligence section. As he enters the main ready room reserved for the Dragon pilots, he finds a full celebration already in progress. Each pilot had destroyed at least three enemy fighters with the gunners from the Hope accounting for the remainder of the Tirgonian losses. Against seemingly insurmountable odds, no one would have ever predicted such a lopsided victory. The Tirgonian Fighting Star, attacked by only sixteen Mark Two Space Fighters and one newly designed Guardian battleship, sustained heavy damage, and withdrew.

CHAPTER SIX

For more than a week, the Guardians maintain their course, crossing the Agreed Zone that once separated the two civilizations.

"Commander," suddenly calls from Nuk-Ma. "I've got a target. It's too far out to get a full scan."

"How far out is it?"

"Right at one million kilometers and it's heading our way."

"Yellow alert," immediately orders Lamminta. "Get Probes Orange and Gold prepared for launch. Hops, have you found out anything about that sister ship of the Landex?"

"Sorry for the delay, sir, it took me more time than I thought," answers Hops as he moves towards the scanner station. "Sister ship is the Napla. Current intelligence reports indicate that she has a new commander by the name of Ge-Kor. No real battle experience. Total service seems to be just under fifteen years. From the information we have, which may not be accurate, it appears that his advancement came from knowing the right people in the right place. He doesn't appear to be as good a tactician as Mular, but we might still have our hands full if that bogie turns out to be the Landex."

"I don't think it could be the Landex. From the damage we inflicted, repairs could not have been completed by now," comments Lamminta. "I also doubt that blip could be the Napla. Mular would need to keep Ge-Kor close for provide protection until he could reach a repair facility. That leaves us with an unidentified intruder for the time being. The only thing we can do is to wait. Nuk-Ma, have you been able to get anything else on that intruder yet?"

"Only a possible course, sir. If it stays on its present course it looks like it will pass us at about forty thousand kilometers to port."

"Helm, come to course six seven two by five four nine. Maintain . . ."

"Too late, Commander. That bogie is a Star and it has family," calls Nuk-Ma.

"Damn! Red alert! Orange and Gold! Launch on command," orders Lamminta. "Engineering! I'm going to need everything you can give me at a moment notice. Trilla! How's the concealment device holding up?"

"Just fine, sir. Ready and on line."

"Is the concealment identification system for the Dragons operational yet," asks Lamminta hurriedly? "If I launch them, will they be able to still see each other if they're hiding?"

"The Dragons can hide and everyone will still be able to see everyone, Commander."

"Nuk-Ma? What are those Stars doing?"

"Not too good, sir. They've seen us are heading this way."

"Okay they've seen us. It looks like it's time to give them a little surprise," acknowledges Lamminta. "Helm! Full stop! Trilla! Get us hid! Launch Control! Launch the Dragons!"

"Full stop and maintaining position," replies Major Cherrick.

"Concealment device activated," answers Trilla.

"Probes out and hiding," says Hops.

"This is what we're going to do," says Lamminta. "I want Orange twenty thousand in front of us and Gold two fifty behind them. As soon as that lead Star is within range, Orange is to show themselves, fire, hide, and move so they can engage their horses as they launch. Gold will do the same thing except they are to concentrate on knocking out the defensive batteries protecting the launch ramps."

"Hopefully," says Hops as a gleam of understandings comes into his eyes, "we can pull this thing off. Once the attack starts, that commander should launch at least a squadron of his best Horses. We ambush their cowboy's with our Indians. We just might have a repeat of the Little Big Horn and Custer just might screw up again."

"Sir," interrupts Nuk-Ma, "that lead Star is six hundred thousand and closing fast. I have Orange and Gold on screen and in position. All orders have been acknowledged."

"I guess this is it then," says Lamminta as he returns to the Captain's chair. "Shields and deflectors up. All batteries hold your fire until I give the order."

"Com-link, this is Orange One. Commencing attack in two minutes."

"Acknowledged," replies the communications officer.

"And good luck," quietly says Lamminta.

The two Fighting Stars continue towards the unidentified blip.

"Telecoup, I no longer have contact with whatever the scanners initially locked on to," reports the scanning officer.

"Send a signal and request identification," orders Mular. "It could be a supply ship with transmitter problems, or it could be a renegade supplying the black market. It could be almost anything this far from the Agreed Zone. Keep trying to contact it."

"Still nothing, sir," reports the Communications Officer. "No response to our requests."

"Closing to within forty thousand kilometers of the last known position," reports the helmsman.

"Launch the fighter," orders Mular! "I want all batteries on line and ready to fire if this turns out to be a trap."

"Twenty thousand to the . . ."

"Telecoup," urgently calls Fighter Command! "Our fighters as being destroyed as soon as they launch! A Guardian Probe is visible for only a moment as they fire, then vanishes!"

"That's impossible," screams Mular as he stares at his monitor! "A concealment device requires more power than a Guardian Dragon could possibly provide!"

"It's true, Telecoup," replies Sprahvic. "I do not have any confirmed targets."

"No targets to lock on to," agrees the senior fire control officer.

"Impossible! There isn't . . ."

"It is true! I can only get a momentary reading on a Guardian Dragon. Each time it is further away," confirms Sprahvic.

"It's a trap," yells Mular! Then, he quietly adds, "But a very impressive trap. The Guardians as definitely here and indeed possess a concealment device for their Dragons." Turning his attention back to the Communications Officer, he orders, "Recall all fighters! Inform the Napla to initiate Attack Sequence Honko."

"Something's wrong," calls Lieutenant Commander Quince over the vehi-com. "The Horses are breaking contact and returning to the barn."

"Can you identify the Star," asks Lamminta?

"You're not going to believe this Commander, but it's the Landex," reports Quince. "How in the hell did they fix that Star so fast?"

"I don't know," answers Hops. "But if that Star's the Landex, then the Napla has to be the other Star. I think we might have bit off a little more than we can chew this time. I think you and Orange better get back here on the double."

"Roger. On our way, out."

"Nuk-Ma, what's the Napla doing," asks Lamminta?

"It looks like the Napla is taking up an orbit around the Landex and is firing into empty space, no specific target or direction, sir."

"Ge-Kor isn't just firing," replies Lamminta. "He's trying to find us. Check the orbit. It should be decaying towards the Landex."

"Aye, sir," says Nuk-Ma as he looks back towards the scanner screen. "Orbit is decaying towards the Landex. They must know that we are definitely in the area even though they can't see us. And with our shields and deflectors up they know that they can't really hurt us."

"Mular does know this," answers Lamminta carefully. "He also knows that if anything hits our shields, it will reveal our exact position. I don't think we could withstand the direct force of two Fighting Stars at once. Mular is letting Ge-Kor drive us towards the Landex because he wants to be the one to claim credit for the kill. Have all probes been recovered yet?"

"Last one just came in," answers Hops.

"Good," acknowledges Lamminta "I want you, all Probe leaders, Trilla and Aflo in my ready room in five minutes."

As soon as everyone assembles in his private domain, he immediately begins.

"All of you know our current situation."

"I think frying pan and fire has a familiar ring to it," mumbles Lammintas Executive Officer.

"Not now, Hops," admonishes Lamminta as he continues, pointing at the scanner screen. "What I propose to do is this. First we move as close to the Landex as possible. Ge-Kor should cease firing in this direction shortly and that's where I want to move to."

"Sounds like a good idea unless Mular begins firing with his own batteries," says Carol. "He may be a Tirg, but I don't think he's a stupid Tirg."

"That is quite true, Commander," says Lamminta "That is exactly what he will do. He wants to trap us between the two Fighting Stars, and he will, almost."

"Sir," asks Hops? "Why don't we just hide behind the Napla? The outside area will be clear in one more orbit. Ge-Kor won't waste unnecessary energy clearing what he's already cleared and should stop firing to the outside."

"Sounds like a reasonable assumption," agrees Lamminta. "But Ge-Kor won't stop firing to the outside. What you suggest is exactly what we did during the last war. It worked until Mular figured out what we were doing. He came up with the tactic of continuous firing in all directions. I nearly lost an entire Task Force because of him."

"The withdrawal from Diglafar," said Williams. "That was you, sir?"

"Yes," acknowledges Lamminta, "And, like Commander Quince said, he may be a Tirg but he's not stupid. He won't open up with his batteries until Ge-Kor has completed his final orbit to conserve his own energy. As soon as Ge-Kor withdraws to a safe distance to recharge the Napla's' weapons system, he'll maintain his firing with his outward batteries while his inward batteries recharge. Then, he'll rotate on his vertical axis and continue firing while he recharges the rest of his batteries. During that time, Mular will clear the area immediately around the Landex until Ge-Kor reaches his original orbit. Once there both Stars will open up with everything they have."

"Forgive me, sir, but I'm not sure of what you are trying to do," says Williams. "I know it isn't too smart to get out of here at maximum power because our distortion trail will be picked up. So how do we move once the Napla stops firing to the inside and Mular opens up at almost the same instant? That doesn't leave much room for error?"

"Once the area is cleared, then the area next to both Stars will be all that's left to clear. Since this area is inside the minimum effectiveness of the defensive batteries, Horses will be used," explains Lamminta. "Mular has a bad habit of using his Alpha ramp for his initial launch, but only his best squadron will use that ramp. All other squadrons launch from the other three launch ramps."

"Why," asks Carol?

"If you see something coming out of the closest ramp, what would you think," asks Lamminta?

"Most of the Horses will be coming out the same ramp because it's the closest exit point to whatever is happening. It's a standard Tirg tactic."

"And if you see something coming out of the closest ramp, what will you normal reaction be?"

"Hit that ramp with everything I have."

"And that's exactly what Mular will want you to do. However, remember what you just said, he may be a Tirg but he isn't stupid. With everything coming out the other three ramps and you're concentrating on only one, I think you just got ambushed and lost your entire Probe," explains Lamminta. "Since I've seen Mular use this tactic before and I know that we can't outrun his energy canons, we're going to need a place to hide that's safe."

"Where," asks Hops?

"There's only one place that I know of that is big enough, and safe enough, for the Hope. We hide in Brave ramp until the initial squadron is launched, then we move to Alpha ramp. Mular uses Bravo, Charlie and Delta ramps for all rearming and refueling. He will not use Alpha until the mission is complete, and all Horses return to the barn. That should give us a few extra minutes to get out of here."

"Why couldn't we move once the initial squadron begins its landing sequence," asks Major Quince?

"They will be landing in a random pattern," says Lamminta. "Whichever ramp is available will be the next one used. There will be too much activity to try to maneuver the Hope through all the Horses while they're trying to land. Remember that they need to get down as quickly as possible. Once the Horses have been recovered, both Stars will open up with continuous firing again."

"I guess that means that we're going to be playing at Mular's back door and we'd better not make too much noise," says Hops. "I just hope this works."

"That's it then. Get back to your sections and make sure everything is ready," dismisses Lamminta. Following Hops back to the bridge he gives the order to begin. "Major Cherrick, maneuver us into a landing position at Bravo ramp."

"Bravo ramp in two minutes," reports the primary helmsman of the Hope.

"Minimum power to maneuvering thrusters Major. Don't waste time turning around and land just inside the ramp entrance," instructs Lamminta. "When we move, back out of Bravo and right into Alpha ramp. We need be heading in the right direction and won't have to waste time turning around later. Trilla, how's the concealment device holding up?"

"So far so good, Commander. No signs of strain at all."

"Bravo ramp in one minute," reports Cherrick. "Reducing power it maneuvering minimum. Maneuvering thrusters engaged. Forty-five seconds."

"Just keep her steady and be prepared to back us out of there as soon as I give the word," orders Lamminta. "Engineering."

"Aflo here, sir."

"I want full power to the engines on a moment's notice. We need to be running a little faster this time."

"Understood, sir. You'll have as much power as I can give you."

"Flight Ops," continues Lamminta as he notifies all concerned sections.

"Major Quince just informed me of what's going on. Major Williams is briefing all pilots," immediately replies Dunlipee.

"Good," acknowledges Lamminta. "We may have to go with a stationary launch."

"From inside the launch ramp," questions Dunlipee?

"Yes. I know that's never been tried before, but if this doesn't work we're going to need as much protection as possible."

"Understood, sir. I don't know how it's going to work, but if you want a stationary launch from we'll be ready."

"Bravo ramp in thirty seconds," informs Cherrick.

"Nuk-Ma, what's the Napla doing," asks Lamminta?

"Maintaining a decaying orbit with continuous firing, sir."

"Fifteen seconds."

"Steady," quietly mutters Lamminta.

"Contact in five, four, three, two, one and contact," says Cherrick with a wavering voice.

As the Napla continues firing and moving closer to the Landex, Ge-Kor contacts Mular.

"I can no longer maintain firing without endangering the Landex. Request permission to cease firing and withdraw."

"Permission granted," replies Mular. "If you haven't found them then they must be close to the Landex. Return to your original orbit and be prepared to engage that ship as soon as I find it."

"Understood, Telecoup. The Napla is clear and returning to original orbit."

"Good." says Mular. "All batteries, defensive barrage! FIRE!"

"What's that," exclaims Nuk-Ma? "Commander, the Landex has begun its firing sequence and it feels like it's coming apart. I can't isolate the vibrations origin point. It seems to be coming from everywhere at once."

"With as much energy as they're using this must be a common occurrence," observes Lamminta. "Maintain a watch for the Horses coming out of Alpha ramp. They will launch the instant Mular stops firing. He doesn't want to hit one of his own fighters inside Tirgonian space."

The defensive barrage of the Landex lasts for a full thirty minutes before it suddenly stops.

"Launch fighters," immediately orders Mular! "Launch!"

"Horses coming out of the barn," calls Hops as she looks over the shoulder of Nuk-Ma. "Initial squadron launching. Alpha ramp is clear and if we don't move fast we're going to have horse shit all . . ."

"Launch," orders Lamminta before Hops is able to finish his analysis! "Major Cherrick, I want you to park the Hope in Alpha ramp as gently as if you're landing on eggshells."

"Understood, sir," acknowledges Cherrick as he begins maneuvering the Hope towards is new hiding place. "But I do have a question. What are eggshells?"

"Damn," softly curses Lamminta. "I've been around Hops too long. I'm starting to sound like him." `

"Pardon me, sir," asks the helmsman?

"Just land as delicately as you can," answers Lamminta. "Then plot a direct course back across the Agreed Zone. Once we are back in what used to be our space, I want an evasive course towards Alpha Cheris. Nuk-Ma, I want a continuous scan and sensor reading. I want to know when the secondary squadrons are launch and when Mular begin his recovery operation. Hops, I want you to ensure everything that can fight is ready for a spontaneous launch. We may have to fight our way of her if this doesn't work."

"You're a day late and a dollar short, sir, that's already been care of that. Williams and Quince are in the tubes and Jo in the waiting room. You know, sir, this is like being an expecting daddy. You know it's going to happen, but you're not exactly sure of exactly when."

"Commander," calls Nuk-Ma. "All Horses are out. It looks like Mular is using a standard search pattern. We should be safe for at least thirty minutes, forty-five at the most."

The Tirgonian search pattern requires the employment of ten full squadrons, one hundred Type Seven War Hawk Class Attack Fighters. This huge formation of fighters extends downwards from the uppermost tip of the Fighting Star, as if is displaying a huge banner. After several rotations around this portion of the Landex, with each fighter continually firing before, changes direction. A huge ball of dangerous energy bursts is now encircling the Landex. Whatever is inside the tangled web has little, or no, chance of survival. For more than twenty-five minutes, the onslaught continues unabated.

"Telecoup, this Zu-Art," calls the Senior Flight Officer of the Landex. "Negative contact. The Guardians seem to have somehow managed to escape. Do you wish to continue?"

"Discontinue and recall you fighters," orders Mular as he maintains his attention at the small view screen on the arm of his command chair. Quietly he begins talking to himself. "Who are these people I am now facing? How do they manage to defy their destruction? Maybe I have underestimated their will to survive."

"Commander, Horses returning to the barn," reports Nuk-ma. "Looks like Mular's decided we aren't where we were supposed to be."

"Helm," calls Lamminta! "Get us out of here! Now!"

"Course locked in and executed," replies a female voice, causing Hops head to turn sharply towards the helm.

Lamminta, knowing of the several women now assigned to the bridge crew, grins at his Executive officer. The shift change had not interfered with any of the normal bridge, or other ship operations.

"Sir," says Hops as he continues to observe the helmswoman. "I know we've worn out our welcome and need to leave, but what are you thinking about this time? Once the Horses are back in the barn, and the door is closed, Mular is going to open up with everything he has, and so is Ge-Kor. We are going to take a couple hits on our aft shields before we can get out of range. I don't think our shields can take that much energy without collapsing."

"First squadron down. Second squadron beginning landing sequence," reports Ensign Brooks, the new shifts female scanner officer, causing Hops, with a confused look on his face, to twist his head in the opposite direction.

"First," begins Lamminta. "How much energy do you think it takes to fire all weapons batteries at the same time? Their engines and maneuvering sections have been on minimum power all this time, and if they haven't changed their tactics, which I don't think they have, the Landex does not have enough power on line to move. Mular wants us personally and isn't going to allow Ge-Kor to come after us alone because of what we've been able to accomplish so far. Therefore, even if we do take a few hits, which may be two or three at the most, the bursts will not be very strong. We will be out of effective range before Mular is able to return to full power and give chase."

"When Mular, or Ge-Kor, hit our shields, they will know our course and exactly where we're heading," argues Hops.

"And that's exactly what I want them to think, for the time being. When you are at a disadvantage, you have to turn that into your advantage. That's why I want an evasive course set for Alpha Cheris. I'm planning on Mular to follow his training and keep doing he's been doing. Hopefully we'll be able to stay in one piece for a little while longer."

"One squadron left, sir," reports Ensign Brooks. "And the next one is heading straight for Alpha ramp."

"Launch," immediately orders Lamminta! "Full power! Let's get out of here!"

The Hope lunges forward as it moves from a dead stop to full acceleration. However, just as Lamminta has predicted, the aft shields absorb the energy from the Trigs weapons. The Hope shakes violently as several energy bursts hits the protective deflector shield sooner than anticipated.

"Let's move it, Lieutenant Roberts," comes an almost serene voice as Lamminta steadies himself in his command chair. "We need to get out of here and we need to do it quickly."

"Aye, sir," answers the young officer. "I've diverted additional power from the forward shields to maneuvering. Speed is steadily increasing by point five. If I could divert a little more power from the weapons systems I should be able to get a little more out of her."

"Aflo! Fab! Did you hear that," quickly calls Hops? "Divert all weapons power to the helm! Lieutenant Roberts has her hands full at the moment."

"Will do, Commander," acknowledges Aflo.

"Diverting power," answers Lieutenant Commander Fab.

"Telecoup," calls out Culmit Sprahvic! "Two hits on a moving target and they are almost out of almost out of effective range. Detonation registered at less than ten percent."

"All batteries! Concentrate all fire in that sector! Follow them as soon as the helm responds," immediately orders Mular! "They will want to get away by the fastest course possible and will not waste time changing course."

CHAPTER SEVEN

The Guardians are once again fleeing from the Tirgonian oppressors. For more than an hour, the Hope races ahead of the pursuing Fighting Stars.

"Full stop," suddenly orders Lamminta.

"Sir? I thought we were . . ." begins Hops.

". . . that we're heading back across the Agreed Zone," interrupts Lamminta. "We are, however, I thought that it would be nice to have an escort. Since Mular and Ge-Kor are heading in the same direction as we are, I don't think it would be polite to refuse their hospitality. Helm, set course, and speed to match the Fighting Stars once they pass. Maintain a distance of twenty thousand behind, and between them. Come to yellow alert. Fab, maintain minimum battle stations and lock all weapons on the Landex and Napla. Hops, keep your pilots ready because if this doesn't work . . ."

". . . doesn't work, we're going to have a serious situation on our hands. Where have I heard that before," interrupts Lammintas' Executive Officer? "Sir, are you ever going to be able to do anything that going to keep us out of trouble?"

"I'm trying," answers Lamminta with a smile. "If we can stay one step ahead of Mular, we might be able to make it. I just hope they haven't fixed that minor flaw in their aft sensor array."

"Fighting Stars closing fast, Commander," reports Ensign Brooks. "Landex to port and Napla to starboard."

"What's the distance between them Ensign," asks Hops as he moves to the scanner station?

"Fifty thousand and steady on parallel course, sir."

"Can you establish our position so we can join them without interfering," asks Hops? "I don't want to stop them from doing the best job they can."

"Position, course and speed plotted and have been locked in the navigational computer, sir," reports Lieutenant Roberts. "No problem with staying out of their way. We won't be bothering them at all, sir."

"Hops, how long has it been since you have had a complete rest period," quietly asks Lamminta?

"I just had . . . sir," questions Hops as it strikes him how seemingly unconcerned Lamminta is with the current situation?

"How long has it been since you have had any decent rest? I think it's a reasonable question that you should be able to answer without too much difficulty," clarifies Lamminta. "The rest of the crew has had several complete rest periods, and if my memory serves me correctly, the last full rested rest period you've had was before all of this started. I believe the crew is fully capable of maintaining the operational functions of the Hope for at least the next two watch periods. So therefore, I would *like* you to take a full, and I do mean a *full*, rest period Commander."

"But sir, I don't think . . ." begins Hops.

". . . that you will be needed on the bridge, or anywhere else that might normally require you talents, for at least the next sixteen hours," interrupts Lamminta. "However, you could attempt to continue working in another section of the Hope, such as maintaining the operational functions of the garbage disposal units, but then that would leave me only one alternative."

"Alternative," asks Hops?

"You do remember that I am still the temporary Council General, and that this ship is still under martial law. You do realize what the punishment for disobeying a directive of the Council General is," asks Lamminta? "I'm sure the new members of our security section would appreciate someone being placed in the Detention Facility so they could further their training on a live crewmember."

"But sir, I . . ."

"A full rest period, Commander," comes the stern advice from Lamminta.

"May I stay long enough to make sure Mular and Ge-Kor pass without interference? They'll be passing close on both flanks," counters Hops. "Ensign Brooks, how long before we end up in a sandwich"?

"In what, sir?"

"In a sandwich, Ensign."

"Sir, I don't quite understand what you mean," states Brooks flatly.

"How long before Mular, Commander of the Landex passes to port . . ." begins Hops as he uses his hands to demonstrate his point, ". . . and Ge-Kor, Commander of the Napla, passes to starboard. They represent the bread, placing us in the middle like the roast beef, cheese, lettuce, and tomato with mayo on wheat, a sandwich, Ensign?"

"Stars passing in two minutes, sir," replies Brooks with icy professionalism in her voice.

"This could get a little interesting," says Hops as he moves from one scanner station to another. "Nuk-Ma, get a full scan as they pass."

"Already set up for that, sir. We've been scanning the interior with a low level intensity beam for that past fifteen minutes."

"One minute to passing," calls out Brooks.

"And they haven't caught on to us yet," asks Hops?

"No, sir. Any interference they might pick up would appear to be normal static from an internal sensor malfunction."

"Thirty seconds to passing," reports Brooks.

"Keep your course and speed steady."

"Passing in ten . . . nine . . . eight . . . seven . . . six . . . five . . . four . . . three . . . two . . . one . . . passing complete."

"Nice job. Let's hope they don't figure out where we are or what we're doing just yet."

The two Fighting Stars continue on course, unaware that the prey they were seeking was slipping silently between them.

"Did you get a good look," quickly asks Hops?

"Sure did, sir," replies Nuk-Ma. "Trilla should have a field day with the information."

"Commander Trilla," immediately calls Hops. "Did you receive the scanner information on the Landex and Napla?"

"Yes, sir. But it's going to take a while before I can decipher everything," answers the Research and Development Chief.

"I'm on my . . ."

"You're on your way to enjoy a full rest period, Commander," again interrupts Lamminta.

"But, sir," counters Hops. "I need to . . ."

". . . take a full rest period Commander" admonishes Lamminta.

"But . . ."

"Commander!"

"Aye, sir," reluctantly agrees Hops. "Request permission to leave the bridge."

"Permission granted for that *full* rest period, Commander," enunciates Lamminta.

For the next nine days, the Tirgs continue towards the former Guardian outpost, unknowingly escorting the enemy they were seeking.

"Commander," suddenly calls Nuk-Ma. "A shuttlecraft is leaving the Napla and heading straight for the Landex."

"What's our current weapons status," asks Lamminta?

"Ready and on line, sir," responds Fab.

"Nuk-Ma, keep a lock on that shuttle. Let's hope Mular hasn't found us yet," says Lamminta as he scans the view ahead through the forward observation portal. "This could be a trick to find out if we are in the neighborhood. We need to back off another ten thousand kilometers. Commander Hoppinzorinski, report to the bridge."

"Second shuttle is launching from the Landex, sir," reports Nuk-Ma.

"This is strange," mutters Lamminta. "Fab, lock onto both shuttles. Nuk-Ma, have you been able to determine what Mular is up to yet?"

"Not yet, sir."

Hops returns to the bridge a few minutes later and immediately goes to the scanner station.

"It seems that Mular is trying to find out if we're in the immediate area, sir," begins Nuk-Ma as Hops looks over his shoulder at the scanner display. "It's beginning to appear the he might be trying to set some sort of trap. We didn't realize what was happening until we saw the two shuttles launch. The patrols have been making subtle changes in their formations, positions, and routes. They initially began in this configuration, following their normal patrol pattern. Now they are like this," explains Nuk-Ma as he overlaps two different displays.

"Then it definitely looks like Mular has decided we are not where he though we were," says Hops.

"That's my thought exactly," agrees Lamminta as he observed the same images on his own small scanner display. "I think we have followed our escort long enough. Helm, set course . . ."

"Too late, Commander," calls Nuk-Ma. "The shuttles are deploying some sort of buoy or probe. I'm trying to get an internal reading but there's too much interference right now. My guess is they might be some sort of sensing or mine probes."

"Full stop," quickly orders Lamminta. "Hops, I want Fab, Aflo, Trilla, Probe leaders, and you too Nuk-Ma, in my ready room for a full analysis in fifteen minutes. Major Cherrick, you have the bridge."

As soon as the designated officers are assembled," Lamminta begins. "What do we know so far?"

"It began two days ago," begin Nuk-Ma. "Mular changed the position and formation of the patrols very carefully. We didn't notice anything at first because the changes were so subtle, until one of Mulars Horses from the Napla landed on the Landex.

"Normal procedure if you want to avoid an open communications that could be monitored," observes Hops thoughtfully.

"Exactly," agrees Nuk-Ma. "Shortly after that both Stars began sending out a low intensity pulsating beam. It's not on any of their normal frequencies. We only discovered it when we did an inverted frequency scan. It seems possible that Mular may have discovered a way of detecting us."

"They were bound to accomplish that sooner or later," states Lamminta as he looks towards Trilla. "Is there any way to change the frequency modulation frequency on the concealment device?"

"We've already changed the frequency modulation, sir, but it's only a temporary solution," explains Trilla. "We're working on something more permanent. If Mular looks hard enough, he's bound to find us again."

"Have you been able to determine what's inside those probes yet," continues Lamminta?

"Not exactly, sir, the readings are still incomplete, but if I were to take an educated guess from the pattern they're in, I would have to say they're some sort of explosive device," says Nuk-Ma. "From what I've been able to understand so far, there's a good indication they contain corlathia. If I'm right, there enough explosive material out there to destroy the Hope and another ship just like her. Other than that, all we can pick up are some very strange readings that we're still working on."

"So you're saying Mular may have definitely found a way of detecting us," sums up Lamminta. "However, since Trilla changed the concealment modulation we may be undetectable for the moment, but I wouldn't count on that for very much longer."

"If it is a trap and if we don't enter it, Mular will definitely know we're on to his little discovery," begins Hops. "It won't take a genius to figure out what we did, or how to locate us again. We're going to need to come up with something in his minefield to throw him off our trail. Whatever we come up with has to be big enough for Mular to think it's actually us in the middle of is minefield and it's has to be concealed. Anyone got any brainy ideas?"

"Commander Lamminta," suddenly calls from Cherrick. "The Landex and Napla have slowed to point five and taking up covering positions of the other side of the minefield. Those buoys are still within their weapons range."

"Understood," acknowledges Lamminta as he looks at the faces of the others in the room. "I need suggestions people. We're quickly running out of time and, as Hops said, we need to put something in that minefield besides the Hope."

"Sir," begins the lone female, "What if Ski could put something together something that would only require the addition of a concealment device? I think . . ."

"Do you have any idea of how long that would take," interrupts Hops sarcastically? "Ski doesn't have enough of anything to make a ship the size of the one we're going to fool Mular! Not to mention the time it would take to put together whatever he could design and build. Along with the propulsion unit, which he probable doesn't have enough spare parts to build, what are you going to do about a navigational, or guidance system, let alone a concealment device? What are we supposed to do? Pick up the telephone and call Mular," placing his hand next to his ears, imitating the ancient communications device, saying, "Hello, Telecoup Mular? We know you're looking for us, but we have a little problem. We're going to need about a week to build a ship that we can put in your minefield so when you detonate it, you'll think it's us. We want to fool you again so we can get our collective asses out of here!"

"I don't think it would take as long as you suggest, High Commander Hoppinzorinski," rebuts Carol angrily. "I believe we have the equipment we need in the hanger bay. This equipment hasn't served any useful purpose so far, except as a training aid for the Academy cadets. Theoretically, it would be possible to connect two of our shuttles together. Ski could then route the aft thrusters from the lead shuttle around the aft shuttle. We strip all unnecessary equipment from the shuttles and reprogram the onboard computers of the lead shuttle to accept the addition of the trailing shuttle. The only piece of equipment we would need to install, if Commander Trilla hasn't already done so, is a concealment device. After that, program the proper course to the minefield and kick it out the launch tube."

"It just may work," praised Lamminta. "What do you think, Commander Williams?"

"I say we give it a try, sir."

"Jo-Ich?"

"Sounds like a good idea to me. Commander Trilla," continues Lamminta, "What about the modifications Commander Quince suggests?"

"It shouldn't take more than an hour, no longer than an hour and a half, to get everything modified."

"Commander Fab, keep you weapons batteries locked on both Stars just in case we have to fight our way out of here. Aflo, if we have to move, I want to be able to outrun Mular and Ge-Kor from a dead stop," orders Lamminta as he accepts the plan. "Does anyone have anything else?"

"Looks like I just got out flanked and out gunned," mutters Hop, still skeptical about the radical idea. "But I guess we give it the old college try."

"Hops, notify Ski to begin work on connecting two of the shuttles. Keep me informed on all progress," accepts Lamminta.

As everyone rises to leave, Lamminta motions silently to one of the officers to remain seated. Neither officer speaks until the door closes silently behind them.

"You presented a good idea," quietly begins Lamminta. "I know Hops is a little outspoken, doesn't fully appreciate your talents and I'm well aware of his feelings towards women in general. Everyone has had a rough time adjusting to these surroundings and the events that have forced us together, especially you and your pilots. I know it's been hard, particularly on you, but you're a damn good officer, and one hell of a good pilot. Hops will eventually come around and when he does, it will be completely unexpected. You'll be surprised at his help. You just need to be patient for a little while longer. If you give him enough time, you'll win the fight on his terms. He won't like it, but it will open his eyes as to who, and what, you are, a damn good officer, who just happens to be a fine young woman. Just have a little more patience."

"I'll try, sir," slowly agrees Carol. "But if he pushes, I'm going to push back just as hard."

"That's all I can ask of you," says Lamminta. "Now I think both of us have a lot of work to do. Mular isn't going to wait much longer.

Carol, knowing that she has the support of at least one male onboard the Hope, rises and departs the ready room. By the time she arrives in the main maintenance bay, Ski has two shuttles connected, and is working on routing the lead shuttles aft thrusters around the trailing craft, without interfering with either ship. Apparently, he is not working as fast as Hops thinks he should.

"Ski? What's taking so long? I've known you to do the impossible, with a lot less work, in less time than it takes most people to wipe their ass. Anything I can help with?"

"Sure is, Commander," yells Ski from under the trailing shuttle! "Get back to the bridge and let me finish! I've never done anything like this and I didn't have time to draw up a proper schematic! I'm trying to do this out of my head! If you think you can do this any faster, grab that electromagnetic collective inducer and the integrated circuit scanner and help Trilla align the primary induction coil on the secondary input circuit that connects the reflective imager to the remote imager primary sensor. I still need to realign the backup release system on the lead shuttle to accept the trailing shuttles backup system. If you can't figure how to do that, get the hell out of my way and let me get back to work! With all due respect of course, sir."

Carol turns to hide her face so that no one will see the obvious enjoyment she is receiving from hearing someone putting Hops in his place.

"Bridge to Commander Hoppinzorinski," calls the voice of Lamminta over the maintenance bay intercom.

"Hops here, sir. Everything's about ready. We should be able to hit the launch ramp in another . . ." Hops pauses as he looks at Ski crawling out from under the trailing shuttle and holding up five fingers. Turning towards Trilla, who, exiting the lead shuttle, nods his head in agreement, ". . . five minutes. Trilla and Ski have just finished with the final adjustments. The navigational computer already has the course to the minefield locked in. Green light just came on. Dun can kick this thing out as soon as you give the word."

"Good," acknowledges Lamminta. "I'm going to need someone to give us a little cover just in case this doesn't work. Inform Commander Quince her Probe has been briefed. As soon as she's strapped in, she's to join Commander Jo-Ich outside. I want you and Trilla here on the bridge to help Nuk-Ma with the scanners before Dun launches."

"We're on our way, sir," replies Hops. "Dun! It's all yours. Clear the bay and launch as soon as the old man gives the word."

"Roger, sir," answers Dunlipee. "Bridge, this is the launch bay. All lights are green. Probes Red is already out and Gold is launching now. Transferring launch control of the shuttles to the bridge. They're all yours."

"Acknowledged," replies Lamminta as he switches off the intercom.

"Probes Red and Gold concealed and identified," informs Nuk-Ma.

"Bridge, this is Orange One. Standing by to assist. In the tube and ready for launch."

"Roger, Orange One," says Hops.

"Commander Trilla," says Lamminta. "You have control. Launch the shuttle, ah, shuttles, ah, whatever you call that thing. Let's see if this is going to work."

"Aye, sir," responds Trilla, "Concealment device activated and on line. Launch sequence initiated. Shuttles have cleared the bay. Course and speed constant. Mular should be picking up a target if he still has tracking capability. The shuttles will enter the minefield in seven minutes."

"The Tirgs have locked onto the shuttles," says Nuk-Ma. "They have an active track. No Horses coming out."

"I doubt Mular will launch his fighters," says Lamminta. "That would be an obvious sign that he knows how to detect us."

"Six minute to the minefield," continues to report Nuk-Ma. "Red and Gold maintaining position. Five minutes to contact."

"Telecoup! I have a concealed ship approaching," calls out Culmit Sprahvic.

"Is it the Guardian ship," challenges Mular?

"It has to be sir. I'm getting the same wavering pattern on the scanners as before."

"How soon before it reaches my little surprise?"

"Three minutes and closing, sir, course and speed consistent with the Guardian ship, two minutes to contact."

"I want a fifteen-second count to the middle of our little gift package," instructs Mular.

"Contact in in sixty seconds . . . forty-five seconds . . . thirty seconds . . . fifteen seconds."

Mular suddenly wonders what it might be like if he does not destroy these few remaining Guardians. He understands that the opportunity to again fight this worthy adversary never arise again.

"Ten . . . nine . . . eight . . . seven . . . six . . . five . . . four . . . three . . . two . . . one."

"Detonate," bellows Mular! "NOW!"

In less time than it take to blink nothing remains where the minefield once been. Mular feels a moment of sadness. If a ship was indeed destroyed the scans the debris field would definitely indicate its size.

"I want a complete scan of all debris," orders Mular. "I want confirmation that the last of these Guardian dogs have been destroyed. The logs must prove that I alone destroyed their last remaining ship. I want complete and undeniable evidence of their destruction. Speculation will not be acceptable."

"The debris is definitely Guardian, Telecoup," reports Sprahvic, "but there is not enough debris to indicate a large ship has been destroyed. The amount of debris indicates a smaller ship entered the minefield. The debris is more consistent with what would be two of their Icarus shuttles."

"Shuttlecraft," explodes Mular! "Where are they? Find Them! I want them found and destroyed! Inform the Napla we will continue towards the Alpha Cheris outpost! We destroyed Status Duo twice. They themselves destroyed Capricorn Seven. They must be heading towards Alpha Cheris! Maximum power! Now!"

"Fighting Stars moving away, Commander," informs Nuk-Ma as he watches the scanner images move away from the present location of the Hope. "Looks like Mular just decided we didn't enter his trap and believes we're heading towards Alpha Cheris, sir. Speed and distance is steadily increasing."

"Hold this position until they are completely out of scanner range," orders Lamminta. "The shuttles may not have completely fooled Mular. I don't want to take any chances that will cause him to suddenly turn around and come back here when we start moving. How will it take them to reach Alpha Cheris?"

"Approximately six days, seven and a half hours, sir," answers Nuk-Ma.

CHAPTER EIGHT

The Tirgonian Fifth Battle Group continues towards Alpha Cheris as the Guardians turn, once again following a course that will take them across the territory of their enemy. Temporary Council General Lamminta decides, now that the Hope and her crew appear for the moment to be safe from attack, to convene the Temporary Council of Elders to select a more permanent ruling body. One of the larger recreation lounges had been transformed it into a Council Chamber where the Council will conduct all official business.

"This session of the Council of Elders is called to order," begins Lamminta. "I do not believe it is necessary for me to give a long summation on how we came to this particular time in our history. Therefore, if there are no objections from those present, or from anyone currently on duty, we will proceed with the acceptance of all current records and section logs that have been maintained aboard this ship, as a factual account of our actions without revision or alteration?" All of the Temporary Council Members nod their head in agreement, as Lamminta continues. "All tapes and official logs pertaining to our actions and incidents are hereby entered into the official Council record as an accurate account of our activities since this war started.

"Our next order of business is in respect to the configuration of the Council itself. As we all know, our laws and traditions mandate that at no time shall the Council be under the control of our defense forces. This however was unavoidable, but now, it appears that for the time being, we have outwitted the Tirgs. Therefore, I recommend that we use this time to return to our normal laws and due process. I suggest we organize a formal vote for the expressed purpose of selecting a permanent Council of Elders."

After a brief pause, Lamminta continues, saying, "I have found that I am unable to perform the combined duties of Council General and High Commander. I therefore submit my resignation as Council General. I will also step down as High Commander once another has been selected."

The entire Guardian population raises its voice as one, shaking the walls of the Council Chamber. It takes several minutes before Lamminta is able to quiet the audience and regain control.

"Sir," begins Hops. "You have to reconsider and think about what you're saying. Who else aboard the Hope has the knowledge, or understanding, of how a Council is to conduct the business brought before it? You're the only one with the ability to preside over this, or any other session of the Council. I can't agree with you on this one and I'm voting against you. I say you must continue as our Council General and I vote against your resignation."

Again, the audience raises it voice in favor of Hops proposal with an uproar more vocal than the first. Only after threatening to clear the Chamber is Lamminta able restore order.

"Commander," says Lamminta once the noise subsides "I appreciate your views but I cannot perform the duties as Council General and High Commander, nor can I agree with your opinion. I request a Council vote on my resignation as Council General. Lieutenant Fa?"

"I must agree with Commander Hoppinzorinski, sir," says Fa. "I reject your resignation and vote nay."

"Thank you," says Lamminta and he looks at Williams. "Commander?"

"I think you're going to remain as our Council General, sir," says Williams. "I vote nay."

Breathing a heavy sigh, Lamminta turns towards the only remaining Council Member.

"Commander Quince?"

"Like the others, sir, I vote nay."

Lamminta remains silent from a moment before continuing. "Even though I will vote in favor of my resignation, it seems that I'm stuck and will remain as your Council General. However, since I am to remain as the leader of this Council of Elders, I can no longer retain the position of High Commander. I submit Commander Gandle Hoppinzorinski as my choice for High Commander of the Guardian Defense Fleet. How does the Council vote? Commander Williams?"

"Aye."

"Commander Quince?"

"Affirmative."

"Lieutenant Fa?"

"Aye, sir."

"High Commander Hoppinzorinski," says Lamminta with a slight grin, "how do you vote on your new promotion?"

"As you so eloquently put it just a couple of minutes ago sir, I guess I'm stuck," replies Hops awkwardly.

"Thank you," says Lamminta calmly. "Now that we apparently have two members chosen for the permanent Council of Elders, we must follow the standard process for the selection of the remaining three Council seats. Anyone who wishes to nominate someone for one of these positions will submit their choice to one of the remaining Temporary Council Members. After a list of applicants has been submitted, and finalized, I will schedule the vote for six days after that day. I know this does not allow us much time, but under the circumstances, I believe the sooner we are able to return to our normal ways, the better things will be. Does the Council agree?" Again, all agreed. "Thank you for your patience during these most difficult times. We will reconvene in five days to present the list of candidates. This session of the Council of Elders is adjourned."

The Temporary Council Members receive a finalized list of sixteen names. Everyone on the list must complete a full background check. Even though the Guardians considered themselves a peaceful society, not everyone was as peaceful as outward appearances would indicate. This background check, though limited due to the loss of the primary personnel records, does narrow the list of names. Finally, on the fourth day, the list of acceptable candidates, containing the names of five qualified individuals, and announced during the scheduled meeting of the Temporary Council. The voting location is once again the only room large enough to accommodate such an undertaking is the Council Chamber, now transformed into the voting location.

The voting is soon competed and the tabulation process begins. Only designated security personnel are authorized access to the small computer chip containing the results. The two apparent members of the Council of Elders, and the three remaining temporary members, return to their quarters, where they monitor the tabulation process via their individual view screens.

"Ready room, this is Lamminta, visual and audio."

"Ready room, this is Hops, visual only, turning off the sound."

"Ready room, this is Williams, visual only."

"Ready room, this is Quince, visual only."

"Ready room, this is Fa, visual only."

"Ready room, this is Lamminta, visual only."

The results of the election is complete in less than five minutes. Lieutenant Commander Bell, the Hopes' Senior Security Officer, reactivates audio communications with the Council members.

"Council General, Council Members, the results are complete and the Council may return to the Council Chamber."

"Acknowledged," says Lamminta.

As the current Council Members gather outside the main inter-ship transport pod, Lieutenant Commander Williams begins to speak, "Council General, if I may. Commander Quince, Fa, and I, did not have out names submitted for the Vote, and are technically no longer members of the Council of Elders. We respectfully submit our resignation from the Council and ask that we be permitted to return to the one thing that we were trained for, fly Dragons."

Lamminta looks into the eyes of the trio with understanding. Even though there had not been any contact with the Tirgonian Empire in the past several weeks, there is still the need to maintain routine patrols.

"On behalf of the people, I would like to thank all of you for your service during these most difficult times," says Lamminta as he accepts the resignations. "I believe everyone will understand you absence."

The three Dragon pilots depart as Lamminta and Hops, accompanied by the security detail, enter the transport pod. Once the group arrives at the entrance to the Council Chamber, Commander Bell hands a small box containing the voting results to Lamminta.

As the two guards assigned as the chamber security detail open the doors to the Council Chamber, an immediate hush descends over the gathered audience. Lamminta and Hops proceeding towards the dais notice several objects that had not been previously present.

Scepters, in small holders, had been on the large curved dais, just to the right of each chair, with the tallest scepter in the center. It stands thirty centimeters tall, topped with the symbol of the Guardians, representing the position of the Council General. The Sword of Arms immediately to the right of the Council General is five centimeters shorter and holds the symbol of the military force, indicating this is for the High Commander of the Guardian Defense Fleet. The remaining three staffs are again ten centimeters shorter than that of the High Commander. Atop these scepters is the Guardian Emblem of Peace. The scepters are located at the upper right corner of small view screens and input panel directly in front of each chair. Also on the table are reddish-brown folders, embossed with the same images as the scepter it accompanies, just to the left of the view screens.

On their way to the slightly raised stage, Lamminta pauses next to the man given the nickname of 'Merlin' and whispers, "Well done, Ski. If I hadn't known better, I would have guesses that you somehow appropriated them from the Grand Council Chamber back home. Thank you."

Lamminta and Hops continue towards the platform with measured strides. Silently, they climb the three steps to the stage, stopping behind their respective chairs. The one reserved for the Council General being slightly taller, and a little more elegant, than the others are. The two men step in front of their respective chair, quietly take their seats, indicating the audience should also return to their seats.

"Guardians, the first thing I would like to do is to complete the Council of Elders," quietly begins Lamminta. Placing the small data disc into a slot just in front of his view screen, revealing the results of the Vote. "You have chosen well. Please allow your new Council Members to come forward and take their place before you. You have chosen William Tro-Ja, Al-Sas Pidera, and Carol Quince."

At the announcement of the last name, Hops turns his head quickly towards Lamminta. The Council General answers with only with a slight smile and shrug of the shoulders.

Two of the newly elected Council Members seated in the chamber and rise amid the heartfelt congratulations of those they passed on their way to the dais. They only have the time it takes them to move to their new positions in front of those gathered to comprehend their new roles.

Lieutenant Commander Quince, monitoring the proceedings from the confines of her Dragons cockpit, does not initially comprehend what has just happened until she receives an unusual request.

"Gold One, this is com-link. The Council General requests the presence of all Council Members in the Council Chamber, congratulations Council Member."

Carol, stunned by the unexpected announcement, returns to the Hopes' landing bay. Though an experienced pilot and Probe Leader, her landing is less than textbook perfect. Still dressed in her flight uniform, she is still in a mild state of shock as she enters the Council Chamber a few minutes later. However, instead of leaving her flight helmet in the cockpit of her ship, as is the normal procedure for all pilots, she has it cradled under her arm. She is also carrying her small flight pad.

"And now the Council is complete," says Lamminta as Carol sits in the only empty chair, next to Hops. Taking a deep breath, he says the words that have begun every general session of the Council of Elders since the very first gathering. "The Council is present and is prepared to give audience. May your faith in our traditions and laws guide you and you your thoughts."

A spontaneous cheer erupts from the audience that quickly subsides once Lamminta raises his hand, silently calling for quiet.

"Our first order of business is to have the Council take the Oath of Office," says Lamminta as he motions for the Council to stand.

Chaplain O'Connell, sitting in the front row, reserved for the senior staff, stands, and moves directly in front of Lamminta.

"Council General, High Commander, and Council Members, will you please raise you right hand and repeat after me" begins the Senior Chaplain.

> *"I . . . state your full name . . . do solemnly swear, or affirm, . . . that I will faithfully discharge my duties as, please state your Council position . . . to the best of my abilities . . . I will protect the laws and traditions passed down by those who have served before me . . . and in accordance with the Charter of Guardian Rights and Privileges . . . I will fulfill my obligations to the people . . . regardless of race . . . ethnic origin . . . personal or religious beliefs or practices . . . To all Guardians I give my first allegiance . . . to all others I give my Honor."*

Again, the audience erupts in a tremendous outburst and again Lamminta quiets the crowd with only the raising of his hand.

"Thank you, Chaplain O'Connell," says Lamminta as he and the Council return to their seats. "Now that we have finally returning to our somewhat normal ways of life, I would like to express the deep gratitude of the Council to everyone during these unsettled times.

"Now, to our next and possible the most important decision we will make today. Our choice will determine the future of our civilization for eons to come. Where do we go from here? We know of only two places within the know sectors and quadrants of space, what used to be our own territory and the territory of the Tirgonian Empire.

As far as we have been able to determine, there is nothing left of that which once belonged to us to which we could possible return and live with any degree of safety. There is also a very distinct possibility that the Tirgonian Supreme Commander would be less than willing to allow us to settle on one of the Empires smallest, unsettled planets. Therefore, I can only find two options at this time. First, we could return to own territory and hope to fine an obscure, uninhabited planet that we currently do not know about where we could attempt to return to our ways. Our second option would be to continue on our present course and try to find the far border of the Tirgonians. If such a border exists, we cross it and continue looking for a suitable planet on which we can settle. I can only hope that whoever controls that area allows us to either settle there, or allows us to continue on our way peacefully. Council Member Pidera, what are your thoughts on this matter?"

"Council General," begins Pidera, a slightly balding, middle-aged man sitting next to Lamminta, "even though we may no longer have absolute control over what is left of our original territory, I do not believe the Tirgs would be willing to conquer more territory than their military forces could effectively control. We have accurate maps and charts of all known star systems within our territory. However, as of now I do not believe we have accurate charts that would allow us to navigate safely through Tirgonian space. If we maintain our current course, we will eventually move beyond what limited information we have. I say we should return to our territory and, as you stated just a moment ago, hope to fine an obscure, uninhabited planet that we currently do not know of and try to return to our ways. There, we would be able to again grow, live in peace, and be safe from future attacks."

"Thank you, Council Member Pidera," says Lamminta. "Council Member Tro-Ja, what is your opinion on this matter?"

Tro-Ja, a man of considerable height and girth, leans back slightly as he begins speaking. "Council General, I have given this matter much thought during the past several weeks of running, fighting and hiding. I am in agreement with Council Member Pidera. We would be safer in familiar surroundings. Eventually we are going to need to resupply our expendable items. We have unlimited knowledge of our territory, but only limited knowledge of the Tirgonian Empire that lies beyond the immediate border sectors. In comparison, the Empire has limited knowledge of our territory that lies beyond the sectors immediately next to the Agreed Zone. We don't know where, or when, we might be able to find what we would need if we are to continue across Tirgonian space. We would be able to find what we will need a lot easier in our own territory. And, as you yourself once said sir, we should use our knowledge to our advantage, not to our disadvantage."

"Thank you, Council Member Tro-Ja," accepts Lamminta as he turns to the other side of the table and asks, "Council Member Quince, where do you think we should go?"

Though still uncomfortable with her new position, Carol slowly, and carefully, chooses her words. "Council General, I am in respectful disagreement with Council Members Pidera and Tro-Ja. With the way recent events have unfolded, I believe the Tirgs have a very intimate knowledge of our territory and star systems. I don't believe we'd be able to find any place of safe refuge within our former borders where the Tirgs couldn't, or wouldn't eventually find us.

"We've been in and out of Tirgonian territory since leaving Capricorn Seven. Our scanners and weapons systems are more accurate and have a greater range than the Tirgs, giving us the ability to detect the smallest artificial energy emission given off by their colonies or outposts. We know they can't detect us since Commander Trilla reconfigured the frequencies for the concealment device. Therefore, finding and crossing the far border of Tirgonia should not be too difficult.

"As far as the re-supply problem that has been raised by Council Member Pidera, we could use concealed Dragons, along with the remaining training shuttles, to raid the Tirgs bases and colonies. They're trying to destroy us, so why shouldn't they provide us with what we're eventually need?"

Lamminta pauses as he considers the opinion of Carol before the same question to the remaining Council Member. "High Commander, what is your opinion?"

"I guess I have to agree with Council Member Quince," begins Hops. "Safety lies where we aren't expected. We've been able to hold our own against the Tirgs so far, but who's to say how long our luck is going to hold? I say we should continue on our present course across Tirgonia. Once we find and cross their far border, we make contact with whoever's running the store, explain our situation and hope they will help. If not, we move on. We know we aren't going to be safe back in our own territory, so that means we have to go where we haven't been or expected to be."

Again, Lamminta pauses slightly before speaking. "We have heard the thought and words from the members of the Council. Is there anyone present, or at their duty stations, who has any other thoughts on where we should go, or how we should proceed on the matter before us today?"

"Council General," calls a voice from the audience.

“Guardian,” acknowledges Lamminta. “Please come forward so that we may hear your words.”

Slowly a woman moves from her seat and walks down the main walkway to stand in front of the Council.

“I am Colette Robison of the Guardian ship Hope,” begins the gray haired woman with a strong and proud voice. “I believe there is a third option the Council may wish to consider. This option would combine certain elements of the first two proposals. A course along and parallel to the Agreed Zone could be followed. We would have the ability to attack the Tirg outposts along the border, as well as any other targets of opportunity we might encounter. At the same time, with the extended range and accuracy of our sensors and scanners, we would be able to gather valuable information about their current defenses. Once we’ve collected the necessary information, we would be in a better position to determine where we would be safe from future attacks and how to get there while having the safety of our own territory as an escape mechanism should the need arise.”

“The Council accepts and respects your opinion,” says Lamminta as the elderly woman finishes. “Please forgive me, madam, but I seem to know you from somewhere other than Capricorn Seven.”

“I only arrived on Capricorn Seven a few days before the attack. I think it would be better if you were to concentrate on the more immediate problem of our survival than where you might remember an old lady,” says the elderly woman as she bows slightly and quietly whispers, “Jughead.”

The word catches Lamminta by surprise but he does not say anything further until the woman returns to her seat in the audience.

“Madam,” begins Hops. “A show of . . .”

He gets no further as Lamminta watches at the woman as she returns to seat. Shaking his head, he quietly whispers to Hops “Forget it. It’s okay.” Returning to his normal tone, he says, “Is there anyone else who wishes to address the Council on this matter?” No one else speaks up, allowing Lamminta to continue. “The Council will address the people after considering all of the options and opinions presented here today. The Council would also like to thank everyone for his or her patience and understanding during these most difficult times. This session of the Council of Elders is adjourned.”

With these last words spoken, the five members of the Council rise and retrieve their scepters and folders. Council Member Quince, still dressed in her flight uniform, has a slight problem. Lamminta, noticing her predicament as she tries to gather her symbols of office, as well as her flight helmet and flight pad, clears his throat in an attempt to gain her attention. It does not initially work, so he cleared his throat a little louder. After clearing his throat for a third time, he is able to get not only to attract her attention, but the attention on the first several rows of the audience. Glancing at the helmet and flight bag, he shakes his head slightly. Carol retrieves her scepter and folder, leaving the objects of her embarrassment where they lay.

CHAPTER NINE

As the Council leaves, the Council Chamber Lamminta informs them that he would like to meet with them in his quarters.

"Please sit and make yourselves comfortable," begins Lamminta as the door silently closes behind him. Turning first to face Carol he says, "First, I would like to apologize to you for your embarrassment in the Chamber. As you know, our process is not as perfect as we would like to believe. I had no way knowing the three names selected by the Vote. I could only announce them and hope for the best. I hope you will forgive our oversight."

"There is no need to apologize, sir," replies Carol. "I'm just a little confused on how I was chosen to be a Council Member. My name wasn't submitted for the vote."

"It's one of the oldest voting traditions dating back several centuries. I'd forgotten this tradition even existed. It has been our tradition that every citizen has the right to write a on the ballot, even though that persons' name was not have been submitted for the vote, with that person receiving that vote. To my knowledge, this method of voting has not been use for several centuries. The last time this method of voting occurred, was for the members of the original Council of Elders. However, it seems that enough of the people remembered because you are now a Council Member."

"Council General, I don't think I'm qualified for to serve as a Council Member," quietly says Carol as she sits next to Pidera.

"The important thing is that the people think you are qualified," answers Lamminta.

"I guess all I can do is to try to do the best I can."

"That is all any of us can do," agrees Lamminta. "I think we need to get down to the business at hand. Hops, it looks like recent events have changed your command structure and you're going to need to make a few personnel changes."

"Don't I know it," mumbles Hops.

"It was one of those things that could not have been foreseen," says Lamminta. "Who will you be naming as your Senior Flight Officer?"

"Williams will take over as Senior Flight Officer and since one of my other Probe Leaders just got voted to the Council, it looks like I'm going to have to promote two of my Dragon drivers instead of one."

"Who are you thinking about assigning as Orange and Gold Probe Leader," asks Tro-Ja, not giving Hops much time to think the replacements?

"Captain Hoblick will take over Orange and Captain Star will take charge of Gold," answers Hops. "Both names will be submitted, along with Williams, for promotion as soon as we finish up here."

"Why, High Commander, I never would have thought that you had it in you," says a surprised Carol, and then quickly adds. "I'm sure you've made a wise choice. My congratulations will be forwarded to them."

"Very well, High Commander," says Lamminta. "The recommendations will be confirmed at the next formal Council meeting. Now, I think we need to decide what our next move is going to be."

The Tirgs have not been idle during the past several weeks. Mular and Ge-Kor complete their journey back to the destroyed outpost without detecting their prey. They arrive at Alpha Cheris and conduct detailed search. Mular orders the outpost destroyed in the same manner that Lamminta used to destroy Capricorn Seven.

"I want to know where they are," screams Mular! "Where are they! Before they were always coming at us and attacking! Now they hide! Before they would use words, then more words, and still more words before they would turn and fight! Now, they no longer talk! They fight without talking! Their actions were once predictable, but now they use treachery, deceit and attack us from inside our own territory! I want to know the name of this man who uses deceit and weapons instead of words! I want the name of this man!"

"Sir," quietly says Ge-Kor after Mular finishes his ranting. "Since we have not had any contact with the Guardians for more than two weeks I believe they have had time to create a new ruling Council. If this has happened, they may have already returned to their way of words. If this has happened, they will debate every possibility before they make the simplest decision. If have created a new Council, it could mean they may again become complacent and vulnerable. We would once again have the advantage."

"IF," screams Mular. "What 'IF' they haven't created a new Council of Elders! What 'IF' they continue to fight! I do not want to hear 'IF'! I want to hear answers! I want to know the name of this man who fights from hiding! I want to know what his options are! I want to know what his next move is going to be! Where will he go! When will he show himself again! We have the information and data from their last attacks and I want that information used to outguess and outfight him. I want him and his ship destroyed! I will not accept failure!"

"Telecoup, I can foresee only three obvious options available to the Guardians at this point," says Sub-Telecoup Zu-Art, the only person in the room bold enough to speak. "First, they could remain in their own territory. Second, they could attempt to cross Tirgonia, and third, they could travel along what used to be the Agreed Zone."

Mular leans forward, crossing his arms on the table in front of him. Staring harshly at Zu-Art, he says, "Continue."

"Considering the first option, there isn't anything left for them here in their territory. They would be helpless without support or a base where they could replenish their expendable supplies. They would be returning to nothing and they understand this. For these same reasons, I do not think they would travel along the Agreed Zone because they would encounter the same difficulties. If I had to make a choice based on this information, I would attempt to cross the territory of my enemy. I would be able to conduct re-supply raids and gather intelligence for future reference. I would be able to learn more about my enemy than they would want me to know. It would also be the last place they would look for me. I would be safer, able to mend my wounds and become stronger to fight from inside my enemies' territory. However, I do not believe they will be willing to continue this fight for much longer. They are a peaceful race and will soon tire of the constant fighting. They will once again become complacent and weak. That will be when they will make their fatal mistake. I suggest we use the information we now possess to plot their possible course across Tirgonia. We set a trap for them before they can make it to the Paporian border."

"Your evaluation is commendable, Zu-Art, but do not underestimate them," says Mular as he leans back in his chair. "We are not fighting an enemy who is complacent, weak, nor humble. These Guardians are stronger than we initially thought. Have you already forgotten how they attacked and destroyed your best Pilinicun squadron? Do you not remember their clever tactic of using this very ship on which to hide? How they used shuttlecraft to evade the minefield? Have you not learned anything," counters Mular? "However, I do agree with what you have proposed. Regardless how far they may travel form a given course, they will always return to one basic direction. Once we know their basic course, we will be able to determine their next target where I be waiting for them. Then I will have the honor of completing their destruction."

"Ge-Kor," continues Mular thoughtfully, "you will proceed to Paporia Two. The Supreme Commander is on an inspection tour there. You will personally inform him of our plans. I will return to the last position where we had contact with the Guardians and will use that point for all future position reports. You will rejoin the Landex as soon as you inform the Supreme Commander and he has given you the orders we require to continue and attack them inside our territory. Are there any questions," ask Mular, not really expecting anyone to answer? "The Napla will depart within as soon as you return to your Star and I will follow in twelve hours. That will give you time to be completely out of the area and not interfere with my scans. Dismissed."

The Tirg officers rise and depart Mulars' ready room. Ge-Kor returns to the Napla and issues his orders as soon as he steps out of his shuttle.

"Contact the Landex and inform Telecoup Mular that we are ready to depart."

"Sub-Telecoup," answers the Communications Officer. "Telecoup Mular orders you to depart immediately. You are also to report all contact with the Guardians."

"Acknowledge the message," replies Ge-Kor. "Helm, set course for Paporia Two, maximum power."

"Sir," calls Nuk-Ma from his position at the scanner console. "I've got a target. It just came into scanner range and it's definitely a Star. Course is six two seven by four eight nine. It looks like they're heading somewhere in one hell of a hurry. They're going to have us on their screens in less than three minutes."

"Red Alert! Engage the concealment device," immediately orders Hops. "It looks like it's time to play hide and seek again. Cherrick, plot a matching course but keep us out of their scanner range. Fab, bring all weapons to standby. Novac, any idea where that Star might be heading?"

"Not yet, sir."

Commander Williams enters the bridge and immediately moves to the scanner station, asking, "What do we have, sir?"

"Looks like a Tirg Star heading this way," replies Hops.

"Sir, if they maintain a constant course there are several planets that could be their destination," reports Lieutenant Commander Novac. "There may be something else out there that we don't know about."

"Nuk-Ma, which Star is it this time? Get a scan on any other Star that might be following," anxiously asks Hops. "I'm getting a little tired of playing cat and mouse with Mular."

"Only one Star so far sir. It's the Napla. Nothing on the Landex so far."

"Then where in the hell is Mular," mumbles Hops? "Did they pick us up before we got hid?"

"No sir, we made it okay," answers Trilla.

By now, the entire Council is on the bridge. With limited space the additional, and at the moment unnecessary personnel is more than Hops wants.

"Council General," begins Hops as he tries to move through the human maze towards the Captains' Chair. "If you please, sir, we seem to have a situation that requires my undivided attention. We don't have anything on the Landex yet. If Ge-Kor decides to take a left turn and head south, I'm going to have my hands full. Right now, it looks like fourth and ten, we're on our own goal line with the score tied, and we have less than five seconds on the clock. I've got one chance to throw a Hail Mary and hope I don't want to get a penalty for pass offensive interference. The Council can monitor all actions and reports from my ready room. I think you might be a little more comfortable sitting there than standing up out here. Now if you will excuse me, I need to figure a way out of this mess."

This is Hops polite way of asking, or as he would have put it, ordering someone, off the bridge, even if it is the entire Council.

"Of course, High Commander, the Council apologizes for such an intrusion at this most inopportune time," says Lamminta. "Council Members, if you will accompany me to the High Commanders ready room. It seems that he requires a little extra room just in case he needs to make a right turn and head north."

Without waiting for the departure of the Council, Hops return to the situation as hand. "What's the distance to the Napla?"

"Three hundred thousand kilometers and closing fast," reports Nuk-Ma. "If we don't move, sir, we're going to get run over. We may be faster and a little more maneuverable, but I think a Star is a hell of a lot bigger."

"I agree. It's not a bad idea to take out a Star but I think there's a better way of doing it than to have it run over us. Cherrick, move us into a passing position. As soon as the Napla passes, execute a following course but don't get any closer than forty thousand kilometers. Nuk-Ma, keep your eyes peeled for Mular coming out of left field."

"Aye, sir."

As soon as the Council enters the ready room, their attention turns immediately towards the view screens on the conference table.

"Excuse me, sir," says Tro-Ja as he takes a seat across from Lamminta?

Without looking up from the view screen, Lamminta replies with a simple, "Yes."

"What did the High Commander mean when he stated the situation could take a left turn and head south," asks Tro-Ja with a puzzled look on his face? "If the Tirgs do find us they would be coming from our port side, not a cardinal direction. I do not understand what he meant by fourth and ten, on our own goal line, with the score tied and only five seconds left on the clock. From what I see in front of me, the Napla is at least an hour away. In addition to that, why would he want to throw someone named Mary just because her name is Hail, and what is pass interference," asks the Council Member? "Are you sure it is wise to have someone in such a position that constantly speaks in riddles at almost every critical situation?"

Still not taking his eyes off the view screen in front of him, Lamminta answers, "A left turn and head south means things could suddenly change for the worse. Something coming out of left field is the High Commanders way of saying trouble could come from any direction. As far as the other terms, I believe they refer to an old earth game called American style football. Apparently, he thinks it's the end of the game and he has time for only one more chance to win. He has to make the right decision the first time because there may not be time for a second try. What he means by pass interference or why he would want to throw someone just because her name is Hail Mary, I'm not sure. I can only guess that it has something to do with our current situation. As far as your concerns about the High Commander and his way of speaking in critical situations, he is definitely the right person for the job. I don't think we could have a more capable individual in command, Council Member, present company included. I have every confidence in High Commander Hoppinzorinski, personally and professionally."

"Is it not our tradition, which you yourself said we must return to, requires the full Council to give final approval before any major action can be taken by our military forces," says Pidera in a sarcastic tone. "The High Commander has apparently assumed the authority of the full Council. He has violated at least three, maybe four of the fundamental laws of our society. These actions require that he surrender his position as High Commander and answer for his crimes against the people. He is unnecessarily endangering this ship and the lives of everyone on board."

Council Member Quince is getting a little upset at the inability of Tro-Ja and Pidera to comprehend the urgency of the situation. She knows that she is not fully comfortable being in close quarters with Hops but realizes that if they are to survive, he is their best chance. Lamminta, sensing Carol's discomfort again speaks in defense of Hops.

"You are correct, Council Member. The Council must approve all major military decisions and the current actions of the High Commander certainly qualify as a major military decision. Apparently, he believes in a course that will take us across Tirgonia. I suggest the rest of us should now consider our position on this matter and make a formal ruling before we get too far and can no longer turn back. Council Member Quince, what is your opinion?"

"Council General, I agree with High Commander Hoppinzorinski. I would also like to add that we should give the High Commander a little more freedom, within reason of course, to conduct military operations without requiring the consent of the Council when a critical situation such as this suddenly develops. If we stop to debate every possible action in a time of crisis we'll never be able to survive or return to a peaceful existence."

"Thank you, Council Member," says Lamminta. "Council Member Tro-Ja, what is your opinion?"

"With due respect and understanding to Council Member Quince, I believe she is still too recently associated with military actions, and thinking, to look at this, or any other critical situation, objectively. I say we should return to our own territory and never forego our tradition of the Council controlling our defense forces. This tradition has served us well in the past and will again serve us in this or any other future situation that requires the use of force. We should remain as we have always been and resolve all situations, as we have in the past, with negations, not weapons. I say that all major military decisions must be approved by the Council."

"Council Member Pidera, what do you have to say on this matter," asks Lamminta of the lone remaining Council Member?

"Council General, I am in full agreement with Council Member Tro-Ja. We should return to our own territory and maintain our traditions. The Council should approve all military decisions, but only after peaceful negotiations have failed."

"Thank you, Council Members. It seems that I must now cast the deciding vote," says Lamminta thoughtfully. "I agree with Council Member Quince and High Commander Hoppinzorinski. We should continue across Tirgonia. I also agree that we should increase the latitude of authority for the High Commander. In difficult times, we do tend to debate too much. If the Tirgs were to suddenly attack, our traditions would require the full Council to convene, discuss, and debate before we make any decision. What are we to do with the Tirgs while we take our time trying to decide what we're going to do? Do we ask them to stop their attack until we make our decision? I think, as the High Commander would say, that would place us in left field. I don't believe our people need a left turn from the Council." Turning he gives Carol with a slight grin, he continues, saying, "It now seems that the High Commander is not in contradiction with the Council, or our due process. Council Member Quince, would you be kind enough to inform the High Commander of our decision? Progress is such a wonderful thing. This meeting is adjourned," concludes Lamminta before anyone could object.

CHAPTER TEN

"Come to Yellow Alert," orders Hops. "Commander Trilla, it looks like it's about time to make sure your baby doesn't fall asleep because it's time to play hide and seek again. Fab, bring you're batteries online and make sure your powder stays dry. We might have to fight our way out of this. Nuk-Ma, what's Ge-Kor doing?"

"Course and speed unchanged, sir. Range twenty thousand kilometers. Passing at ten thousand in two minutes."

"Helm, engage and follow in five minutes," continues ordering Hops. "Maintain forty thousand kilometers separation. Nuk-Ma, let me know if there's any change in the Napla's course or speed. Trilla, you might want to get yourself an extra babysitter. I don't think we need any temper tantrums because you miss a feeding. Commander Williams, the bridge is yours. I need to brief the Council on why I just did what I did and hope they don't put me in front of a firing squad."

"Aye sir, and good luck," acknowledges Williams. As Hops leaves the bridge he moves to the scanner station occupied by Lieutenant Commander Nuk-Ma and quietly asks, "What in the hell is he talking about?"

"He just wants an extra set of eyes on the concealment device just in case there's any malfunction. He doesn't want any surprises."

"If that's what he wants, why doesn't he just say so," asks Williams? "Sometimes I'm not quite sure exactly what he's asking me to do or what he really wants."

"Don't worry, Commander, if he says anything you don't understand just ask him what he means," says Nuk-Ma. "You'll figure that out what he's talking about the longer you're around him."

"I hope we're all around that long," says Williams as he pats Nuk-Ma on the shoulder.

Council Member Quince, on her way out of the ready room to complete the task given to her by the Council General, is not expecting the High Commander to be at the doorway and is moving at a slightly quicker than normal pace.

"Whoa," exclaims Hops as he collides with Carol, grabbing her arm to keep her from falling backwards. "Who are you running from?"

"Excuse me, High Commander," says Carol as she releases her grip from his arm and regains her balance.

"No need to apologize," says Hops. "If you'll excuse me, I think I have some explaining to do."

"Of course," says Carol as she returns to the ready room.

As the door closes behind Hops, he is a little puzzled at the quick return of someone who was just leaving. Not waiting for any explanation he begins, "Council General, Council Members, I apologize for making such a hasty decision without requesting approval from the Council. I ask for the Councils' indulgence so I can explain my actions."

"High Commander," says Lamminta. "The Council does not disagree with your actions. Nor does the Council understand why you feel it is necessary to submit an apology. The Council has already discussed your actions, along with the options available, during our recent meeting. The Council agrees with your decision and the option of continuing across Tirgonia. Therefore, I am a little confused as to why you have left the bridge during this critical situation to explain something that the Council is in full agreement with."

"I wasn't told of any Council meeting, sir," replies Hops who appears more confused than before. "By our laws, I'm required to get Council approval for any major military action before that mission can be executed? I'm still required to explain my actions to the Council for making any major decision, and taking action on that decision, without Council approval?"

"I tell you again, High Commander," says Lamminta with a slight grin on his face. "You did act without Council approval. With your actions, you placed the immediate situation, and your vote, before us. The rest of the Council merely proceeded with the process you began. In addition, the Council has, if you agree, to allow you, and all future High Commanders, to have a little more freedom in making critical decisions and take action on that decision without receiving prior approval from the Council."

"I think that would be a good idea, sir," answers Hops, still a little confused.

"Then that's the way it shall be," says Lamminta. "Now that that has been settled, I think you should return to the bridge."

"Yes, sir," says Hops as he turns and departs the ready room, still unsure of what has just transpired.

"No change in the Napla's course or speed," reports Williams as Hops enters the bridge. "Maintaining a following course at forty thousand, concealment device holding steady and weapons are on line and standing by."

"Maintain heading, speed, and separation," orders Hops. "Nuk-Ma, have you been able to determine if Mular has the Landex hidden anywhere in the neighborhood?"

"No sir, nothing to indicate the Landex is anywhere close by. Mular wouldn't let the Napla go off on her own without something up his sleeve."

"I agree, maintain a long-range scan behind us. Orin," continues Hops, "I'm going to need all Dragon drivers standing by just in case Mular shows up and decides to crash our party. Trilla, what are the chances of Mular finding us again?"

"Slim to none, sir. I set the concealment frequency to continually automatically oscillate the frequency modulate. If they did happen to find any of the random frequencies, they would have it for only a microsecond before losing it. The frequency selection is strictly random. Without any set pattern to detect, I don't think I could find us if I had to. We should be safe for quite a while."

"That's what scares me," says Hops. "If you can figure out something like that, Mular will probable figure out a way to compromise it and find us again. Just keep those scans going behind us. Fab, is there any way to increase the strength of the rear deflectors? I don't like heading in one direction while being kicked in the ass from the other. I want you to get Ski and Aflo to figure out something that will give us some better protection aft."

"I'll get with them and we'll figure it out, sir," replies the senior weapons officer. "I'll keep you posted on what we come up with."

"Good," acknowledges Hops. "Orin, after you get your pilots moving, I want you and all Probe leaders in my ready room. Trilla, Novac, I'm going to need both of you there as well. The Council should be out of there by now. Nuk-Ma, you have the bridge."

As three of the four men requested leave the main bridge, they see the Council walking down the corridor. Within a few minutes, Commander Williams and the Probe Leaders enter the ready room.

Not wasting any time, Hops immediately begins his briefing. "Grab a seat. As you know, we have a slight problem and I'm going to need some help figuring out what exactly we're going to do. Orin, I want you to get the Intel and Security to go over every scrap of information we have on the Tirgs since this nightmare began. If we end up in another fight, I want to know the best way to win. I'm also going to need a course we can follow without depending on any help. I don't think it would be a good idea to get too close to any of their outposts or bases unless we intend to do a little raiding of our own.

"Next, and this is why you Probe leaders are here, I want specific information on the damage the Landex suffered during every encounter we've had with it. I want to know what's inside that damned Star at the damaged point and exactly how bad was Mular hurt. Coordinate everything with Trilla.

"The reason for putting Probe leaders on this is for your own information. When we get into our next fight, you're going to need as much specific information as possible, as quick as possible. Briefing work, but when you need something you need it right then. It doesn't do anyone any good to need something and find out you're going to have to wait for an answer, especially when you have a herd of stampeding Horses trying to trample you to death. I don't like losing anyone, especially because someone forgot to get a piece of vital information when they needed it the most.

"In addition to all that, we're going to need to know where their supply and support bases are located. I don't want to get a surprise from one of them. Start with the known locations around Tirgonia and work out from there. They have to have something somewhere out here that is able to re-fit a damaged Star. I want everything, regardless of how insignificant or crazy it sounds, to be coordinated with Trilla, and I want updates on anything you find. Are there any questions?"

"Sir," asks Lieutenant Commander Hoblick? "I understand what you want us to do and from an intelligence standpoint we should be able to determine their obvious strengths and weaknesses. We should also be able to determine the internal damage we may have caused to the Landex and the possibly location their supply bases but, may I speak freely, sir?"

"Of course, Hobby, anytime."

"I've known you for a long time sir and I know that you don't always go for the obvious. What exactly are we looking for this time?"

"I don't know," answers Hops carefully as he slowly moves about the room. "There's something we've missed. Something just doesn't feel right and I want as many eyes looking at everything and go over every scrap of information we have. With everyone going over the same information and data from different angles, we should be able to find whatever it is that we've missed. Anyone got anything else?" All remain silent as Hops ends the meeting. "Okay I guess that's it then. Everyone knows what to do, so let's get it done."

"Okay guys and gals," says Williams as he pushes his chair away from the conference table. "I'll meet everyone in Probe Ops in fifteen minutes. Be prepared for some long nights. Inform your second-in-command they're in charge until further notice."

Hops remains in the ready room after the others leave. After almost half an hour of quite thought, he returns to the bridge, still wondering how he can help these few remaining Guardians to survive long enough to find a new home where they will return to their peaceful ways.

CHAPTER ELEVEN

Telecoup Mular maintains his position at Alpha Cheris as the Napla disappears from the scanner screen. He, like his adversary, is trying to find a weakness in his opponents' armor.

"Helm, bring the engines on line and follow the Napla. Maintain an exact matching speed and course. Culmit Olderin, you have the bridge. I want constant scans on all frequencies and, as soon as we find these Guardians, you will be notified me immediately." quietly orders Mular as he activates the ships intercom. "Sub-Telecoup Zu Art, this is Mular. Report to my ready room."

"Telecoup," says Zu-Art as he enters Mulars' private domain.

"I have changed my plan," begins Mular as the Senior Flight Officer stands before him. "Only the bridge crew, and now you, know of this at this time. I do not believe the Guardians have returned to their side of the Agreed Zone. I have decided to follow the Napla sooner that I previously ordered. If these whore-dogs have become as capable as I believe they have, once they detect the presence of the Napla and determine her destination is Paporia Two, they will not be able resist such an escort across the Empire.

"We will maintain a distance just beyond the scanner range of the Napla. If the Guardians do follow, as I suspect they will, they will be well within our scanner range. As soon as we have detected their presence, you will launch every fighter you have and engage their covering patrols. I will then move the Landex close enough to engage their ship."

"I understand your plan, Telecoup, but their weapons have greater range and accuracy than before. How do you plan to get close enough to their mother ship to engage it without suffering additional damage to the Landex," asks Zu-Art?

"By using the fighters, I believe . . ."

"My fighter squadrons are . . ." interjects Zu-Art.

"Do not interrupt me! I am in command of this Battle Group and I will give the orders that my fighter squadrons will follow," bellows Mular! "When the Pilinicuns attack, the sheer number of fighters I will send to conduce the initial attack will cause the reaction time of these infidels to be slightly slower. They will be distracted, but for only a moment. Their forces will be engaging over two hundred fighters at once. Their scanners will be so full of targets they will not notice the Landex moving to attack until it is too late. The fighters will provide me with the advantage I need to destroy them. Assign the pilots as necessary to make a coordinated attack. Their aft deflectors and energy absorption shields are their weakest defensive point so plan your strongest attack there. The attack must be swift to deny them the opportunity to come about. Ge-Kor will be concentrating strictly on his forward scans, his energy batteries will not be on line, and his fighter squadrons will still be in the hanger bay. I will not be able to contact the Napla for any assistance because the Guardians will be monitoring all frequencies. I will only be able to recall the Napla once the attack begins, therefore, the primary duty of distracting them will be your responsibility. Do not fail me again, Zu-Art. Do you understand?"

"Yes, sir," replies a humbled Flight Officer. "I understand your requirements."

"Good," replies Mular sarcastically as he dismisses Zu-Art. "Go prepare my squadrons for the attack."

The mission High Commander Hoppinzorinski has given his staff and Probe Leaders seems impossible. There is very little available information on the internal configuration, or design, of a Fighting Star. However, Lieutenant Commanders Jo-Ich, Star, and Trilla work on determining the internal configuration of the Tirgonians most powerful battle platform. They know that certain sections had to be placed is specific areas. Certain areas are therefore easy to plot. The primary command center, main bridge, hanger and launch bays for the Horsehead squadrons, are the easiest to plot. Areas such as the secondary fighting bridge, defensive fire coordination center, attack squadron command, main engineering and propulsion control, and the concealment array generators should be located in accessible areas of a Fighting Star. The computer generated holographic image automatically rearranges the projection with the addition of each area. However, areas previously plotted suddenly appear outside the ships structure. Nothing fits where it should be logically located.

The task for locating the Tirgs supply and support bases, assigned to Lieutenant Commanders Hoblick and Novac, is more difficult than first anticipated. Whenever a possible position is located, Novac enters the suspected coordinates into the navigational computer. With every possible location plotted, the results are the same as the group working on the configuration of a Fighting Star. The Tirgonian supply and support bases are not where they should be. They only discover the emptiness of space. The endless circle of frustration soon takes a toll on everyone.

"Commander, I think we need a break," requests Star. "We're not making any headway and we need to get away from these view screens for a little while. We can take everything we have and go over the information in different surroundings. I think it might help clear our heads, sir."

"Good idea, Star," says Williams as he rubs his own tired eyes. "I think everyone could use a break. Hobby, let the computer work on that last set of variables and bring what you have to the relaxation lounge on deck seven. I'll notify Trilla to get his people to join us."

"You got it, Commander," acknowledges Hoblick. "Thanks."

The four officers gather their computer notepads and head for the Lounge. As they seat themselves, with a refreshing beverage, they prepare for the informal informational briefing as they wait for Commander Trilla to arrive with his small group.

"I guess we should begin with what we know for certain," begins Williams as he nods towards Hoblick to begin.

"First sir, we know, or think we know, that a supply base has to be located on solid ground or at least a stationary station of some sort. We know the location of the bases immediately surrounding Tirgonia." Activating the holographic generator, Hoblick produces an image of Tirgonia along with the location of the known support bases as he continues. "They have three successive tiers that we can positively identify. From the information we have in the computer bank, the first tier is one light year from Tirgonia. The second tier is one and a half light years from the first and the third tier is two light years from the second. Therefore, using that formula as a starting point, we went out two and a half light years from the third tier but couldn't find anything. We reconfirmed everything, rechecked the computers and sill came up with the same results. Then we went out three light years from the third tier. We still can't find anything that even remotely resembles a supply or support base. We know that a Fighting Stat is only capable of operating for eighteen to twenty-four months without returning to a base somewhere, if for nothing else to give the crew some shore leave. Also, they have to recalibrate their engines every twenty-four months if they go faster than light five for more than a cumulative total of six months, which isn't hard to do."

"Then how did they manage to cross the Agreed Zone and follow us at almost light seven for as long as they did, conduct who know how many other missions, and never slow down long enough to recalibrate their engines," asks Williams?

"They must have some sort of super sophisticated support system," replies Novac. "We haven't been able to find anything except empty space whenever we entered a suspected location into the navigational computer."

"If there aren't any fixed bases out here, what about a mobile base," asks Williams. "Something that could move about freely to go where it's needed, when it's needed?"

"Good idea, sir," answers Hobby, "but the only problem with that is that the mobile support ship would have to be at least two-thirds to three-quarters of the size of a Fighting Star. Even with a minimum number of personnel on board, the re-supply ship would have to not only carry whatever supplies it would take to sustain itself but also carry whatever would be needed to re-fit a Fighting Star. One resupply ship for every Fighting Star? So far sir, we've only had contact with the Landex and Napla, which indicates that we should have discovered at least two supply ships. Next, I don't think a supply transport would be able to move as fast or travel as far as a Fighting Star. If your theory is correct, then either the Napla is the support ship for the Landex or it's the other way around, but with the fire power she demonstrated when we hid on the Landex, would that be possible?"

"I don't know, it is a possibility but would that be a realistic option? Why don't you run that through the computer when you get back down to navigation control," replies Williams? "Trilla, has your group been able to come up with anything on the internal damage we might have caused to the Landex?"

"Not much, sir," answers Trilla. "From the damage we know we inflicted on the external hull we had to have damaged something pretty important to force Mular into withdraw and leave his Horses the why he did. Our guess is that we somehow managed to damage their fire control and defensive suppression system. We could have damaged four or five of their defensive fire control units because their firing pattern changed drastically just before Mular withdrew. Other than that we're still working on square one."

"It looks like we're not making much headway today," says Williams as he reaches up and massages the back of his neck. "I want everyone to take what they have back to where you got it and knock off for the rest of the day. Everyone is to be back on duty at zero seven hundred tomorrow."

"Commander," says Trilla. "Hops wants . . ."

"I know what Hops wants, and he'll get it, but only from people who are able to find answers for his questions," interrupts Williams. "Everyone in tired and needs a rest. I'll inform him of what we've accomplished, which isn't much. All I want for now is for everyone to get some rest. We can get back to work first thing in the morning. Now get out of here and take a break."

The next day begins much like the previous day ended. Returning to his or her duty station, everyone tries to appear to be fully rested and refreshed. Speculation and conjecture again result in nothing new discovered about the internal configuration of a Fighting Star. After a few hours of fruitless searching, everyone takes a short lunch break. No one is hungry, but the change of scenery is a welcomed relief. Within an hour, all are back at their workstations. For the most part, they just sit in front of the input terminals and display screens, staring listlessly at the information displayed. Meanwhile, Hops sits nervously in his command chair on the bridge, quietly contemplating his next move.

"I've got a target behind us," suddenly calls Nuk-Ma. "It keeps coming in and out of scanner range. I can't get any decent readings on it, but from the readings I can get, it has to be a Star. It's not trying to hide and it's not trying any contact with the Napla."

"Keep an eye on it," orders Hops. "Try to establish a pattern so you're ready on the next sighting and try to get anything you can to identify which Star it might be. I just hope it isn't Mular again. Commander Williams, Commander Trilla, report to the bridge."

Hops realize that it is happening again. No matter how hard he tries, he is unable to avoid a confrontation.

"What's going on, sir," asks Williams as soon as he enters the bridge.

"I think we just found the Landex, or to be more precise, Mular's trying to find us. Nuk-Ma has a target that keeps floating in and out of scanner range. He's trying to get a positive identification on it. If it isn't the Landex, it could be another Star trying to put a notch on his gun."

"That's it," exclaims Williams. "If it is Mular following the Napla, the Landex should be concealed if he's trying to set a trap for us. If that's his intention, the only way he can do it without engaging his concealment device is to stay out of effective scanner range of the Napla. If Mular can't hide his concealment array must have been . . ."

"Bingo," yells Hops! "Trilla! Get down to your section. I want everyone you can spare to go over the latest information on the exterior configuration of the Landex before and after our last encounter. Pinpoint the exact location of all damaged areas. There has to be some sort of anomaly on the outer hull. Concentrate only on those areas. Look for anything that doesn't fit their normal structural design. If push comes to shove, our Dragons are going to have to fire everything they have at that point. Maybe if we can cause enough damage additional to the Landex, Mular will have to head for a repair base to get his wheels fixed and he'll have to take the Napla along for protection. That should give us a starting point to find the rest of their supply bases. If we can pull this off maybe, they won't be so eager to come after us again.

"Orin, give everything you have to Trilla and get your Dragon drivers ready. They may have to go without much warning. I want all information that Trilla finds transferred to the Dragons' navigational and targeting computers as quickly as possible. I want you to put together a simple scenario that you can use to hit whatever target Trilla can find. Your hotshot driver are going to have to get in and out fast. They need to hit that target before Ge-Kor can get back here with his weapons ready for a fight"

"On my way," calls Williams as he races off the bridge.

"Helm, come to an outside parallel course so that the Landex passes fifteen thousand kilometers to port. Slow by one-quarter," orders Hops. "If it is the Landex shadowing the Napla, I want to be able to engage before Ge-Kor has a chance to get back here and join the fight."

"Commander," calls Nuk-Ma. "It is the Landex, I don't think Mular has any clue we're actually in the area. Speed and course are matching the Napla. Passing in nine hours. Fifteen thousand to port."

"Trilla," calls Hops over the Hopes' intercom, "you've got about eight and half-hours to find that flaw."

"Understood, sir," acknowledges Trilla. Lieutenant Commander Trilla has already put his section to work. He constantly moves from one workstation to another, monitoring the information displayed on each individual view screen.

"Anything yet," is the constant question from the Research and Development Chief.

"Nothing."

"Anything unusual?"

"Zilch."

"Find anything we can use?"

"A left over sandwich from lunch."

Trillas' team finds nothing for the next two hours. Then three hours, four, and just as quickly the five-hour mark slips slow by. The time passes quickly for the small group. Within another two hours, the Landex will be close enough for the Hope to attack. The team finds nothing to indicate the location of the concealment-imaging device.

"Trilla, I need a target. Mular is getting close and I need something for the Dragons to hit," anxiously pleads the High Commander.

"We're doing the best we can, sir," answers Trilla. "I'll let you know as soon as we have anything."

"Yell out as soon as you find anything," acknowledges Hops as he switches intercom channels. "Commander Williams."

"Williams, sir."

"How you coming with you're planning?"

"It would be a little easier if I had a specific target to hit. I've put together a basic scenario that can become operational as soon as Trilla gives me a target location."

"Understand. Trilla hasn't been able to find with anything yet," says Hops as he tries to control his anxious anticipation at the pending attack against a superior force. "You'll get the information as soon as he can figure what he's looking for."

The Research and Development Section continues their desperate search with increased fervor. In less than thirty minutes, the Landex would be passing the Hope.

"Commander Trilla," suddenly rings out! "I think I found it!"

"Where," yells Trilla as he rushes towards a monitoring station at the opposite end of the room!

"Here, sir," points the Image Interpreter as Trilla manages to work his way through the small crowd that has gathered at her station. "This is the area before the attack and the same area after it was hit. Some sort of modification seems to have been made."

"I don't see anything," says Trilla as he looks at the split image screen.

"I didn't either at first, sir. I didn't see anything until I overlapped the images," explains Ensign Germick as she touches a blinking input control sensor and points to the small area. "Right here is a slight hull blemish that's probably less than five meters square. I've gone over every damaged section in this area and it's the only thing that I can find that doesn't fit the design of a Fighting Star."

"Good work, Germick," congratulates Trilla as he gently pats the young woman's shoulder. "Now let's hope this works." Reaching towards the input panel, he activates the ships intercom. "Bridge, this is Trilla. I think we just found Mulars' Achilles Heel. Transferring coordinates to Commander Williams in the launch bay."

"Outstanding! Orin! Did you monitor," rapidly calls Hops!

"Affirmative, sir," acknowledges Williams just as hurriedly. "It's already downloaded to the Dragons. Final briefing in two minutes. Ready to launch in ten."

"Better make your launch in five. Tell your drivers to be careful out there this time. Mular isn't likely to be caught with his britches down again."

"Understood, Williams, out."

The Pilots ready room is jammed with anxious pilots. Twenty Dragon pilots are about to attack the most feared and destructive force in the galaxy.

"Let's grab a seat," orders Williams as he moves down the center aisle way and activates the main holographic image projector. "We don't have much time. Specific coordinates are already in your ships. Hobby, you have the primary target area right here. It's only about five-meter square," explains Williams as he points to the small highlighted area on the computer generated three-dimensional image. "It's their concealment device imaging array. Jo-Ich, you'll be lead Probe and target Alpha Ramp. Star, you'll be next and target the main defensive batteries here and here. Lucas, you'll be in reserve here. Be ready to support the attacking Probes, but only if necessary. Any questions?" Commander William scans the faces in front of him, wondering how many of them is he looking at for the last time. "That's it. Get to your ships and good luck." As the pilots rush out of the room Williams again activates the ships intercom system. "Bridge, this is Williams. Launching in two minutes. Has the Napla deviated from her course or speed yet?"

"Negative," replies Hops. "Speed and course unchanged. Eleven minutes to intercept with the Landex."

"We'll be ready," acknowledges the Senior Flight Officer as moves towards the main exit to return to the main bridge. As the doors silently close behind him, he hears launch control inform the High Commander the launch sequence has begun.

"All Dragons are outside and hiding," reports Nuk-Ma as Williams moves to the main scanner console.

"Raise the shields and deflectors slowly. I don't want any energy spikes," quietly orders Hops as he painstakingly monitors the small screen on the arm of his command chair. "Lock all batteries on the Landex. I want to give our people as much protection as we can. Turn the Hope around and close on the Landex at dead slow speed."

"Course reversed. Dead slow," acknowledges Lieutenant Roberts. "Landex dead ahead, course and speed is constant"

"Maintain this distance and will someone please turn off that damned alert siren? I think we all know what's going on." The alert siren suddenly goes silent, allowing Hops to continue, "Ski? Have you been able to get the shields and deflectors to full strength yet?"

"No quite yet, sir. Mular just screwed up my repair schedule," reports the Chief Maintenance Officer. "I still have a skeleton crew still working but it's going to be at least another six hours before they'll be at full strength. Right now they're at eighty-three percent and should hold if you can keep the forward deflectors angled to take the majority of the hits."

"Do the best you can," replies Hops, knowing that Ski was doing just that under less than desirable circumstances. "Commander Williams, what's the status of the Probe? It looks like it's about time we give Mular our little surprise."

"Probe Leaders are reporting in now, sir."

"Orange on station."

"Good luck, Hobby," acknowledges Williams.

"Red ready."

"Watch yourself, Jo."

"Gold Ready."

"Watch your six, Star."

"Why Commander, I didn't think you noticed," reply a sweet, half-joking voice over the open communication channel.

Not about to let a comment such as the one just made by Williams to pass without comment, Hops quickly says, "I think it would be a good idea to keep your eyes on everyone's buns, Commander, not just Commander Stars'."

Lieutenant Commander Nuk-Ma, sitting next to Lieutenant Brooks, leans back in his chair and tilts his head back slightly, looking at the back of the junior officers' helm chair.

"Nuk-Ma," says Williams questioningly, "would you keep your eyes on the scanner and not on Lieutenant Brooks . . .?"

"Just following the example of my superiors, sir," answers Nuk-Ma.

"Look," says a slightly red-faced Commander. "I think everyone needs to get back to situation at hand."

"Purple on station," reports Lucas. "And Commander, I think I'm in a better position to keep an eye on Stars' six that you are. Would you mind if I kept an eye on her for you?"

"Hope, this is Orange One. Does that mean I can't delay the mission so Gold One can check out my buns?"

"Orange One, this is Gold One. Just stay in front of me. I have a great view of your six. Besides, I should be able to get a much better view if I hold position behind you and watch you hit Mular from here."

"Enough of the chatter," admonishes Williams! "There's a specific target out there that needs your full attention, and it's not the exhaust thrusters on Commander Stars' Dragon. It's time for all of you to forget about whose backside you want to watch and get back to concentrating on your target areas. Once you start your attack run, those Horses aren't going to stay in the barn for long. Red One, you're on lead."

"Roger," acknowledges a more serious Probe Leader.

CHAPTER TWELVE

The Landex is within full visual range of the Dragon pilots as they turn their attention back to their mission.

"Orange, this is Orange One, confirm visual on target," quietly instructs Hobby.

"Orange Two, I have a visual."

"Orange Three, got it."

"Orange Four, no problem with visual confirmation."

"On my lead," orders Hobby. "Let's see what we can do to that tin can."

Lieutenant Commander Hoblick moves his thruster sensor to full power as he leads his Probe into a single file formation towards the unsuspecting Fighting Star. No longer surrounded by the emptiness of space, the five Dragons are now skimming along the surface of the Landex. Flying less than fifteen meters above the exterior hull of the Fighting Star does not leave much room to maneuver, and no room for error.

"Have you located the Guardians yet," questions Mular as he enters the bridge after a short rest period?

"No, sir," replies Culmit Olderin. "All scans are still clear."

"Keep trying on all frequencies."

"Yes, sir."

"Is the Napla still maintaining course and speed?"

"Yes, sir."

"Keep me informed . . ."

"Orange initiating attack," reports Williams as Hobby dives towards the small target area and fires the first volley, barely missing the location of the main command center as he pulls up and speeds away.

"Telecoup! We're under attack! No visible targets! Quadrant twenty-two! Forward battery two," suddenly calls out the Weapons officer of the Landex!

"Impossible," bellows Mular! "There isn't any way they could know! Fire all batteries! Defensive barrage! Close absorption shields! Raise the energy deflectors! Launch all fighters! Recall the Napla!"

"Shields closed and deflectors are at full strength," reports the Weapons Officer.

"Fighters launching," responds Zu-Art.

"Damage report," bellows the commander of the targeted Fighting Star!

"Quadrant twenty-two! Battery two sustaining severe damage and appears to be the only target," reports Olderin! "Extreme external hull damage in that quadrant. Severe breech in the secondary hull. Sections forty-six through fifty-three on levels fifteen, sixteen, and seventeen are sealed. Ninety-three confirmed dead, twenty-eight in sickbay, nineteen unaccounted for."

"Horses coming out," yells Jo-Ich as soon as the lead attack probe begins the initial assault on Alpha Ramp. "Aw hell! They've changed their launch tactic! They're all coming out at once!"

"Don't worry about that," quickly orders Williams. "They can't see you. Just take out as many as you can. Orange is going to need as much help as they can get! Watch out for that cannon fire!"

"How are we doing," quietly questions Hops as he monitors the progress on his small chair arm screen?

"Red reports a massive Horsehead launch from all ramps. We're holding our own so far. I don't know how long that advantage is going to last. Red's targeting the Horses coming out of Alpha Ramp. Gold's hitting as many defensive batteries as it can. Purple has gone from reserve to helping counter the Horses."

"Has the Napla turned back yet?"

"Affirmative, sir," reports Nuk-Ma. "Ge-Kor received as signal from Mular as soon as the attack began. We should be able to get out of here before Ge-Kor is close enough to provide any effective support. The Napla still too far out to scan for weapons."

"Don't worry about her weapons. Ge-Kor will have them armed and ready long before he gets here."

"Have our fighters or the defensive batteries been able to find any confirmed targets yet," demands Mular!

"Negative, sir," reports Olderin. "They must be using the concealment device of their mother ship to hide the Dragons."

"Idiot," screams Mular! "Remember our previous encounters! Remember you couldn't find them then! These Dragons have a concealment device of their own!"

"We have a target," calls out the Weapons Officer!

"All batteries! Concentrate on that sector," orders Mular!

Lieutenant Commander Hoblick, making his second attack run, tries to get a damage assessment when he sees the cannon fire. A ball of highly charged particles barely grazes the deflector shield protecting the stubby wing and weapons pod of his Dragon. It was not much of a hit, but it is enough to cause the trajectory of the particle ball to veer off course just enough to reveal his position.

"Get out of here! I'm hit! Don't wait . . ."

The vehi-com goes silent as an uncounted number of Tirgonian energy cannons immediately concentrate their fire on the small enemy fighter.

"Orange! This is Three! On my lead," calls Captain Penicutt in an unhesitating voice. "We've done our damage! Let's get out of here!"

"Sir! Probes detected," yells Nuk-Ma from the main scanner station!

Suddenly a second is hit, then another, and another. In less than a minute of the first hit on Lieutenant Commanders Hoblick's' stubby wing pod, four Guardian Dragons are destroyed.

"Casualty report coming in, sir," reports Williams who is sitting next to Nuk-Ma.

"Sir! Second Star approaching," calls Lieutenant Commander Nuk-Ma suddenly.

"Damn! That was fast," says Hops as he begins to move towards the scanner station.

"It's not the Napla, sir, and it's not concealed."

"Orin! Get our Dragons back here," orders Hops!

"Where in the hell did that Star come," from rapidly asks Williams at the unexpected report!

"Can't tell you right now, sir," says Nuk-Ma. "All I can say is that it's coming in with a full head of steam. All weapons are online and armed."

"Recovery in progress," reports Dunlipee. "We should have everyone back aboard in less than ten minutes."

Leaning over Nuk-Ma shoulder to get a better look at the scanner screen, Hops quietly asks, "How soon before that Star gets here?"

"Ten minutes fifteen seconds, sir," says Nuk-Ma. "That's not much of a margin, sir."

"Cherrick, set a course to pass the Napla as close as possible without hitting it. As soon as the last Dragon is secure, get us out of here as fast as this thing can move. I don't want to be around three Stars at the same time," orders Hops.

Having already disengaged the Landex, the Dragons rapidly return to the Hope. Abandoning the normal landing sequence, the reduced time interval between the returning Dragons turn the landing bays into a seen of organized confusion. Without the automated systems to move a Dragon once it completed the landing sequence, several of the returning fighters would have collided, causing more damage to the Hope than it may have already received.

"How much longer before we can get moving," questions Hops?

"Four minutes," reports Williams. "Nineteen seconds ahead of that Star."

"Nuk-Ma, do you have any identification on that Star that just ruined our party?"

"No, sir, the only thing I can pick up is that it's still heading this way in one hell of a hurry."

"Orin, how many are still out," asks Hop?

"Purple is landing now," replies Hops executive Officer. "Just picked up another four seconds."

"Keep it smooth," instructs Hops. "We don't need to damage the Hope just because Mular hasn't hit us yet."

"That Star is definitely going to cause a problem, sir," calls out Nuk-Ma. "I don't like the look of the signature readings I'm getting. They're trying to jam the concealment device frequencies."

"Block out the interference," orders Hops. "We need to stay hidden as long as we can."

"Lucas just landed, sir. All Dragons accounted for," reports Williams.

"Cherrick! Get us out of here!"

"Telecoup Mular, this is Telebisque Teka of the Palup. I have been monitoring your situation. How severely is the Landex damaged," calls the Commander of the fast approaching Fighting Star? "Do you need any assistance with repairs?"

"Not at this time," answers Mular. "The Napla is returning and will have everything required to make the necessary repairs. Is the Junnack with you?"

"Yes. If these Guardians remain as dangerous as they have recently become, I will need her facilities sooner than I may wish," answers Teka.

"I am relaying my battle reports to you. These devil dogs have damaged my primary communications antenna and I need the reports relayed to the Supreme Commander. I have also severe damage to my concealment antenna."

"I have your reports and will relay them to Paporia Two," acknowledges Teka. "You should have your new orders. Join me as soon as your repairs are complete."

"Affirmative," answers Mular.

"Good luck, Palup, out."

"Sir," calls out Nuk-Ma. "I just found out why we can't find any of their supply or repair bases. I also have a positive identification on that Fighting Star."

"Orin, get all Probe Leaders in my ready room in five minutes. Nuk-Ma, notify all Section Chiefs that I want them there also. They are to bring everything they have concerning their actions during the attack. Major Cherrick, you got the bridge."

The Hopes' ready room quickly becomes very crowded as everyone quietly files in and takes a seat. Wasting no time, Hops quietly begins the meeting.

"Okay, first things first. How many did we lose?"

Taking a deep breath, Commander Williams begins slowly. "A total of five, sir. We lost Hobby from Orange."

"Damn," softly mutters Hops. "Please, continue."

"Captain Penicutt has command," resumes Williams. "Lichtner and Budlar from Gold, Maprick from Purple and Brock from Red. We still have the extra Dragons, but no replacement pilots yet. It will be at least another ten or twelve weeks before we'll be able to confirm the few remaining cadets we have and they can join the regular Probes."

"Realign your pilots as necessary," says Hops as he tries to maintain control over his emotions at the loss of his friend. "Nuk-Ma? What all did you get from that Tirg communiqué?"

"That third Star is the Palup. Commander is a person by the name of Telebisque Teka and his sister ship is the Junnack, commanded by Sub-Telecoup Envela. Teka has been in command for the past seven years. He replaced Vice Telecoup Cublas who was relieved of command for attempting to lead a coup to overthrow their Supreme Senate."

"I'll be damned," mumbles Hops.

"I know, sir. I already started the computers working on getting any additional information we might have on Teka and Envela. I'll let you know as soon as I get anything."

"Is Teka following us?"

"Last scans were negative, sir."

"You said that you found out how they refit a Star. How in the hell are they able to repair or re-supply without fixed bases?"

"They carry their supply and repair facilities with them, sir," explains Nuk-ma. "It seems that the Landex and Palup are the main fighting force. The Napla and Junnack serve as the supply and maintenance facility. Ge-Kor and Envela can still fight, but has less to do it. Their main function is to support the Landex and the Palup. That's how Mular was able to repair the Landex so quickly after our last meeting and it explains why we couldn't find any fixed bases."

"How'd you decode the message and get that information so fast," asks Hops?

"The message wasn't coded, sir. Everything was sent in plain language over an open frequency."

"Why would Teka do that," says Hops quietly. "Commander Williams, were you able to determine how much damage we did to do to the Landex?"

"I'm not really sure at the moment, sir. Hobby was hit when he when in for the damage assessment scan. The target was so small that we're going to have to go over the information we have very carefully before we'll be able to complete an accurate report. We should have a preliminary damage assessment in about an hour."

"Okay," accepts Hops. "Now I'm going to need a complete analysis on the defensive tactics they used and what everyone saw. Captain Penicutt, if you will begin."

"Hobby was in the lead and Capernia went in second, I was third and Ensign Pen went in last. Hobby was going in for his second run at the target area when he took a hit on his wing pod. Instead of getting out of there, he still went in to get the damage assessment scan. That's when he was hit the second time. He told us to get out of there when his vehi-com went silent. We were able to get through the hole they left when they concentrated their fire on him. I'm sorry, sir."

"Thank you, and no need to apologize. You did your best. Captain. Jo? What did you see?"

Hops listens as each Probe Leader and section Chief gives their detailed report on the action of their respective areas of responsibility. The briefing lasts for more than three hours. Hops wants to know everything that happened. What were the actions of the Tirgs just prior to the mass Horsehead launch? How did they deploy after the initial launch? What was the damage, if any, sustained by the launch ramps of the Landex? What did the Probe leaders think all this meant in terms of a military advantage, or disadvantage? Hops concentrates on each report carefully, occasionally asking for additional details. After the last Section Chief finished her report and the analysis of her sections actions during the encounter, Hops gives his orders.

"What I'm going to need now is for you to go over every scrap of information we have on the Landex and Palup. I not only want the normal computer enhancement, but also as much personal input as possible. We're going to need a new set of parameters under which we can develop an effective battle plan that we can use the next time we get into a fight. What are we going to do if we face four Fighting Stars at the same time? What's the best way to defend the Hope, stay in one piece, and while at the same time creating a little chaos and destruction our own? I'll be damned if we get into another fight we're just going to roll over and cry 'Uncle'. Also, the Junnack is out there somewhere and we need to know where she is, and get me as much additional information on all four Stars as possible." Pausing, Hops looks at the weary faces in front of him before continuing, "If no one has any questions, it looks like it's time for everyone to get back to work."

Hops sits quietly as his senior officers leave the ready room. Moving to one of the large portals, he stares into the vast emptiness through which the Hope silently glides. After a few minutes of quiet thought, he returns to the bridge and instructs Cherrick to alter course and slow to quarter speed. Now he wants to be alone.

"Good evening, High Commander," greets Lieutenant Johns, the Landing Bay Officer of the Watch as Hops enters the main hanger bay. "Is there anything I can help you with?"

"Yeah. You don't have a spare bird that needs to get out of the nest and get a little flying exercise," asks Hop without stopping at the small room reserved for the Duty Office.

"Sure do, sir," answers Johns as she quickens her pace to catch up with Hops. "We still have the extra Dragons that haven't been flown since we left Seven. Over in the back corner, sir. Just pick out the one you want and I'll get it ready for you. By the way, sir, you Dragon is in the front row on the left."

"Thanks. How long before you think you could have her ready?"

"It shouldn't take me more than ten minutes to complete the pre-op and . . ."

"You know, I think I'll do all that. I'm a little out of practice," interrupts Hops. "I'll just give a yell when I'm ready to move to the launch ramp."

"No problem with that, sir. Just give me a few minutes to get the cover off," says Lieutenant Johns as she moves towards the High Commanders Dragon. "You can wait in the Watch Office, sir. I just duplicated a fresh pot of coffee and you're more than welcomed to have a cup."

"Thank you," solemnly replies as Hops walks slowly towards the small room reserved for the duty officer.

A short while later, and sipping on a hot cup of coffee, he is quietly interrupted. "Sir, your ship is ready for pre-flight. Since we don't have anything scheduled for launch, I had her moved to the launch rail. I thought it might be a little easier for you to do your pre-flight there."

"Thanks you, Lieutenant," says Hops as he takes a final gulp of coffee. "I guess my flight plan will be within ten thousand kilometers of the Hope. I'll be using the concealment device, and I don't know how long I'll be outside."

"Stay out as long as you want to, sir. Fuel and weapons systems are charged. All you'll need to do is to give a yell if you run into anything that isn't on our side. Orange is on standby for the next hour and Purple comes on duty after that."

"Sounds good to me," answers Hops. "After I launch, would you be kind enough to notify Commander Williams that I'd like to see him . . ."

"I thought you might be heading down here," calls Williams as he walks up behind Hops. "I've told Jo that you might want to take a trip outside. He and George will be going outside with you and, since this is one of your own rules, there's no use of arguing against it. They're just going out with you to provide a little extra protection. They understand to give you plenty of room."

Understanding that any argument would be useless, Hops silently nods in agreement as he walks towards his waiting ship.

After climbing the access ladder and lowering himself into the once familiar, cramped, cockpit, Hops has to begin the pre-flight checklist. Several times, his mind wonders from the task to the memories of his friend, causing him to restart the checklist several times. Finally, he finishes the pre-flight checks and tightens the safety restraints. As the clear bubble canopy slowly closes, he hears a faint, almost distant voice over the vehi-com. Quickly putting on his flight helmet he answers the launch notification as if nothing is wrong.

"This is Red One. Prepared for launch."

"High Commander, we already have a designated Red One," answers the com-link operator. "You're going to need a new call sign."

"Old habits are hard to break," mutters Hops.

"Sir?"

"Nothing," quickly answers Hops. "Sorry about the confusion. Just give me one I can use. It really doesn't matter what I go by."

"Roger, sir. I guess call signs aren't that important right now. You're cleared for launch."

"I'm going to need something to go by," says Hops as he reaches out to activate the ignition sensor. Suddenly stopping he grins, saying, "Well, since we're lost, I guess that's as good as anything. I'll just go by Lost One."

Jo-Ich, monitoring the exchange, quickly asks, "Lost One, does that mean I just became Lost Two and George is Lost Three for this trip?"

"Affirmative, Lost Two," acknowledges Hops. "I'll meet you outside, out."

Activating the ignition sensor, the force of the sudden acceleration thrusts Hops violently against the padded seat back as his ship accelerates from a dead stop to almost half the speed of light. One second he is sitting inside the launch tube, and the next moment he is hurling through the darkness of space. Slowly, he moves his hand to his face to wipe away a lone tear trickling down his cheek. Softly he speaks his words of farewell to his friend.

"You got stupid on me. You forgot how to fly. You came down with a real bad case of dumb ass on me. Damn it, Hobby, you just forgot how to fly."

"Lost One, this is Lost Two," yells Jo-Ich as he watches the High Commanders Dragon make a series of erratic maneuvers! "Is there a problem with your control sensors?"

Pulling out of a steep dive, Hops answers, "Nothing's wrong, Two. Just getting the kinks out of them."

"Don't do that again without warning me, sir. You scared the hell out of me."

Hops didn't answer as he peers out into the dark emptiness surrounding him. After several minutes of more normal flight maneuvers, he quietly whispers, "You got stupid on me, Hobby, but I guess you knew what you were doing. You saved quite a few lives with your stupidity, and I guess that's what counts. Looks like I won't see you until this war is over and it's my turn to get stupid. Thanks, my friend, I'll see you then."

CHAPTER THIRTEEN

For the next several weeks, the Guardians continue their trek across the Tirgonian Empire. Everyone understands that another fight could be no more than a few minutes away, but slowly, everyone begins to relax, everyone except the High Commander.

During this time of relative peacefulness, Hops is able to convince a vast majority of the crew that a centuries old Earth adage is still true. For a reason he can only speculate about, Murphy's Law, as it is called, simply states, 'If something can go wrong, it will go wrong, and at the least opportune time'. No matter what task the crew performs, someone always comes up with a 'What if . . .' situation. Every briefing, conference, or seminar also contains the 'What if . . .' question.

Daily educational classes, not only for the children aboard the Hope, but also for the newly inducted crewmembers, have begun. Training classes for the surviving Guardian Defense Fleet Training Academy also continues.

With limited training facilities aboard the Hope, the cadets training schedule becomes even more challenging. These soon to be pilots now receive their training at an even greater pace than before. In addition to the already rigorous textbook and classroom assignments, the intensified training includes two simulated Probe flights per day. Each cadet is also required to participate in at least one weekly patrol with a regularly scheduled Probe to replace a simulated mission. Additionally, they are now responsible for all daily maintenance of their assigned Dragon.

In his capacity as the Senior Flight Officer and Academy Commandant, Commander Williams keeps a watchful eye on the progress of the cadets. In his spare time, which is almost nonexistent, he, along with the High Commander, Council Member Quince, and the remainder of the Probe leaders and pilots, instruct the cadets in such areas as Emergency Procedures and Communications, Launch and Landing Bay Operations, Advanced Battle Tactics, and Tactical Simulations.

As a regularly scheduled Council meeting is about to end, High Commander Hoppinzorinski poses one of the long awaited concerns of the Guardian Fleet Flight Training Academy Cadets.

"Council General, I've decided to conduct the Commissioning Ceremony for the Academy cadets. Commander Williams has informed me they're ready to get their wings. I just need to let them know when."

"Commander," says Lamminta, "have the cadets completed all necessary requirements and do you feel that they are ready to join the fleet?"

"Yes, sir," answers Williams. "They're ready and anxious to graduate from the Academy. The only requirements that remain are their final examinations and Probe Qualification Flight."

"When do you think this could be completed?"

"Two weeks, sir, and one more to complete the preparations for their Commissioning Ceremony."

"And you agree, High Commander," asks Lamminta as Hops nods his head?

"I do," says Hops.

"I also think they have been called 'Cadet' for long enough. So, if there are no objections from the Council, I propose that the Fleet Flight Training Academy Commissioning Ceremony be conducted in three weeks from today." All Council Members silently nod their heads in agreement. "Commander Williams, it now seems that you are about to get a few replacements you need. If you would please notify the Cadet Commander of our decision."

When Commander Williams informs the cadets they are about to get their wings and join the rest of the Fleet, a spontaneous roar erupts from the main training room, echoing through several corridors surrounding the training area. Hops, returning to the bridge after a short trip to the engineering section, pauses at a communications panel.

"Commander Williams, this is the High Commander."

"Williams, sir."

"What in the hell is that racket?"

"I just informed the Cadets when they will be joining the Fleet."

"Okay," says Hops. "Just tell them to keep the noise down to a mild roar or I'll find a way to keep them there for another three weeks. The Tirgs haven't bothered us for a while and we don't need their noise to let them know where we are."

"Understood, sir."

"Good. Hops, out."

The entire Corps of Cadets begins studying, and working, even harder than before. On a daily basis, Commander Williams orders most, if not all, of the cadets out of the training room to get their required rest. In another attempt to force the cadets to get their much-needed rest, Commander Williams restricts the use of all reference tapes and logs to normal duty hours. However, once in the privacy of their quarters, these enterprising cadets promptly retrieve any item they were able to smuggle out of the training library. Whatever one cadet needs, whether it is the Battle and Tactical Scenario, or Emergency Personal Hygiene Procedures, the required material mysteriously appears. No one wanted to graduate with the unofficial title of Academy Retro-Jet, the Cadet with the lowest point total, and the last one to receive their wings.

Commissioning Day finally arrives for these anxious cadets. First Cadet Ashford Seeret, responsible for conducting the official inspection prior to any formal function, enters the training room carrying a handful of small armbands and holds them up for all to see.

"Do we all agree," asks Seeret?

"Yes," is the only answer given.

Silently he hands an armband to the twenty-nine Cadets. As he hands armbands to the last few cadets, one of the soon to be commissioned pilots quietly says, "You know you're going to get one hell of an ass chewing by Commander Williams, and who know what the High Commander is going to say."

"Don't worry, Televy, I've got everything figured out, I hope" says Seeret as he hands her one of the last the two armbands.

"You know this could get you kicked out before you get your wings," says the cadet as he accepts his armband.

"Look Craig, like I just told Televy, Commander Williams and the High Commander will follow protocol. That should give me the one chance I need. Besides, Williams needs all the pilots he can get, so I doubt there's any chance of any of us not getting our wings," explains Seeret. "Now, everyone fall in and prepare for inspection."

The only room large enough to accommodate such an event is once again the Council Chamber. The only noticeable change to the Chamber is the placement of small nameplates on the back of the first several rows of chairs. Each cadet has a chair reserved to include those who died during the attack upon Capricorn Seven. A slender black ribbon drapes the chairs reserved for these cadets whom died during the attack against Capricorn Seven. The arrival of the Council brings an immediate hush over the audience as the five leaders mount the dais and step in front of their respective chairs.

"Allow those to be honored to enter and take their rightful place among us," says Lamminta solemnly.

The doors at the rear of the Council Chamber open slowly, allowing the cadets, dressed in their formal uniform, to enter. Several members of the audience quietly whisper as the cadets silently march down the center aisle. As the cadets stop in front of their chairs on the front row and turn to face the full Council, they see Commander Williams is visibly irritated.

"First Cadet. Center. Post," quietly, but stern order from Williams.

Stopping in front of Commander Williams, the cadet leader responds in a sure, steady voice "Sir, First Cadet Seeret reporting as ordered."

"What is the meaning of this," harshly whispers question from Williams? "Why is the Corps of Cadets wearing a Probe designation when Probe assignments have yet to be made? And since when was Probe Black authorized?"

"Sir," begins Seeret with the same confidence as before, "Guardian Defense Fleet Regulation Four Six Seven Four, Section Three One Two, Paragraph One Six, Sub-Paragraph Bravo Seven Alpha states, may I quote sir?"

After a slight hesitation Williams nods his head slightly, saying, "Continue."

"Sir, this regulation states, and I quote:

> *A Cadet, or group of Cadets, from a specified Class from the Corp of Cadets assigned to, and/or attending the Guardian Defense Fleet Training Academy, may individually, or as a group, request assignment to a specific command, if, within that command, a current, or expected, vacancy is known to currently vacant, or is expected to become vacant due to unforeseen circumstances, or uncontrolled, events. To correct such vacancies, the assignment of qualified personnel shall occur as soon as such personnel become available for reassignment. Such request, or requests, shall be written, and, at the earliest possible time, prior to the official commencement of the Commissioning of Cadets Ceremony, in accordance to Section Three One Six of this regulation, and submitted to the Council General of the Guardian Council of Elders, through the appropriate Guardian Defense Fleet Headquarters, to allow sufficient time for the determination of the final disposition of said request.*

"Sir," continues Seeret calmly, "as First Cadet, and Cadet Commander of the Corps of Cadets, I submit to you, for your submission to the High Commander of the Guardian Defense Fleet, for presentation to the Council of Elders, our formal request to fill the vacancies which currently exists within the Guardian Defense Fleet. This request is in accordance with all current and applicable regulations."

"Very well, First Cadet," says Williams as he begins to understand what is taking place. "Do you have the written request?"

"Aye, sir," replies Seeret as he reaches under his tunic and withdraws the requested documents. "In addition to our request, I would like to also present the Motto and Creed of Probe Black."

"Then you're requesting what I think you are," quietly mutters William?

"Aye, sir."

"I see why you were selected to be First Cadet," says Williams as he accepts the and small scanner and information pad. "Return to your post, Cadet."

Commander Williams, waiting until Seeret is back in his proper place, first chair on the first row, turns to face the Council.

"Council General, High Commander, and Council Members. In accordance with current regulations and traditions, the entire Corps of Cadets has requested an assignment to fill the vacancies that currently exist within the Guardian Defense Fleet with the formation of a new Probe. They have requested to be designated as Probe Black and to be assigned collectively to this Probe."

"The entire Corps of Cadets," questions Hops?

"Yes, sir," answers Williams as he takes a few steps forward and hands the documents to Hops. "I would like to present their petition, along with the Motto and Creed of the proposed Probe Black."

"Commander Williams," says Hops as he accepts the documents "I'm quite aware of the regulations concerning these matters and by these same regulations, as so adeptly quoted by Mister Seeret, these documents are to be presented to me before the Commissioning Ceremony begins, not after."

"With due respect, sir, and to the rest of the Council," rebuts Williams, "the Commissioning Ceremony has not yet officially begun. As you can see sir, you and the Council are still standing and the Council General has not yet stated the official purpose of this special Council meeting. Therefore sir, the petition has been presented in accordance with all applicable regulations, though just barely."

"I believe Commander Williams is correct, High Commander," says Lamminta who has been quietly listening to the unusual beginning of the Commissioning Ceremony. "We are still standing and I have not yet called the Council to order. Therefore, as Commander Williams has stated, the Commissioning Ceremony, technically, has not officially begun. So it looks as if we should accept the request of First Cadet Seeret and make a formal decision before we proceed with the Commissioning Ceremony."

A sigh of relief escapes from Seeret's lips as Lamminta, looking directly at the future officers, continues as he taps a small gavel on the dais. "Please, may we be seated? I call to order this special meeting of the Council of Elders. It seems that we have a petition before the Council in which the entire Corp of cadets is requesting to be assigned to a newly proposed Probe and that this new Probe is be designated and Probe Black. I will begin with the reading of their proposed Motto and Creed.

> *MOTTO: Defend - Protect - Preserve*
> *CREED: Probe Black will defend the Honor of all Guardians. Protect all Guardians against all aggression as well as all we encounter who require the same. Preserve all Guardian traditions through our thoughts, our words, and our actions. To fight for the preservation of the oppressed and to never become the oppressor. To the Guardian people, we, as members of Probe Black, pledge our allegiance and our lives. By our words, we pledge our Honor.*

"The entire Corps of Cadets has signed this Motto and Creed. It now seems that we have a very unique situation before us, and an equally unique decision to make," continues Lamminta as he leans back in his chair and again looks directly at Seeret. "This type of request is not unknown, as Councils in the past have been presented with similar requests, which I can see has been thoroughly researched. However, a specific request of this type is unprecedented. All twenty-nine cadets are requesting to be assignment to a single Probe, which this Council has not yet authorized, and this new Probe be designated as Probe Black. I do not see how the Council could accommodate such a request as this. High Commander, what is your opinion on this matter?"

Hops, shaking his head slightly and raising an eyebrow, begin speaking slowly. "Council General, since this request seems to have been submitted, just barely within the confines of current regulations, I believe the idea just might work. Our regular Dragon drivers have been on constant alert status, not to mention being engaged in actual battle, ever since the Tirgs started this war and tried to annihilate us. They can't maintain such a state of readiness much longer without suffering more stress on themselves, or the additional strain on the Dragons as well. They have to get a break. Therefore, this is what I would suggest these soon to be hotshot pilots do. First, they should have their request honored, and for now, be assigned to a single Probe with three sections of four pilots each. That would be twelve out of the twenty-nine cadets. They will then need to reassign the remaining nine pilots, and the eight non-combat cadets, to what we have left of Fleet Headquarters. The reassignment of those individuals will then be at the discretion of Commander Williams. First Cadet Seeret, who apparently came up with this crazy proposal, will have to be the one who figures out the details, and just like any other Probe Leaders, report to Commander Williams. Probe Black could then relieve the regular Probes on routine patrol around the Hope. That would get these new driver accustomed flying on a constant basis and give our normal pilots a much needed rest. It's a little unorthodox but, under the circumstances, it just might work."

Seeret breathes a slight sigh of relief as he realizes that his plan just might have a chance of success.

"Unusual situation call for unusual solutions," says Lamminta as he nods, indicating that he might approve of the solution. "Thank you, High Commander. Council Member Quince, what do you have to say concerning this proposal presented by First Cadet Seeret and the solution offered by High Commander Hoppinzorinski?"

"As a former Probe Leader, I can sympathize with the stress our pilots have been forced to endure. I agree with the recommendation of the High Commander. Commander Williams will now have fifty-seven pilots, including the ones who have returned to active and have completed their requalification training. I would suggest that he realign his personnel to have a more even distribution of personnel and Probe assignments. I believe the Council should not only authorize the formation of Probe Black, but also increase the total number of authorized Probes, including Probe Black, to eleven with five pilots each. Eleven Probes would make for a much easier duty rotation in the future. The remaining two pilots would have duties that require a qualified pilot to perform, and could be rotated between the regular Probes to maintain their qualifications."

Again, Seeret breaths a silent sigh of relief at the additional support he just received from Council Member Quince.

"Thank you, Council Member," says Lamminta. "Council Member Pidera? Your opinion?"

"I believe the High Commander and Council Member Quince are more knowledgeable in these areas and I support their recommendations."

"Thank you. Council Member Tro-Ja?"

"I also agree with the recommendations of the High Commander and Council Member Quince."

"Commander Williams," says Lamminta as he leans slightly forward, leaning against the Council table. "How long would it take before you would be able to institute this proposal now before the Council?"

"It should only take three days to complete the realignment and begin implementing this plan, Council General."

"Very well, Commander," continues Lamminta as he looks directly at the senior ranking cadet. "It seems that First Cadet Seeret has indeed learned has not only how to successfully pilot a Dragon but, a great deal about Council protocol as well. First Cadet, you have presented a viable solution to a most stressing situation. Please, come forward."

Seeret looks about nervously. Standing alone before the Council General was not part of his original plan as he slowly steps forward to stand next to Commander Williams.

"You may uncross your fingers, Mister Seeret," continues Lamminta. "It appears that your plan has worked, although not exactly the way you may have anticipated. Protocol now requires that we proceed with our traditions."

"First Cadet Seeret, it appears the High Commander and Commander Williams have granted your request pertaining to the formation of Probe Black. It is therefore, by the authority of this Council that, upon the completion of the Oath of Allegiance, and the acceptance of your commission, that you, Captain Seeret, be given the authority to activate and implement the operations of Probe Black. Captain Seeret, it shall now be your responsibility to divide your pilots and reassign those pilots not selected for assignment to Probe Black, to the Defense Fleet Headquarters for reassignment to other Probes. Do you understand your responsibilities and duties, Captain?"

"Yes, sir," answers Seeret nervously.

"Very well. You may return to your post Mister Seeret," dismisses Lamminta as he nods to Williams, indicating that the Commander may now proceed.

Seeret return to his place with the other cadets in a mild state of shock. Never before has a graduating Cadet been promoted to any rank higher than Lieutenant, which has happened only twice before in the history of the Academy.

Clearing his throat and waiting until Seeret is back in front of his chair, Williams announces the purpose for the special meeting of the Council. "Council General, High Commander, Council Members, I would like to present Guardian Defense Fleet Training Academy Corps of Cadets Class Three Two Nine Seven."

"Why do you do you wish to present this class from the Corps of Cadets to the Council of Elders," asks Lamminta as he maintains the tradition of the Guardians?

"Council General, it is my recommendation that this class from the Corps of Cadets, be permitted to take the Oath of Allegiance and join our Space Defense Fleet. I recommend that all, with the exception of First Cadet Seeret, receive a commission with the rank of Ensign in the Space Defense Fleet. First Cadet Seeret, through the unusual abilities and unique capabilities he has demonstrated during his training and the recommendation of the Council of Elders, that he receive a commission as Captain. In addition, as endorsed by the Council, I recommend that selected members of this class establish a new Probe to be designated Probe Black. I give me word and my honor as to their competency in all required," turning his head slightly towards Seeret before adding, "and a few not so required areas of responsibility. High Commander," continues Williams and he again looks directly at the Council, "I hereby request, with the approval of the Council, that you administer the Oath of Allegiance to this Class of Cadets."

Hops stands and turns slightly towards Lamminta saying, "With your permission Council General, I will administer the Oath of Allegiance to this Class of Cadets."

"You have the Councils permission," solemnly says Lamminta.

Turning to face Commander Williams, Hops says, "Commander, you may prepare you cadets."

"Aye, sir," acknowledges Williams as he snaps his heel together with a resounding click signaling each cadet to raise their right hand.

Hops, raising his right hand and speaking in a loud, clear voice, begins the Oath, saying,

> *"I, state your full name . . . do solemnly affirm to abide by the laws and traditions of the Guardians . . . To obey the orders of the officers appointed over me . . . with loyalty, dignity and honor . . . To perform all duties . . . in*

accordance with all current and future regulations . . . To protect and defend all life . . . regardless of personality, race or creed . . . To give my life in defense of the same . . . and in the pursuit of freedom for all . . . To all Guardians I pledge my only allegiance . . . so help me God."

As each Cadet receives their commission, the gathered assembly remains quiet. After the commissioning of the last Cadet, Lamminta says, "Before ending this special meeting of the Council of Elders, I would like to invite everyone to the Forward Observation Lounge where a reception is to be held for our new officers," says Lamminta. "This meeting of the Council of Elders is adjourned."

CHAPTER FOURTEEN

The reception for the newly commissioned officers is the first celebration enjoyed by the Guardians since their first, and only successful, victory against the Tirgonian Empire. As the celebration settles into a joyous routine of mingling and laughter, Commander Williams slowly maneuvers his way over to Captain Seeret.

"Captain, you played a very clever hand in the Council Chamber. May I offer my congratulations to you, and your officers?"

"Thank you, sir," accepts Seeret and he shakes Williams's hand.

"Now you need to finish the game you started."

"What game, sir? I'm not sure I understand what you mean."

"The one you started when you presented your proposal to the Council. You do understand that you now have the responsibility to finish forming a completely new Probe and establish a covering force for the next few weeks. You have twenty-eight pilots, twenty-nine including yourself, and now you need to decide whom are you going to keep and whom are you going to assign to Fleet Headquarters? Whom are you going to assign as your Probe Section Leaders? In addition, since you now have three Sections using the same designation, how are you going to distinguish one from another? How are you going to coordinate everything with Probe Operations? Are you going to make any recommendations for your Section Leaders for promotion due to their increased responsibilities? What is your rotation schedule going to be? These are just a few of the questions and initial problems that you will have to have answered in the next two days. It looks like you have a lot more work to do than you thought, and not much time to get it completed. I, along with the other Probe Leaders, will be available to help you with anything that we can. Now, enjoy the rest of you Commissioning Day, and good luck, Captain."

"Thank you, sir," answers Seeret. "Probe Black will be ready on time."

"Just remember, you have the entire crew to rely on if you run into something that you might need a little help with, so don't be afraid to ask."

"Understood, sir."

Williams moves away as Seeret looks about the room until he locates a small group of Ensigns sitting at a table next to a large portal. Walking past the small table Seeret barely nods his head, but it is enough to get the attention of two of the young officers.

"Excuse us," says Ensign Craig as he and Ensign Televy rise from their chairs and silently follow Seeret.

The three of officers depart the observation lounge so quickly no one notices their departure. The three officers do not speak as the walk silently along the corridors and passageways that would indicate their intention, or their destination. Only when they are back inside their old classroom is the silence broken.

"I think you know why we are here," says Seeret.

"Yep," answers Craig.

"What's first," asks Televy?

"I guess we start with Section designations," says Seeret.

"Well, sir," says Craig. "Why don't you take Black Alpha, Televy can be Black Bravo and I'll be Black Charlie."

"Okay, that's settled," agrees Seeret. "Now whom do we keep and whom do we give to Fleet Headquarters?"

The three Probe Leaders begin working on the list of names, trying to decide who would join Probe Black, and who would go to Fleet Headquarters. Within a short while, without much success, the list remains incomplete as they address the other problems brought up by Commander Williams. They work through the night and are almost finished by the time Commander Williams enters the Operations Center the following morning. He immediately notices the officers are still dressed in their dress uniform, and two of them are in desperate need of a shave.

"Captain Seeret," begins Williams, startling the three officers. "I didn't mean for you to begin work yesterday. It would have been just as acceptable for you have begun today. You do understand our tradition of not assigning any duties to any . . ."

". . . to any newly commissioned officer on their Commissioning Day," interrupts Seeret. "Yes, sir, we fully understand but it was our choice to begin yesterday, which is acceptable. We did not have any family at the reception so we thought no one would miss us. We should be able to submit a complete roster, duty assignments, and Probe rotation schedule no later than fifteen hundred hours. We believe that two weeks should be enough time for the normal pilots to rest and recuperate. After that, the three Sections of Black can be included in the normal Probe rotation. Also, sir, here are the recommendations for promotion to Lieutenant for Ensign Craig and Ensign Televy and their assignment recommendation as Probe Leader."

"Very well, Captain," says Williams as he accepts the computer note pad. "Now I think you, and your Lieutenants need a break. I'll give your recommendations to the High Commander for his approval, which I'm sure he'll give."

"Thank you, sir," says Seeret. "As soon as we get cleaned up we'll get back here and finish the last few details that still need to be worked out, along with a few normal housekeeping chores that need to be finished."

"Not so fast, Captain," admonishes Williams. "You, and your Musketeers, are not going anywhere on this ship, except to you quarters until zero eight hundred tomorrow morning. I'm sure that by then the High Commander will have approved you requests. The three of you need your rest before you fall asleep on your feet. Therefore, as far as I am concerned you, and your work, are finished for today. Is that clear?"

"Yes, sir," answers Seeret, "very clear."

The three officers leave the Operations Center as quietly as they had entered the day before. Only after they are on the deck where their quarters are located does anyone speak.

"I thought when we graduated from the Academy things would be different," softly mutters Televy.

"What do you mean," asks Seeret?

"When we were cadets, how many times did Commander Williams order us out of Ops? And just in the last month how many times did he tell us we had to leave?"

"More times than I can count," answers Craig.

"Exactly," continues Televy as she begins grinning. "I'm beginning to think that we're not supposed to be in the Ops Center whenever Williams is there."

"I don't think that's the real reason," says a voice from behind them."

Turning around they see the High Commander walking down the corridor towards them. They immediately move to one side to allow him to pass.

"Stand easy," says Hops as he stops in front of them.

"Thank you, sir," says Seeret as he tries to relax.

"I'd like the three of you to come with me," says Hops. "I've got something I'd like to talk to you about."

"Of course, High Commander," says Seeret. "As soon as we get changed and cleaned up, we will . . ."

"Captain, I think I'd like to talk with you at my convenience, not yours," admonishes Hops.

"Yes, sir," answers the young Captain as he and his officers walk behind the senior military officer aboard the Hope.

"Please, come in gentlemen," says Hops as he stops in front of his private quarters, "and ladies, of course."

Televy smiles politely as she enters first. Being fresh from the Academy the young officers move directly towards the small conference table in the formal area of the main room and, as protocol demands, remain standing as they wait for the High Commander to take his seat.

"I think you might be a little more comfortable over here," says Hops as he moves towards the informal area of the primary living area. "And before I begin, let me just say that none of you are in any trouble, at least none that I know about yet. This is not what you would call an 'official visit'. I've wanted to talk to you before, but knew it would be better to wait until after you received your commission."

The three newly commissioned officers, exchange confused glances as they walk to the more comfortable area. They sit quietly together on one of the couches next to the outside portal.

"Would the three of you relax," again says Hops as he tries once more to ease their fears. "Like I said before, you're not in any trouble, I think. I'd like to talk to you about a few things as just another officer, not you're High Commander."

"Yes, sir," says Seeret as he glances nervously at Televy sitting next to him.

"Good," says Hops as he looks as the trio. "Would any of you like a cup of coffee or something to snack on?"

"A cup of coffee would be fine, sir," says Seeret. "Thank you, sir."

"What about the rest of you?"

"Coffee would be fine, sir," answers Craig.

"Coffee also, sir," answers Televy.

Hops walks to the duplicator, requesting, "Four fresh cups of coffee, with cream and sugar on the side." Turning to the new officers, he asks, "How about a nice hot apple pie."

"Is this request to know if hot apple pie is available or is hot apple pie ordered," replies the computer synthesized voice?

"Requested," says Hops with a slight hint of irritation in his voice.

"Regular hot apple pie, deep-dish hot apple pie, regular hot Dutch apple pie, a deep-dish Dutch apple . . .?"

"Hot deep dish Dutch apple pie," answers Hops as he interrupts the unseen voice. Within a few moments, the requested items appear in the dispensing area of the duplicator. After retrieving the refreshments, and returning to the living area, he softly mutters, "Damn computers just don't have the personality of a good waitress."

"Here you go, grab a piece of pie while I get started," says Hops as he reaches for a cup of coffee and a piece of pie for himself. "First, I'd like to tell you to stop trying so damned hard. You've already proved yourselves and don't anything to prove to anyone, including me. Your little surprise to the Council yesterday was very ingenious. I had never heard of anyone putting the entire Council on the spot the way you did and get away with it. It sure caught everyone off guard. If our defensive systems back at Seven had worked as well, maybe we would not be in the fix we are in now. My personal congratulation, Captain."

Seeret nods silently as he quietly sips his coffee.

"Now for the real reason you are here instead of being where Commander Williams ordered you to be. First, we all need your talents and capabilities more now than ever before. At the same time, you don't need to burn yourselves out before you complete you're first combat patrol. Eight hours a day for the fourteen to twenty-one days straight in a Dragon is going to be a lot longer than you might think. You have to slow down and quit trying to finish every task, or mission, in record time. The Tirgs are going to be here for a long time to come. I'm quite sure you'll get your chance to try to stop a stampede sooner than you might think. Just take your time and slow down before you end up doing something stupid that might get yourself, or someone else hurt, or even killed. We need every Dragon driver we have. You can do just as much as anyone can, without too much of a problem. You just have to learn how to pace yourself. Okay?"

Again, the three of junior officers nod their heads in understanding.

"Another cup of coffee for anyone," asks Hops as re returns to the duplicator.

"No thank you, sir," answers Seeret, as Televy and Craig shake their heads no.

"Don't be embarrassed. If you want another cup just say so," says Hops as he places his order. "One cup of coffee."

"Hot coffee? Cold coffee? Iced coffee? Decaffeinated . . ."

"One cup of hot coffee. Black. No cream, no sugar, no ice, just regular caffeine. Just a damned cup of regular hot black coffee," says Hops angrily as he returns to the informal seating area and the three officers. "Damned computers. I need to talk to Trilla about giving that damned thing a better personality.

"Like I was saying, you can do anything that's asked of you. If at any time you feel like you're getting in a little over you're heads, all you have to do is to slow down, and don't be afraid to ask for help. Everyone on this ship is here to help everyone else, and that includes Commander Williams, the Council, and me.

"Now this might sound a little crazy, but after you make it through you're first combat mission, and you make it out with a whole skin and your ship is still flying, you might understand. If you're actually looking forward to taking someone's life, whether it is Guardian or alien, you're a damned fool. Every living being has a right to exist, unless they're trying to hurt another living being without just cause. Just remember that while you're trying to put someone, or something, into the realm of non-existence, that same entity is trying to do the same thing to you. So don't try to do anything fancy. Being that stupid just might get you, and possibly someone else, killed. If you come up with an idea on how to do something better, run it through the simulators, Use your pilots to bounce it. You know as much about Tirg tactics as anyone. In addition, since you were the first ones to use our new concealment device, you had the chance to use it while still in the development stage. In addition, no one aboard this ship knows the systems aboard the Hope better than the three of you. You know this ship better than anyone does. That includes Commander Williams, Council Member Quince, or even me, and you already know that we've already put it to one hell of a test. Just don't take any unnecessary chances because it's going to be a long time before we get any more replacement pilots and we can't afford to lost the ones we have."

The young officer listen with great interest as Hops continues.

"Next, talk to your people. Just because you outrank them, doesn't necessarily mean you're smarter than they are. They're people just like you. They have feelings and ideas just like you. Don't ever shut any of them down. Listen to them. If you learn to trust them, just as you trust each other, you'll find out that they're going to be a lot more willing to cooperate. You're going to end up getting the job finished a lot faster and a lot easier. Don't always give them orders. Ask them to do something, or to help you with whatever you are doing. If they don't take the hint, then make it an order. Just remember don't ever tell someone to do something that you can't do, won't do, or haven't done, yourself. If they see you're willing to get just as dirty as you expect them to get, you'll earn their respect a lot faster than if you're always standing around afraid to get a little dirt under your fingernails," Hops grins as he glances towards Televy and says "No offence meant."

"None taken, sir," replies the young woman with an equally wide grin.

"If that don't make too much sense," continues Hops, "just think of how you would feel is if you're always being ordered to do something, and Commander Williams wouldn't do anything except stand over your shoulder drinking a cup of coffee. Would you be willing to do your best, or just enough to get by? I think you might be more willing to do your best if Commander Williams would ask you to something and get just as dirty as he would expect you to get.

"I hope you understand something of what I'm trying to say. I can't order any of you to follow my personal views on how to command, or how to finish a job. A long time ago, someone who was once trying to kill me, told me what I just told you here today. At first, I didn't understand what he was trying to say but, when I did finally understand, the advice he gave me has gotten me out of quite a few tight spots since then. You can learn a lot more by listening, regardless of who's doing the talking. Any of you have any question?"

The three young officers are speechless.

"Aw, come on now," says Hops. "I've never heard of you three Musketeers not having something to say. From what I've seen and have been told, the three of you usually have something to say about everything."

"Sir," begins Seeret slowly. "It's not that we don't have anything to say, it's just that I, we, didn't think any of us ever expected to be spoken by any High Commander as you just have."

"Well, Captain," replies Hops. "I wish someone would have said to me what I just said to you when I first got out of the Academy. It might have kept me out of a lot of trouble."

"Sir," says Televy?

"Yes," answers Hops.

"You said that someone who was trying to kill you gave this advice to you?"

"Sure was."

"If I may ask, who was that?"

Thinking carefully Hops answers slowly "Just someone who I thought would do whatever it would take to end my life, instead of actually saving it."

Knowing that there would not be any further explanation, Televy nods, accepting the vague answer.

"If there are no more questions, I think I need to get back to work and the three of you need to get to your quarters to get some rest before Commander Williams decides to check in on you."

During this same, Telebisque Teka spends every waking moment scrutinizing the battle reports received from Telecoup Mular, trying to find a weakness in his enemies' armor. He is also trying to find anything that might indicate the next move of the Guardians. While spending a rare rest period in his quarters, the door chime interrupts him.

"Enter," orders the tired Tirg officer.

"Pardon the intrusion, Telebisque," begins Culmit Raccesia, Tekas Aide-de-Camp, as she stops just inside the open doorway. "Culmit Cudrosia requests your presence in your ready room. He has obtained information concerning the Guardian ship."

"He could have used the intercom," admonishes Teka.

"He said he did not want the crew to know about the information just yet, Telebisque," explains the Raccesia. "He has learned that several unauthorized interceptions of intercom communications have been attempted. He is quietly attempting to learn the identity of the individual, or individuals, responsible."

"Very well," says Teka as he slowly rises, placing the book he had been reading on a small side stable. "Inform Culmit Cudrosia I will be there shortly."

A few minutes later Teka enters his ready room. In addition to the Executive Officer of the Palup, the Senior Security Officer Culmit Tomdoc, and Sub-Culmit Jollickma, the Palups' Senior Weapons Officer, are also present.

"What new information have you found," asks Teka, as he acknowledges their presence, moves to the head of the briefing table and motions for everyone to sit.

"Telebisque," begins Cudrosia, "I believe we have determined the basic size and weapons configuration of this mysterious Guardian ship."

"Very well," says Teka. "Proceed."

"First," says Cudrosia as he presses a small sensor button, causing a three-dimensional rectangular holographic image to appear in front of Teka, "if we are correct in our assumptions, this is what we have found. Based on the distance between this ship and the Landex, and the relative effectiveness of the energy bursts that struck their aft deflectors, we believe the ship to be approximately three hundred meters wide and eleven to twelve hundred meters long."

The holographic image displays the recorded hits on one end of the rectangular shape causing a slow change in its appearance.

"From what we have been able to analyze so far, this is definitely the aft portion of their ship," continues Cudrosia as he begins to point out several specific locations. "We believe these to be the engine exhaust ports. These side projections are, or could very possibly be, the launch ramps for their Dragons."

"Very interesting. This ship does appear to be larger than we first anticipated from Mular's reports," comments Teka as he leans forward slightly and begin studying the image in front of him. "Continue."

"Again, sir, if our assumptions are correct, they should have defensive batteries along each side of the ship from here to here," says Cudrosia as he points to various locations that magically change to the shape of the mysterious Guardian vessel. "Additionally, there would also be weapons batteries over, and under, the launch ramps themselves. Of course, sir, this is only the suspected aft portion of the ship, presumably, the aft third, or maybe the entire aft quarter.

"From the size of these ramps they could conceivably have had as many as twenty full Probes before their attacks against the Landex." Cudrosia activates a holographic image of a Fighting Star in direct proportion to the suspected Guardian vessel. "Judging from the location of the five Guardian dragons destroyed during the latest attack against the Landex," continues Cudrosia as he activates a third image sensor, "we believe that five or six full probes conducted the main assault against the Landexs' Alpha Ramp. One or two of the Probes penetrated the primary defenses along the Alpha arm to attack the primary concealment array, with the remainder of the Probes held in reserve.

"Using their tactical history, they have never sent their entire Probe force into battle. They have always held approximately one third of their strength in reserve to guard against any possible counterattack. Based on the location of the destroyed Dragons, we believe that seven or eight Probes participated in the actual attack, with possibly two or three more held in reserve. Again, using their previous battle history, they could possibly have a total of fourteen to sixteen Probes, or seventy to eighty Dragon. If we subtract the five Dragons destroyed by the Landex, they should have no more than sixty-five to seventy-five, Dragons remaining. When we find them, we should be able to destroy their remaining Dragons. If that can be accomplished, their mother ship shall be left defenseless."

"An admirable assessment, Culmit," says Teka as he studies the holographic images before him. "I would not be so sure that the defeat of these remaining Guardians will be as easily accomplished as you suggest. They possess less than a third of the fighting strength or firepower of a single Fighting Star, yet they have still managed to inflict enough damage to the Landex to render her, and the Napla, temporarily ineffective. An impressive achievement for such a peaceful race, so do not be so sure they will surrender so easily. However, now that we know their possible strength, we still need to know where they are likely to be heading."

"It is my guess, sir, that when the Napla returned to assist the Landex, they set a passing course," says Cudrosia. "It would have been the fastest route away from the engagement area. If they did indeed slip past the Napla, they could very well be on a course towards Paporia Two."

"That course does not make any logical or tactical sense," replies Teka. "What could they possible gain by such a move. As far as any intelligence they might have, they will know there is no strategic value on continuing towards Paporia Two. What could they possibly gain by such a move?"

"I believe such a course does make logical and tactical sense, sir," rebuts Culmit Tomdoc carefully. "It would be the last place we search for them. That, and the confidence that we would not ordinarily be looking for them in that sector, would give them more time to plan their next move. So far, they have not followed their traditional battle doctrine. They attack when logic would dictate they should withdraw. I do not believe they will do anything that would be as logical, or as tactically sound, as staying close to the border to conduct raids on small targets of opportunity. Since they have not followed their traditional tactical doctrine, where would the last place we would look for them, which should be the first place they would attempt to go? Considering everything they have, and have not done, this is the only logical decision they could possible make."

After a few moments of quiet thought, Teka says, "It would appear they may be more reasonable in their tactical thinking than they would have us believe. I believe that we are about to see if your estimate of their ability is as accurate as you think, Culmit. Set a course for Paporia Two at maximum speed. We just may find them when they least expect us."

Cudrosia, Tomdoc, and Jollickma return to the main bridge of the Palup and the orders age give to proceed to Paporia Two. For several more hours, Teka remains in his ready room studying the battle reports, observing the recorded action of each encounter between the Landex and the strange Guardian ship. Finally, he enters the bridge, quietly moving from one monitoring station to another, pondering the current situation and the next possible encounter. Only when he stops to gaze out one of the large view ports is he actually able to think clearly. He remembers a Guardian he met so many years ago. Had he been on one of the Guardian outposts? Had he survived the devastation?

CHAPTER FIFTEEN

"High Commander," calls Cherrick from his helm station. "I'm starting to get automated course corrections."

"What," asks Hops?

"I'm getting erratic control inputs from the forward maneuvering thrusters, then when I compensate, the aft maneuvering thrusters activate."

"Check all systems. Start with the secondary system protocols. If that does not fix the problem, something has to be wrong with the redundancy protocol in the emergency backup system. Check it out," orders Hops. "Orin, get down to Engineering and find out if Aflo or Trilla has any idea on what's causing this malfunction and how long it's going to take to work the bugs out."

"On my way, sir."

"Launch Control," says Hops as he activates the intercom.

"Captain Seeret here, sir," is the immediate reply. "I monitored and have relayed the information to the standby Probe. No problem with launching on your order, sir."

"Who's up in the launch tubes?"

"Lieutenant Televy with Black Two, sir."

"Good," acknowledges Hops. "If we have to launch, you need to make sure your drivers take it easy."

"Understood, sir."

"High Commander, this is Williams."

"Go ahead, Commander," answers Hops.

"I'm in Engineering and there's a glitch in the navigational systems. It seems that the emergency backup system is giving override commands to the primary system.

The secondary system is caught in the middle and it's trying to compensate with its own correction commands."

"You're telling me that all three navigational systems are trying to come on line at the same time?"

"Affirmative, sir."

"Is it safe to keep going or do we stop to get the problem fixed?

"High Commander, this is Aflo. I recommend that we stop. We'll just have to take the chance that no one stumbles over us."

"What's the worst thing that can happen if we keep going at minimum speed?"

"I can't say for sure, sir. We could possible keep going using manual control commands, but each time the correction needed would continually increase exponentially. The corrections would increase until eventually we wouldn't be able to maintain any stability or directional control. The structural stress could tear the Hope apart. Whatever you decide to do sir, make it fast. We're only going to have stability control for another ten minutes at the most."

"Okay," answers Hops. "Engage the concealment device. Cherrick, come to a full stop. Ease into it nice and slow. Don't make any sudden course corrections. Scanning, I want constant monitoring on all frequencies. Launch bay."

"Captain Seeret, sir."

"I want Televy outside now, and then get the rest of your hotshot drivers out there to help her. Institute a three-quadrant cover. Commander Williams will be there shortly to take over."

"Understood, sir."

"Heading to launch control," replies Williams immediately.

"Engineering," calls Hops without acknowledging the action of Williams.

"Trilla, sir. I still haven't been able to track down the source of the malfunction. I've gone over every circuit in all three systems and still can't find out why all three navigational systems are counteracting the commands from the others. When I take one of the systems off line, everything checks out. However, as soon as I try to put it back on line, the other two automatically kick in. I don't know how long it's going to take to isolate the problem."

"Keep working on it," says Hops as he turns off the intercom channel. "Scanning? Anything being picked up yet?"

"All scans are still clear. There's nothing within normal scanner range that can do us any harm," answers Ensign Germick, now assigned to the bridge crew.

"Just keep a sharp eye on your screens, Ensign."

"Aye, sir."

Arriving in the launch bay operations center, Commander Williams receives a briefing from Seeret. After the quick explanation, Seeret leaves to join his probe, ready to launch and provide protection to the Hope.

"Captain Penicutt," calls Williams as several pilots from the original Probes begin entering the Operations Center. "Get everyone down here. If Black gets into a jam, we are going to need one hell of a big pry bar to get them out. We are going to need a few more Probes out there. Briefing is in five minutes."

As soon as the pilots are gathered Williams begins outlining his plan.

"I want an eight-quadrant defense established. Red, you'll replace Black Charlie and cover the lower aft quarter. Black Charlie will cover the upper aft quarter. Blue, establish the same cover on the starboard beam. Black Brave will cover the port beam. Gold, you'll take the lower forward bow. Black Alpha will be responsible for the upper section. Orange and Green, the two of you cover the upper and lower center beam respectively. Indigo, Violet and Purple will rotate with Black Alpha, Bravo, and Charlie in one hour. After that, we will use a three Probe rotation every two hours. I don't know how long we're going to be in this configuration, so get whatever rest you can whenever you can. Get to you ships and prepare for launch."

"Launch control, this is Hops."

"Williams here, sir. I'm reinforcing our protective cover as we speak. First rotation is in one hour, then every two hours after that."

"Good," says Hops. "Engineering."

"Trilla, sir."

"Any luck locating that gremlin?"

"No, sir. Every test I run comes back normal, but I still can't get a single system back on line without the other two trying to override. It looks like I am going to have to rewrite the control input initiation protocols. It's going to be at least another two or three hours before I might be able to get the primary system on line. It's the best we can do down here."

"Hopefully the Tirgs won't bother us and you'll have enough time to figure everything out. Bridge, out," says Hops. "Ensign Germick? Anything out there besides our Dragons?"

"No, sir," answers Germick. "At least there's nothing out there that can get to us in less than ten hours. I haven't had anything except training targets for so long I think I may have forgotten what to do . . . This doesn't look good sir!"

"What's that," rapidly asks Hops as he points to the small blip on the scanner screen.

"I don't know yet, sir. It's in plain sight and it is not Tirg. Energy signatures appear to be similar to ours but there's just enough difference that I can't be sure."

"If it isn't Tirg, then what in the hell is it? They don't let anyone cross their territory without permission or escort, and as far as we know, they don't have any alliances or pacts with anyone that we know of. Germick, inform Commander Williams that we have a bogie. Tell Commander Trilla that he just ran out of time to fix that navigational glitch. Nuk-Ma, bring us to Yellow Alert. You have the bridge. I have to let the Council know what's going on because this is one decision they are going to have to make."

A few minutes later Hops enters Lammintas' quarters.

"There's a problem and you need help," says Lamminta as the door closes silently behind Hops.

"Uh-huh," agrees Hops.

"Then whatever it is, it must be serious. You have a free hand when it comes to dealing with the Tirgs, so this problem must be something else."

"To say the least, sir," answers Hops. "First, the entire navigational system decided to take a hike. The next problem is that that now we have a bogie on a definite intercept course and Germick's trying to find out whom it is. Trilla's trying to find out what's causing the navigational glitch and Williams is circling the wagons because we can't run. We don't know who or what this bogie is, so what do we do if they stumble over us? I need help on this one."

"Quite right," agrees Lamminta as he activates a sensor on wall mounted communications panel. "I'll get the others in here."

A calm synthetic female voice begins a ship-wide call. "The Council General requests the presence of the Council in his quarters. Hotel One."

Within a few minutes, the remaining three Council Members are present.

"This emergency meeting is called due to some unusual information I have just received. High Commander, please tell the Council what you have just told me.

"About five minutes ago an unidentified ship appeared on the scanner. The only information we know is the ship is on an intercept course and it's not using any type of concealment technology. This would not be much of a problem because we could've just altered course. However, we can't do that because the entire navigational system decided to go haywire. Therefore, if this ship does turn out to be a new Tirg design we don't know about, I know what to do. If it turns out to be someone else, what then? I need help on this one."

"High Commander," says Council Member Quince, "what's the distance between this ship and the Hope and how much time do we have before they actually become a possible danger to us?"

"Right now they should be a little over six hours out."

"And you don't have any idea who this ship might belong to," continues Carol?

"Nope."

Suddenly, a completely unexpected question from the female Council Member. "Could this vessel possible be another Guardian ship"?

"What," exclaims Hops! "Pardon me, Council Member, but correct me if I'm wrong. A couple months ago, the Tirgs started trying to annihilate us and damn near did. We barely got off Seven by the short hair of . . ."

"High Commander," admonishes Lamminta.

"Excuse me, sir," says Hops, never taking his eyes off Carol. "We barely made it away from Seven. So far, we have only had contact with Mular, just recently with Teka, and now you think that this ship might be one of ours! Do you know what the odds are that any other ships from the Fleet survived? The Tirgs conducted a coordinated attack, against all our outposts and so far, they haven't left anything capable of maneuvering, let alone fighting, in any serviceable condition, except a few Dragons on Seven. I'm sorry Council Member, but you need to start using your brain for . . ."

"High Commander," again admonishes Lamminta. "This is neither the place nor the time for one of your infamous Probe lectures. We must all work together. I believe Council Member Quince has a valid point. We did manage to escape, so there is a possibility, though slight, that somehow others may have survived. Just because we have not had any contact with anyone, besides those here on the Hope, does not mean that there may not be others who also managed to escape. If this mystery ship is not of any Tirgonian design that we know of, then who is it? Can you definitely say this ship could not be another Guardian design that Fleet may have been working on before the fighting began? Since this ship is not within the normal design parameters of the Tirgs, then it could possibly be friendly, not just another enemy ship that we need to avoid. It this is true, I think we should maintain a more neutral position until we have more detailed information. Council Member Tro-Ja? What would you suggest our next move should be?"

"I believe as you do, Council General. We should proceed with caution. I'm also wondering if it would be possible to contact this ship in such a manner as not reveal our exact position, or current situation."

"A very interesting idea, Council Member. High Commander, would this be possible?"

"I don't know," says Hops. "We do have the capability to create a bogus signal and it might work. I need to get with Nuk-Ma and Trilla to see how fast if it can be done."

"Good. Council Member Pidera?"

"I agree with Council Member Tro-Ja. We should maintain our current defenses while we attempt to covertly contact this ship, if it is at all feasible."

"Thank you," says Lamminta as he again turns to the High Commander. "Do you have any other suggestions on what we might be able to do if this is a new Trig design?"

After a few moments of careful thought Hops says, "First thing we need to do it to move over just a bit and I think we need to do it as soon as possible. We need to be in a position that would give us a tactical advantage if this ship does turn out to be Tirgonian after all. If we don't move, we're going to need to make more repairs than Ski could handle. If Trilla is able to find a way to move us out of the way by at least three thousand kilometers, we should be in a better position to get a decent scan of this ship when it passes.

"As far as contacting it, I think we should wait until it passes, we get a better look at them, and possibly try to determine their intentions before we do that. If it does turn out to be a new Tirg design, we just let it go on its merry way. It if turns out to be someone else maybe we could risk a short message at close range to avoid interception and wait for their reply."

"That sounds like a reasonable approach," says Lamminta. "Does anyone have anything else that they would like to add?"

"Yes," says Carol. "If we can't move to a reasonable distance to facilitate a safe passing, how close would this ship actually come to the Hope?"

The question catches Hops off guard as he answers, "What are you thinking about this time?"

"How close, High Commander," again asks Carol in a slightly harsher voice?

"Current indications are that this ship will pass with less than a seventeen kilometers separation."

"Then they would pass extremely close to the Hope and the Probes, right?"

"Yes," answers Hops skeptically. "The Probes are maintaining their protective cover at ten kilometers out. That bogie would clear them but without much room to spare."

"What would be the closest distance this ship would have to be before it would be unsafe for us to move to a safer passing distance and at what speed would they be traveling at when they pass?"

"If we don't move by the time they're at a distance of one hundred kilometers, I'd be extremely hesitant to move if Trilla hasn't got the navigational system fixed. As far as their passing speed, our last report indicates they're maintaining three point five light, which is real slow considering whose backyard they're playing in."

"If we can't move, and this ship just keeps getting closer, what do you plan to do?"

Hops is getting a little irritated at the questions and tries to maintain his composure as he asks, "Exactly what are you trying to get at, Council Member?"

Slowly Carol, with a slight grin on her face, begins to explain her idea. "If Commander Trilla cannot maintain navigational control enabling the Hope is able to move out of harm's way and Commander Nuk-Ma is unable to send a false signal, would it be possible for one of our Probes to get close enough to get a visual identification? The Dragons are all equipped with a concealment device and apparently, this ship does not have the capability to detect a concealed ship. They haven't discovered our presence, at least not that we know of. I believe we could take a reasonable risk by having a small Probe move close enough to this ship to obtain a positive identification, without risking the Hope. We could disguise our communications with the Probes as subspace static. Would this option be possible?"

"A very sound suggestion, Council Member. It could very well save time, and lives," says Lamminta. "High Commander, what do you think?"

"I'll be damned. This hair-brained woman actually came up with one hell of a good idea," races through Hops, but says aloud, "It just might work. With the approval of the Council, I'll get things started on both ideas. Plan A, we move and Plan B, we use a small Probe."

"Does anyone disapprove of these suggestions," asks Lamminta? When no one offers any concerns, he continues, "Good. High Commander, you have the recommendations of the Council."

"Thank you," says Hops as he and the three Council Members rise to leave the Council Generals' quarters.

In the hallway Hops turns and heads towards the transport tube.

"High Commander."

Startled by the voice behind him, Hops turns sharply, bumping into Council Member Quince.

"My apologies, Council Member," mumbles Hops as he tries to hide his embarrassment. "Excuse me."

"We have got to stop meeting like this, High Commander," says Carol as she grabs Hops arm to keep her balance.

"Is there something I can do for you," asks Hops as he relaxes his arm from around the Council Members waist. "Again, I apologize. I didn't know anyone was following so close behind."

"I'd just like to know if I could walk with you to the Probe Ops. It's been quite a while since I've been down there, or for that matter seen, or been in a Dragon," says Carol as she regains her balance. "And there's no need to apologize. It was an accident, wasn't it? And, I do have a first name, High Commander."

"Of course, Council Member," says Hops.

"It's Carol, not Council Member," replies petite female as she turns to face Hops directly. "Look, we're both on the same team, and I'd like to work with you, not always against you. We're both professionals, and we both need to forget our differences. We just need to work together. Of course, we're not going to agree on everything, but at least on this one thing, we both gave each other a chance and it worked out damn good if you want my opinion. So how about it?" Holding out her hand she asks, "Truce?"

Pausing for a moment, Hops finally accepts the offered gesture. "Okay, but just remember, you're not in the Defense Fleet any longer. You're a member of the Council of Elders, just as I am. That means I have control over the fleet and what the fleet does. Technically, you're not even a Dragon driver any longer."

"Like I said Hops, we won't always agree on everything," says Carol. "Besides, right now I think we need to let Orin know what he's about to get into."

Both remain silent until the doors to the turbo tube close.

"May I ask a question," asks Carol?

"For that you don't need any permission, Council . . . Carol."

"I know Orin will work out something so that enough Probes take care of this mission and still have with a few Probes held in reserve. It will be a little tricky, but he will pull it off. What are you going to do if Trilla can't get the navigation system back on line? How are you going to handle the passing?"

"Very carefully, Carol, very carefully."

It takes another ten minutes to reach the Operations Center. They find Commander Williams at the main com-link console, monitoring the position of the Probes and the unidentified ship.

Glancing back over his shoulder he says, "It's been a long time since I've had the pleasure of a Council Member down here and now I get two at once. Something tells me that I'm not going to like what I'm about to hear." Straightening up and turning around, he motions towards a doorway several feet away saying, "We can talk in the ready room. I need a break anyway."

The trio enters the ready room where Hops explains the purpose of the surprise visit.

"I knew I wasn't going to like it," says Williams when Hops finishes outlining the proposed idea.

"It will work," says Carol. "And just to insure we're ready for Hops version of Murphy's Law, we need to do this hopefully without too many things going wrong."

CHAPTER SIXTEEN

The Guardians were not the only ones to see this new intruder.

"Telebisque! I have an unidentified ship! Position five four seven point six by three two eight point nine. Course seven six four by five eight seven. Speed three point five. Weapons and propulsion signatures appear to be Guardian. It's them!"

"Relay the scanner image to my view screen," quietly instructs Teka. "How did you find them?"

"They are not using their concealment device, Telebisque."

"Then where are their Dragons," asks Teka as he begins to study the image in front of him. "If their concealment device in not operational they would have surely launched their Dragons for protection."

"No Dragons detected, sir, just the mother ship."

"Idiot! This is not the Guardian ship. Look at the size of this ship! It's too small to be them! We have often used the same basic design for our transport and supply ships," yells Teka! "Under-Culmit Matilosk! Send a signal on all primary channels. I want to know who is in command, where they came from, their destination, what cargo are they carrying, and what is their transit security authorization to be in this sector. Have they have had any contact with the Guardians and if they have, I want all information regarding that contact regardless how insignificant the commander may think it is."

"Understood, sir," acknowledges Tekas' communications officer. "That ship is not responding to our request."

"They're changing course away from us, sir," reports Under-Culmit Dramek, the Palups scanner officer. "Increasing speed. Five point two. Six point five. Holding steady at eight point five. Weapons systems are on line. I do not believe this ship belongs to the Empire."

"You may be correct," says Teka thoughtfully as he continues to watch his small screen. "The ship is running which indicates they have something to hide. Helm, change course and overtake that ship."

"Course plotted and engaged, sir."

"Weapons. When we get within range to disable their engines. I do not want that ship destroyed."

"Fire to disable only," acknowledges Sub-Culmit Jollickma. "Weapons at one-third power.

"Sub-Culmit Matilosk, notify the Junnack to follow and advise them of the situation. They are to remain in support unless they receive orders to do otherwise."

"High Commander," calls Nuk-Ma as Hops enters the bridge. "We've got another problem and you're not going to like it. That ship is definitely not Tirg."

"Why wouldn't I like that kind of news," asks Hops as he nears the scanner station?

"The Palup just came into scanner range and Teka is trying to contact it, sir. That ship is trying to outrun a Star and it doesn't look like it is going to make it. The Palup is beginning to close on it. Weapons armed and on line."

"Damn," mutters Hops. "Your right, Nuk-Ma, I don't like it. Send a brief signal and tell them we may be able to help. If they respond, try to get them to head towards us. From the way things are shaping up, they're going to need all the help they can get. Just make sure your message is short and to the point. I don't won't Teka to get a fix on us if that ship turn out to be one of ours."

"Aye, sir. Message sent."

"Any reply?"

"Nothing yet, sir. That Captain may think this is a trap and doesn't want to answer."

"That's what I was thinking. How close is the Palup?"

"It will be within weapons range in about six hours. That ship is still maintaining course and its weapons are armed."

"Have you been able to determine the configuration of their weapons systems?"

"I'll be damned, sir," answers Nuk-Ma. "Just got the final readings. The weapons systems are definitely Guardian, sir. At least we know their strengths and capabilities if they turn out to be someone else."

"What about their power source? Can you get any reading on their exhaust signature?"

"Just barely, sir. They're trying to diffuse the exhaust stream, probably trying everything they can to hide," says Nuk-Ma as he and Ensign Germick adjust the sensitivity of the scanners. "Got it sir. Zithium! They have to be Guardian survivors from another outpost."

"I'm beginning to think you're right," says Hops as he continues to monitor the scanner image. "Cherrick, how soon would we be able to intercept at full power?"

"Just under four hours, sir," replies Cherrick.

"Set an intercept course . . . Damn! Engineering! Is the navigational system back on line yet? Can we move under manual maneuvering power?"

"This is Trilla, sir. I just found the problem with the navigation systems. There isn't anything wrong with our navigational protocols. I found the source of the interference. It's an external signal and I traced it back to that ship. They are sending out a signal that's interfering with the navigational control protocols. It's going to take me at least seven hours to get the primary system back on line."

"You don't have that long," warns Hops. "The Palup is six hours behind that ship. Seven hours put us there too late to give them any help. Can you get anything on manual maneuvering?"

"I might be able to get minimum power to the helm for manual maneuvering in about twenty minutes or so. I've got to rewrite the startup protocols."

"Just get me something as fast as you can," replies Hops. "This ship may be one of ours and they're going to need help. Hops, out. Cherrick, as soon as you have helm response kick this thing in the ass and get this tub moving."

"One ass kicking coming up as soon as I have helm response."

"Nuk-Ma, send another signal. Tell that ship that we are going to try to intercept the Palup, or at least try to slow Teka down. Maybe if we give them the name of that Star, and who's chasing them, they might reply. I need to brief the Council so you got the bridge."

"Aye, sir. Message sent, waiting for their reply."

Once again, Hops enters the Council Generals quarters.

"Come in, Hops, I've been expecting you," says Lamminta. "I've been monitoring your actions regarding this mystery ship and it appears that Telebisque Teka has an interest as well. What do you propose to do if you can't move the Hope close enough to offer direct help?"

"I don't know yet, sir but I'll come up with something. I briefed Williams and told him to come up with a plan we could implement if we do manage to get there in time. Right now, the only thing we can do for certain is to send out a limited number of concealed Dragons to verify the ships identity."

"Sounds like a reasonable approach. How much more time do you think he'll need to finalize this plan and have it ready for presentation to the Council?"

"He might've already finished," asks Hops as he reaches out to activate the intercom sensor. "May I, sir?"

"Of course," answers Lamminta with a slight grin.

After conferring with Williams. Hops again faces Lamminta, saying, "I guess his plan is ready for presentation, sir."

"Very well, if you will inform the Council."

Hops, standing inside the door, activates the ships automated intercom. Within a few minutes, Commander Williams, accompanied by the remaining Council Members, enter Lammintas quarters. The only non-Council member takes his place conspicuously between Hops and Carol.

"Commander Williams," begins Lamminta with a slight grin, "I believe you have a plan that may help identify this mystery ship."

"Yes, Council General, I do," says Williams. "Council General, if I wish to present what I believe to be the only viable option for an accurate identification of this ship."

"Please precede, Commander," says Lamminta with a slight grim and in his usual calm voice.

"Council General, Council Members, as you already now, when we reach this mystery ship we are going to need to have a positive identification to whom this ship actually belongs to. Current indications are that this ship is possibly one of ours and this is where we encounter our biggest problem. The Palup is going to be in the immediate area, which will require our entire fleet of Dragons to maintain the protective cover around the Hope. All pilots will be engaged in this single operation. That leaves only three other qualified pilots to investigate and provide the positive identification that we need."

"And just who are these three remaining pilots," asks a still grinning Lamminta?

"Council General, the only three qualified pilots who are available to conduct this secondary mission are me, the High Commander, and Council Member Quince."

Council Members Pidera and Tro-Ja gasp in horror at the mention of not just one, but two Council Members. Tro-Ja recovers from his shock first.

"Council General! I must protest! To allow two of our Council Members to participate in such a dangerous mission is unthinkable! What are we going to do if something should happen to one, or both of them? I say this plan of Commander Williams is not only unfeasible, but also completely ludicrous. I cannot support such a recommendation."

"I understand," accepts Lamminta as he looks towards Pidera. "Are you of the same mind as Council Member Tro-Ja?"

"I am not sure how I feel about this proposal, Council General. I understand we must keep our Dragons close to protect the Hope against any attack launched by Telebisque Teka. I also understand the need to identify this mystery ship. I acknowledge that the High Commander, Council Member Quince, and Commander Williams, are the only remaining qualified pilots whom the capability of conducting this mission. I only wish we did not have to depend on such important individuals to conduct it. Are the no alternatives to this plan that would not endanger their lives?"

Lamminta, the smile gone from his face, looks at the three former pilots before him, says, "If there were an alternative, I would agree with Council Member Tro-Ja and object to such a proposal. However, as Commander Williams has stated, the Palup will be in the immediate area, we need to protect the Hope, and we still need to identify this mystery ship. I cannot find any alternative that would provide us with the positive identification that we need."

"Engineering to High Commander," suddenly explodes over the intercom.

"This is Hops, go ahead."

"Helm should have manual maneuvering," says Trilla. "I've been able to override the interference but I still have a problem with transferring control back to the computer. Cherrick should have manual helm control."

"Keep working on it. Hops, out. Bridge."

"Nuk-Ma here, sir."

"Tell Cherrick to engage manual helm control. Trilla has it back on, line. We need to be within Dragon range as soon possible."

"Understood, sir. We have helm response. Intercept time is down to about three and a half hours."

"Good. Tell Dunlipee to recall our security blanket. As soon as everyone is back onboard we need to get moving so we can give that ship a little help."

"Aye, sir. Anything else?"

"Negative. Hops, out." Turning his attention back to the Council saying, "It looks like we're going to intercept this ship about a half-hour before Teka shows up. Is Commander Williams's proposal approved or not?"

"I believe Commander Williams had a little help in coming up with this particular plan," says Lamminta quietly. "High Commander? Do you vote to authorize the proposal before the Council?"

"Damn right . . . excuse me, sir. I vote in favor of accepting Commander Williams's recommendation."

"Council Member Tro-Ja?"

"With grave reservations, I agree."

"Council Member Pidera?"

"In favor, and as Council Member Tro-Ja has stated, I also went to express my reservations."

"I understand," says Lamminta. "Council Member Quince?"

"I vote in favor of the proposal."

"And reluctantly I am also in agreement with the plan," says Lamminta as he looks directly at Williams. "Commander, it appears that you have a mission to conduct and not very much time to complete you planning. Good luck to all of you."

The meeting ends as the three pilots return to their own quarters to change into the once familiar flight uniforms. Carol is the first to arrive in the hanger bay and immediately begins the preflight inspection of her Dragon. After completing the external visual inspection, she climbs into the small cockpit. Sitting quietly for several minutes, she glances over the various sensor panels and digital readout display screens, insuring each system is still operating properly. Slowly climbing out of the restrictive confines of the cramped cockpit, she senses someone watching her from behind.

"How long have the two of you been standing there?"

"Long enough to know that you haven't forgotten how to conduct a preflight," answers Hops as he and Williams turn and begin walking towards the other end of the hanger bay, saying, "I think we need to figure out our flight plan."

As soon as the trio is inside the briefing room normally reserved for regular Probe briefings, Williams activates the holographic image projector, producing a basic image that resemblance of the mystery ship.

"This is the best design that we can come up based on our current scans. It appears to be quite a bit smaller that the Hope and as far as I determine there aren't any blind spots that we could use to our advantage. We're going to be using the concealment device, so that should not pose any problem. As far as our approach vector, I suggest that we come in from the aft port quarter."

"Sounds okay to me," says Carol. "It looks like they have a majority of their weapons systems positioned forward which means they can head straight into a fight with maximum firepower and minimum hull exposure. This might indicate a new class of attack Cruisers or battleship. High Commander, what do you think?"

"First, this isn't the Council Chamber so there's no need to be so damned formal, and I'm not so sure that would be the best way to go," says Hops as he picks up a small laser pointer. "These appear to be ion cannon weapons batteries."

"I agree," says Williams.

"Then what are these projections here, here, here, here and here? Could they be another type of weapons array, a new design for a defensive system? If they are, how accurate are they? Do they have the ability to detect a concealed ship and don't want to divulge that information yet? We might be safer going in directly on their six. If they do turn out to be friendly, we would be in a better position to land if we're invited aboard."

The planning continues until they receive the message they have been waiting for.

"Bridge to High Commander."

"This is Hops."

"Within maximum Dragon range in five minutes, sir."

"Thanks, Hops out," acknowledges the senior officer as he takes a deep sigh. "Well gang, I guess looks like show time."

They look at each other, nodding their heads in silent agreement, and just as silently, they leave the ready room.

CHAPTER SEVENTEEN

"Culmit Cudrosia, I want all fighters launched as soon as we are within effective range of this mysterious ship," calmly orders Teka as the Palup slowly gains on the unidentified vessel. "That ship may have communications problems or the commander may be involved in the black market. Either way, I want to know why he is attempting to out run a Fighting Star. If this ship belongs to anyone except the Empire, I want all fighters to be ready to launch and identify that ship. If the Captain refuses to be boarded they are to fire only to disable the engines."

"They are already on standby, Telebisque," replies the Palups, Executive Officer.

"Sensing," continues Teka, "have you been able to determine if the Guardians are in, or possibly near, this sector?"

"No, sir."

"Maintain a positive lock on that strange ship, but keep all long-range sensors set for the Guardians. They've developed a nasty habit of showing up at the most inopportune time. I want to be notified the moment you detect the slightest wavier in the scanner beam. That was the method Mular to detect them. Maybe they haven't been able to correct this slight design defect yet."

"Nothing indicated on any long-range scan, sir. No waiver in the scanner beam. The unidentified ship is maintaining a steady speed of seven point five. Course unchanged."

"Telebisque," says Under-Culmit Dramek. "We will reach maximum fighter range in one hour."

"Then brief your pilots and crews. Insure they understand they are not to engage that ship, only identify, but be prepared to disable it if necessary."

"Understood, sir," acknowledges Cudrosia as he leaves the bridge.

"Helm. Full stop," orders Lieutenant Commander Nuk-ma. "Maintain position. I don't want to get too close to that ship just in case it turns out to be another trap. Germick, what's the Palup doing?"

"Still heading this way, sir," reports Ensign Brooks. "Maintaining full power and will be here in fifty-five minutes. Weapons are armed and on line."

"Hopefully we'll be long gone by then," says Nuk-ma as he opens the intercom channel. "Launch bay, this is Nuk-ma."

"Dunlipee, sir."

"Launch the cover Probes. I want a complete covering force out there before you launch the High Commanders Probe. Inform all pilots to engage their concealment device."

"Aye, sir," acknowledges Dunlipee as he stands between the launch control and com-link officers. "You heard the orders. This is a concealed launch. Launch Red and Gold. Blue and Orange are next."

"Transferring launch control," says the young female officer in a calm, steady voice. "Red and Gold are cleared to launch. Blue and Orange in position."

The launch bay becomes alive with activity. To anyone not accustomed to seeing, or hearing, the organized confusion, the entire launch area appears to be nothing short of complete chaos. Everyone is yelling without anyone acknowledging what anyone else was saying.

"Clear those fuel lines!"

"I need that collective inducer," yells Lieutenant Commander Gallaski in his unmistakable voice of over the hubbub!

"Watch out! Purple needs to get in line!"

"Red and Gold have cleared the ramp," reports the com-link officer in her sure and steady voice over the Launch Bay address system. "Blue and Orange are in position. Transferring launch control. Black Alpha and Black Charlie are in position. Blue and Orange are cleared to launch."

"Damn it! I need that collective inducer" again yells Ski!

"Green and Indigo ready."

"Blue and Orange have cleared the ramp. Transferring launch control to Black Alpha and Black Charlie. Green and Indigo are in position."

"I need that inducer," again yells Ski! "Purple Four isn't going to make it!"

"Get that charge cable out of here!"

"Black Alpha and Black Charlie have cleared the ramp." The voice of the launch control officer never falters as she continues to maintain her solid control over the launch operation. "Green and Indigo have launch control. Black Bravo and Violet are in position."

"Get me that inducer! This bird is going to fly if I have to kick it out the tube myself," yells Ski, as he turns, almost tripping over a maintenance cart. "Move that damn thing out of here! I need some room to work!"

"Get me that hatch cover"

"Can't get this canopy locked!"

"Where in the hell is Purple," yells Dunlipee! "They're up next!"

"It's about time," yells the maintenance chief as he snatches the inducer for a crewmember! "Where in the hell was it! Next time put it back in the tool chest where it belongs!"

"Green and Indigo have launched. Black Bravo and Violet have launch control. Purple is in position. Purple four is not in position."

"Damn it! I know Purple Four ain't in position," comes the graveled voiced of Ski over the organized confusion. "She's got a bad inter-collector release coil. Give me two minutes and I'll have it fixed!"

"Black Bravo and Violet have launched. Purple is in position. Purple Four is not in position."

"Dun! Go ahead and launch Purple," shouts Ski. "Four ain't going to make this mission!"

"How long before you can get it fixed?"

"I don't know. I thought it was just a stuck release circuit but it ain't," yells Ski! "I'm not sure where the problem is. Purple will just have to fly one short."

"Okay," answers Dunlipee as he pats the shoulder of the woman in front of him. "Launch Purple and get the High Commanders' Probe ready. Also, inform him that Purple is one short but that everyone else is out and covering. As soon as Probe . . . What's the High Commander Probe sign?"

"Com-link to High Commander."

"This is Lost One," answers Hops with a slight chuckle.

"Does that mean I'm Lost Two," asks the former leader of Probe Gold?

"Yep," quickly answers Williams. "He's One, you're Two, and I'm Three."

"I think that you and I should swap call signs," says Carol. "I know where I am so I can't be lost too."

"Transferring launch control," interrupts the launch control officer. "Lost. Launch when ready."

"Okay Lost, let's get this over with," calls Hops as the three pilots press the ignition sensor. Within the blinking of an eye, Probe Lost hurls down the launch tube and into the emptiness of space.

"Com-link! This is Black Alpha Two! I'm coming back! Concealment device just went out!"

"Damn," yells Ensign Germick from the main bridge scanner station! "One Dragon visible! Just made it to the landing ramp."

"Do you think the Palup picked up on that," quickly asks Nuk-Ma as he stands looking over Germick's shoulder?

"Telebisque! Contact! Guardian Dragon! Positive identification! Sector six three seven by nine two five! The Guardian mother ship is definitely within effective Dragon range of the unidentified vessel."

"Get that scan enhanced," rapidly orders Teka! "I want that Guardian ship found! Send another signal to that unidentified ship and order the Captain to come about and to stand down! All fighters will fire to disable their engines! Prepare all boarding parties!"

"Telebisque," calls Dramek. "If we send such a message the Guardians will know we are here and in pursuit of that ship."

"They already know we are here! Why do you think they launched their Dragons and are using their concealment device? They are considerably closer to that ship than we are. If they're able to identify that ship before we can and it turns out to be one of theirs, they will be prepared to fight and defend it. We only have the ability to destroy the ship we can detect. After that, we must withdraw for our own safety because we cannot fight what we cannot see. I suggest you analyze that last sensing scan and find a way to detect that Guardian ship."

"Yes, sir."

"Fighter Command," continues Teka as Dramek leaves the bridge with the computer chip. "I want all fighters launched. You are to engage the unidentified ship."

"Sir, we are too far away for our fighters to be able to engage that ship and safely return," says Culmit Bassicloe. "My fighters will not be able to . . ."

"They are my fighters," yells Teka! "You will launch as ordered! The Palup will continue on course, which will enable you to recover them when necessary. Launch all fighters now!"

"Yes, sir. Initiating launch sequence."

"Sir," calls Germick. "We have a problem. The Palup just opened her doors. Horses coming out all four launch ramps but they're still too far out to be effective. The High Commander should be able to identify that ship and be back on board the Hope with about ten minutes to spare."

"Think again, Germick," says Nuk-Ma. "Has the Palup stopped?"

"No, sir."

"Then those Horses could engage that ship and not have to worry about being too far from the barn. What do we do if that ship actually turns out to be one of ours that somehow survived just as we did? What then?"

"I see, sir," says Germick.

"However, I do agree that we definitely have a problem," says the temporary commander of the Hope as he activates the communications channel. "Launch bay, fire control, this is Nuk-Ma. Inform the Probes and defensive batteries that we're moving closer to that ship. The Palup just launched her Horses and it looks like we may end up in a fight. I don't want the Probes to arm their weapons systems until the last possible moment. The Tirgs may not be able to see them, but with the transfer of that much energy, there's going to be one hell of an electromagnetic field generated. They will definitely be able to lock on to that. Teka may already know we're here when Black Alpha Two couldn't stay hidden."

"Understood. Message relayed."

"Also, I want all communications with Lost One transferred to the bridge. Hops may need information without depending on the middleman."

"Transferring channel," says Dunlipee. "Contact Lost One to verify."

"Lost One, this is Nuk-Ma."

"I got you're last message," says Hops. "It doesn't look too good for the home team. Have you been able to get anything on that ship yet?"

"Not yet, Hops . . . Lost One."

"Well it's obvious that Teka knows we're here. Send another message to that ship and tell the Captain that he's got Teka breathing down his neck and that if he wants any help he'd better answer."

"I'll try again," asks Nuk-Ma. "Anything else?"

"Yeah, I just remembered how damn tight this cockpit is. Lost One, out."

As soon as Hops clears the vehi-com channel a strange, he hears another familiar voice.

"Lost One. This is Commander Victor Freslof of the Guardian Battleship Revenge. What is your personal identification?"

"Vic! This is Hops," he yells as he recognizes the voice of an old friend!

"Negative," replies Freslof tersely! "Request positive identification. What happened at Crelos Five that . . .?"

"Look Vic! We aren't got time for all that bullshit! You're about to get your ass in a sling and I don't have time to go back and get a crowbar big enough to pry your ass out of this mess!"

"Lost One, this is the Revenge, if you're whom you say you are, just answer the damn question!"

"I got into a fight with four Crelosites and lost! You bailed me out and all it cost me almost two months wages," yells Hops! "Now can we . . ."

"I'll be a son of a bitch," shouts Freslof! "How in the hell did you manage to survive! Where in the hell are you! I can't get . . ."

"Stop you're squawking, Vic! Teka's heading this way and he's looking up our collective asses. I'm coming in with two more birds on my tail. We'll be landing in two minutes. You'll see us just before we hit the deck. Break. Hope, this is Lost One."

"Roger, Lost One," acknowledges Nuk-Ma. "We monitored and holy hell just broke out around here. What do you need for us to do?"

"First, get the Council off the bridge and into my ready room so I can talk to them in private if I need to," begins Hops. "Get our umbrella closed and move over here as quick as you can. Those incoming Horses aren't going to wait until we finish our celebration before they hit us. Keep the channel to the Revenge open."

"Recovery underway," reports Nuk-Ma. "Dun says it will take only a few more minutes to get everyone down. We should be there in seven minutes."

"Good," acknowledges Hops. "We're going in."

Just before the three Dragons land on the Revenge, the concealment devices are disengaged. The landing bay crew of the Revenge is surprised as the three Dragons suddenly appear in the emptiness of space. As soon as the ships are maneuvered into empty maintenance stalls, the Captain of the Revenge, almost knocking over several crew members, enters the landing bay at a dead run.

"Hops," yells Commander Freslof! "Where in the hell have you been!"

"Take it easy, Vic," calls Hops as he climbs down the access ladder. "We still have the Palup out there and Teka don't take kindly to strangers playing in his back yard. I think that we need to . . ."

"Don't worry about Teka. He has about another ten minutes before his navigational system goes on haywire. That's how we are able to stay in one piece for this long," interrupts Freslof. "Bridge, this is Freslof. Engage the navigational interrupter on command."

"Wait a minute," yells Hops! "That's how we found you. If you turn that thingamajig on you'll stop the Hope."

"No, not this time," answers Freslof. "How close is your ship?"

"Should be within ten thousand in about three minutes if everything went okay with getting our Dragons down. Why?"

"If you're within a fifteen thousand kilometers, the interrupter doesn't have any affect any ship and somehow, and I don't know why, but the Dragons aren't affected at any range. The interrupter doesn't have any effect on the Horseheads either. I can get you a full briefing for you and you ships' captain on how the thing . . . and who is this," asks Freslof as he sees Quince and Williams walking towards them.

"Vic, this is former Major, now Council Member Carol Quince, and my Executive and Senior Flight Officer, Commander Orin Williams."

"You're telling me that she's an actual Council Member?"

"Yep."

"And Commander Williams is you Executive and Senior Flight Officer?"

"Yep."

"So what kind of promotion did you get?"

"We didn't know if anyone else survived so we elected our own Council as soon as we got the chance. I got stuck as High Commander and given command of the Hope," explains Hops. "I think we need to stop with all of the explanations get to work. Is there someplace we could talk?"

"Sure. We can go to my ready room," answers Freslof. "Captain Rasnole, get these Dragons refueled. The High Commander may want to return to his ship as soon as we finish."

"Aye, sir," replies Rasnole. "Already started on it and should be finished in another fifteen minutes."

The four senior leaders depart the landing bay and move towards the bridge of the Revenge. As they first enter the bridge, Freslof begins his introductions.

"I'd like all of you to meet High Commander Hoppinzorinski, Council Member Quince, and Commander Williams of the Battleship Hope."

"What," exclaims one of Freslof's officers!

"Hops, this is Lieutenant Commander Wester, my Exec," says Freslof as he turns to face the officer. "Wes, tell scanning to keep a close watch on those two Stars out there. As soon as the Hope gets within the safety margin, activate the interrupter. You have the bridge."

"Aye, sir," replies the still stunned officer.

"You can detect the Hope," asks Hops?

"Just barely," answers Freslof. "That's how we knew to turn the interrupter on."

"Telebisque," calls out Sub-Culmit Dramek, the scanner officer of the Palup! "Three Guardian Dragons have appeared and landed on the second ship!"

"Culmit Bassicloe! Launch all fighters and attack," immediately orders Teka! "Culmit Cudrosia! Inform them . . ."

"Telebisque! The helm is not responding," reports the Palups' helmsman.

"Engage secondary system," orders Teka! "Maintain speed and course!"

"Secondary system on line. Navigational control still not responding," reports the helmsman. "Taking primary and secondary systems off line. Engaging primary manual control and still no response. Engaging secondary manual control. Still no response."

"What," screams Teka! "What do you mean no response?"

"I don't know, sir. The helm does not respond to any control inputs. Automatic course corrections occur without any control commands from helm control. I do not have control over any navigational commands."

"Disengage all helm computers," orders Teka. "Maintain complete manual control."

"Unable to disengage navigational computers."

"Shut down the engines," yells Teka! "Inform the Junnack to continue with the attack!"

"The Junnack reports the same problems, Telebisque," reports Cudrosia. "They have taken their engines off line."

"Recall the fighters," screams Teka! "If we cannot maneuver we are going to need their protection here. Sensing! Has that ship move? What is the current range? Have you been able to locate the original ship?"

"Position of second ship unchanged. Separation is steady at one hundred and fifty thousand kilometers. Unable to locate the primary Guardian ship."

"Telebisque," calls out Cudrosia, "all fighters are reporting they still have navigational control and are moving into defensive positions around the Palup."

"Thankfully, our fighters are not as dead as we are," says Teka. "This interference must be originating from that ship. Isolate the frequencies they are using and override the interference. I want navigational control as soon as possible."

"Inform all squadron leaders to maintain their defensive posture around the Palup until further notice," orders Teak as he slowly regains control over his emotions. "Sensing, maintain a positive lock on the Guardian ship we can see. If that ship moves a micrometer, I want to know about it. How long before the fighters are in their defensive formation around the Palup?"

"Lead squadron is within fifty kilometers. All squadrons will be in their defensive positions in forty-five seconds," reports Cudrosia."

"Aye, sir. Engineering is already working on the problem."

CHAPTER EIGHTEEN

"Okay, Vic," begins Hops as soon as the doors to the ready room close, "where in the hell did you get this ship and how in the hell did you make it this far alone?"

"Take it easy, Hops," says Freslof as he moves towards the lounge area of his quiet domain. "I'll give you a full briefing as soon as you calm down and take a take a seat. Refreshments?"

"We don't have time for an ice cream social," continues Hops as he settles into a soft chair. "Just tell me how in the hell you got this far."

"Settle down, Hops, and I'll start from the beginning," says Freslof as he sits down across from the High Commander. "The Revenge was still in the construction docks when I was given command. I was at Pine Tree Five for a little shore leave when I received word that the original skipper felt that he was too old to accept another command and decided to retire. I only had a skeleton crew and ordered to proceed to Uri Two to pick up the remainder of the crew and begin the shakedown cruise. The first day out of Uri Two we received a distress call from Alpha Cheris."

"Cheris got a message out," hastily interrupts Carol?

"Yes ma'am, and I'm glad they did," answers Freslof. "The shakedown was scrubbed and we were ordered to investigate. However, when we reached Cheris there wasn't anything left except a destroyed outpost. I tried to notify Fleet Headquarters but couldn't get any response. I decided to head for Capricorn Seven, but by the time we got there, we couldn't find anything except space dust. If it hadn't been for a few faint scanner readings, no one would have ever known that Seven ever existed. The Tirgs really must have wanted to destroy Seven pretty bad to leave nothing but dust."

"The Tirgs didn't destroy Seven," says Hops. "Lamminta did. He didn't want to leave anything that the Tirgs might be able to use against us."

"Smart move," continues Freslof. "I started to head back towards Uri Two but ran into the ass end . . . excuse me ma'am."

"That's okay," says Carol. "I've used worse when I had my own Probe."

"You were a Probe Leader," asks Freslof?

"I was."

"Must have been heck of a Probe."

"About getting back to Uri Two," interjects Hops.

"They weren't looking behind them," continues Freslof, "which gave me enough room to back off without letting them know we were so close. I couldn't raise anyone so I guessed the war on. I crossed the Agreed Zone and raised as much hell as I could, but I did have a slight advantage. Whenever anyone got too close I just turned on the navigational interrupter."

"How much damage have you been able to do so far," asks Hops?

"A little so far. We've been able to take out one cruisers, three battle destroyers, two hunters, and seventeen Horses. I haven't quite found the handle on how to go after a Star yet."

"How many Battle Groups have you counted so far?"

"Four as of right now, four that I've been able to identify," answers Freslof. "We've had contact with the Fourth, the Costic, and Baylough. The Sixth Group with the Tablor and Wissicle. Seventh with the Gissoc and Zobak. Then the Loksija and Frema of the Tenth almost tagged me. What about you? How many Groups have you encountered?"

"Only two groups so far. The Fifth was our first contact."

"Landex and Napla," says Freslof.

"Yep," agrees Hops "and now Teka with the Eleventh is chasing us."

"And his support Star?"

"The Junnack," answers Hops. "We have managed to figure out how to cripple a Star without getting run over by it but like you, we haven't figured out how to take one out completely. I'll give you the details later. Right now, we need to get back to the Hope and brief the Council to let them know we just had a population explosion. I'll let the Council know that you'll be paying you're respects in what, about an hour or so? Would that be enough time for you to prepare you're briefing?"

"More than enough," answers Freslof. "I've kept complete logs on everything we've done. All I have to do is to get it from the computers. I could download everything to the Hope to make things easier."

"Good idea. I'll let my communications chief coordinate with yours on that," says Hops as he looks towards Carol and Commander Williams. "Well gang, I think that does it for now. I'll meet the two of you in the Launch Bay."

"Commander," says Carol as she rises and moves towards the door.

"Council Member," returns Freslof.

"Commander," says Williams as he follows Carol.

"Commander," acknowledges Freslof.

As the door closes silently behind the departing guests Hops turns, directly facing Freslof, saying, "Okay, Vic, now I want you to tell me exactly what you're doing here, and I want the truth."

"I just told you the truth, Hops," rebuts Freslof. "There wasn't anything left on our side of the Agreed Zone so I came through the back door and, if I might add, just like you apparently did."

"I don't think so, Vic. You're telling me that you took out twenty-three ships without getting a scratch. How'd you let them get that close when you could've stopped them dead in their tracks with that interrupter thing? If you were out of weapons range, you would've had to move damned close to do that kind of damage. If your 'secret weapon' only interferes with navigational control, they still had control over their scanner and weapons systems. I think you better come up with a better story than that, and fast."

"I just told you everything that happened and how we did it, sir," says Freslof hotly! "You can have your own people go over my logs and they'll give you the same information I just did."

Still not completely satisfied with the explanation, Hops turns to follow the others saying, "I'll see you on the Hope in about an hour."

A short while later Commander Freslof and Lieutenant Commander Wester arrive aboard the Hope and are immediately escorted Hops ready room.

"Council General Lamminta," begins Hops as he begins the formal introductions "Council Member Pidera, Council Member Tro-Ja, and Council Member Quince, I would like to present Commander Victor Freslof, Captain of the Battleship Revenge and his Executive Officer, Lieutenant Commander John Wester."

"Gentlemen," begins Lamminta as he extends his hand, first to Freslof and then to Wester. "You honor us with your presence. Please, be seated."

"Thank you, Council General," says Freslof as he and Wester accept the offered chairs at the side of the briefing table. "The honor is ours to be in the presence of the Council of Elders."

"Thank you, Commander," says Lamminta. "High Commander Hoppinzorinski has informed us that your tapes and logs have been transferred to the Hope."

"That is correct. The transfer should be complete by now so I will try to be as brief as possible," begins Freslof. "As the High Commander may have already informed you, we initially received a distress call from Alpha Cheris. When we arrived, we only found the destruction left behind by the Tirgs. Capricorn Seven was our next destination and we found the same thing. Only High Commander Hoppinzorinski informed me that you were the one who gave the order to destroy Seven. I figured the war was on so I crossed the Agreed Zone to return the favor and do whatever damage I could.

"From what High Commander Hoppinzorinski has told us, we have a firm count on six Battle Groups. Twelve Fighting Stars, fourteen cruisers, seven battle destroyers, twenty scouts, and forty-eight hunters. To date the Tirgs have lost one cruisers, three battle destroyers, and two hunters and seventeen Horses. The High Commander has informed us that we can add one Star to that count."

"Not taken out completely, only severely damaged, Commander," corrects Lamminta. "I'm afraid that it will be operational in a relatively short time and once again pose a threat."

"Of course, sir," says Freslof.

"Now, what are your shortages Commander," asks Lamminta. "How many crew members do you currently have, or may need?"

"I still have a full complement, Council General, nine hundred and twenty-four. As far as supplies, all I actually need is basic medical and some minor repair supplies. I believe that we have been as fortunate as the Hope when it comes to any actual battle damage."

"High Commander, would you see to the needs of Commander Freslof and his crew? I believe that we should be able to share our supplies as best as possible," says Lamminta. "Now, do any of the Council Members have anything they would like to ask Commander Freslof or Commander Wester?"

"I have but one question for Commander Freslof," says Pidera. "When we first identified ourselves to you, why did you not immediately respond? It would have saved everyone concerned a great deal of time, and not have endangered us with the approach of the Palup and Junnack."

"I will not apologize for my actions, Council Member," says Freslof cautiously. "I just finished an engagement with a reinforced Battle Group. Two Fighting Stars, one Cruisers, three battle destroyers, four hunters, and six scouts. They found the Revenge and I was running from them with everything I had. I finally managed to lose them in the Decatas System. I've been running from them for as long as you have, Council Member. I wasn't exactly ready to accept a signal from an unknown ship just because it says it's friendly and hasn't fired at me yet. Besides, with your concealment device engaged I could barely detect your presence, but you expected me to answer someone who calls out from hiding under those circumstances?"

"I understand," says Pidera with a sight bow of his head as he accepts the explanation.

"Commander," says Lamminta as he looks about the table, waiting for any further questions. "It appears that you have satisfied the Council with your briefing and explanation. It seems that you need a concealment device installed on the Revenge and we need a navigational interrupter installed on the Hope. Has work already begun, or must the Council give its approval before anything can be started?"

"I already gave the job to Trilla and Nuk-Ma, sir," replies Hops. "They're already coordinating with the folks on the Revenge. Everything should be ready for us to get under way in about an hour or so."

"Very good, High Commander. Before we all return to work, I would like to suggest that High Commander Hoppinzorinski now be responsible for our small Task Force and, if the Council agrees, Commander Williams shall take over the duties as Captain of the Hope, leaving the High Commander to concentrate on his own duties." No one at the conference table offered any objection, allowing Lamminta to continue, "I believe everything needs to be completed as quickly as possible. The Palup and Junnack may not be able to move but their communications system is still operational and Telebisque Teka may already have informed their Supreme Commander concerning our current location and his current situation. Reinforcements may already be heading here. Everyone needs to work as quickly as possible so we can get out of here."

Freslof and Wester immediately depart and return to the Revenge as Hops and Williams towards the main bridge of the Hope.

"Commander Williams has full command of the Hope as of this date and time. An entry will be in the ships log to reflect this change of command. Good luck, Orin," says Hops as he relinquishes his authority to the new ships captain. "I'll be in the ready room going over the information on the Revenge that Freslof sent over."

Williams, assuming the duties as Captain of the Hope, immediately goes to work as if nothing out of the ordinary has happened.

"Nuk-Ma? What's the status of the Palup and Junnack?"

"Unchanged, sir. It seems that they haven't figured out where the interference is coming from. They did send a message to their Supreme Commander of their situation. No indication of any reply as of yet, or that reinforcements have been ordered here. I haven't been able to detect any communications between Teka and anyone else except their Supreme Commander."

"Thank you," says Williams as he sits in the captain's chair. "Commander Trilla, this is Williams. How's the installation of the navigational interrupter coming along?"

"It should be operational in about another fifteen minutes."

"Let me know as soon as it is on line."

"Aye, sir."

"Nuk-Ma," continues Williams. "Open a secure channel to the Revenge."

"Channel open and secure, sir."

"Revenge, this is the Hope."

"This is the Revenge," answers Freslof."

"Commander Williams, here. How soon before you will be able to get under way?"

"The concealment device should be operational in about another half hour, sir," replies Freslof. "We should be able to follow you as soon as the basic operational and all protocol checks have been completed."

"Good. As soon as it's operational, turn it on. The High Commander will want to get out of here before Teka has any help show up. As soon as he comes up with a course, I'll let you know."

"Understood."

"Williams, out," acknowledges the Hope new Captain as he nods towards Nuk-Ma, indicating the open frequency should be closed. "Nuk-Ma, inform Commander Jo-Ich that I would like to see him in my ready room."

"Aye, sir."

As he departs the bridge, Williams cannot help wondering what was actually bothering Hops.

"Come on in, Orin," says Hops as Williams enters the room that is now his place of sanctuary. "Grab a seat and I'll be right with you."

Williams, taking a seat next to Hops, stretches his neck to look over the High Commanders shoulder to see the information sent on the travels of the Revenge displayed.

"How'd he do that without us finding him before," quietly mutters Hops? "Course changes for no apparent reason. He makes contact at long range, then moves closer but doesn't launch any Dragon cover. Then he reverses course and stays just far enough ahead to stay out of weapons range for six hours before he takes off like a bat out of hell. He does the same thing at almost every encounter. It's almost as if he actually wants the Tirgs to chase him."

"Why would he intentionally make, and then maintain, contact? Why didn't he use his navigational interrupter," asks Williams? "What was he trying to do?"

"I don't knew, but I intend to find out what in the hell he's trying to hide," replies Hops as he looks at Williams. "What's up?"

"Just wanted to let you know that Trilla is just about finished installing the navigational interrupter and the concealment device we sent over to the Revenge should be ready in about another twenty minutes or so. We can to move any time after that."

"What about Teka?"

"He sent a message to their Supreme Commander but hasn't received any reply yet. It seems that he still hasn't figured out that his problem is originating from the Revenge."

"So far, so good," says Hops. "I want you to get a complete copy of these logs down to Commander Bell. Tell her to go over everything with a fine toothcomb. She's to go over everything manually as well as the normal computer analysis and enhancement. If Nuk-Ma can spare her, I'd like Ensign Germick to help. She found what we were looking for the last time and she might be able to do it again.

"As soon as everything is ready set a course for Uri Two, I want to see what's left back there. If we don't find what we're looking for there, we'll head for Pine Tree Five. Something isn't right and I want to find out what it is before we get too much further into Tekas' backyard."

"I'll get our people ready and inform Freslof," acknowledges Williams.

"No, not yet" comes a stern warning from Hops. "Just send a short message to have him tag along. Let's take our time on this one. Don't set a direct course because I don't want Freslof to know too much just yet. Put a lot of static in the signal but let him get just enough to know that he's to follow us."

Being more than a little confused Williams asks, "What are you actually intending to do? None of this makes any sense to me."

"Just get us moving, Commander. I want to get out of here as soon as possible. Once we're under way, I want a quite meeting with you, Quince, Lamminta, Jo-Ich, Trilla, and Seeret. Don't tell anyone . . ." says Hops the door chime interrupt him.

"Come in," says Williams.

"You sent for me, sir?"

"Yes I did, Jo," answers Williams. "As of now you're rated as a full Commander and are my Executive and Senior Flight Officer."

"What's going . . .?"

"Jo," interrupts Hops. "I just told Orin, but since you're here, there's something I need you to do."

"Sure Ho . . . sir."

"Quietly inform the old man, Quince, Trilla and Seeret that I need to see all of them in my quarters as soon as we get under way. I'll explain then. Make sure no one finds out about this meeting."

"You got it, sir."

"I guess I'll find out what's going on later," says Williams as he and his new Executive Officer leave the ready room.

"No change with Tirgs," reports Nuk-Ma as soon as Williams enters the bridge. "Trilla just reported that the navigational interrupter is on line. He's not exactly sure how it works but should be able to give you a full briefing as soon as he goes over the complete schematic."

"Good," says Williams. "What about the Revenge?"

"Commander Freslof says he should be ready in another five minutes."

"Okay. Novac, plot a roundabout course for Uri Two. Don't make it obvious that's our destination."

"Sir," questions the Navigational Officer?

"Just do it, Commander. I don't have time to explain."

"Aye, sir," replies Novac.

"Nuk-Ma, send a message to the Revenge. Keep it short and put a lot of static in it. Give our course. Initial speed is deal slow so we don't leave any disturbance trail. Let Freslof understand that he is to follow at ten thousand kilometers."

"Basic course plotted and locked into the computer," reports Novac. "Manual course corrections will be made on your orders."

"Message sent, sir," reports Nuk-Ma. "Commander Freslof is requesting a confirmation. He didn't understand the entire message."

"He wasn't supposed to," answers Williams. "Send the same message only put a little more static in it. All he needs to know is that he is to follow us at ten thousand. Tell him to keep his interrupter on line and engage the concealment device. We leave in one minute."

"Aye, sir," replies Nuk-Ma as he sends the message a second time. "Revenge acknowledges course, speed, and distance. Still requesting confirmation."

"Disregard the confirmation request. Cherrick, let's get out of here."

"Helm responding, speed dead slow."

"Any reaction from the Palup," quietly asks Williams?

"No, sir," says Nuk-Ma. "The Palup and Junnack are maintaining position. It looks like they don't know we're moving."

"Is the Revenge following?"

"Yes, sir, concealment device engaged, interrupter is operational but off line. The navigational interrupter on the Revenge is still on line. Maintaining a distance of ten thousand, dead slow speed. Palup and Junnack maintaining current position."

"Telebisque! I just lost contact with the Guardian ships!"

"What are they up to this time," asks Teka in an amazingly clam voice. "Inform the Junnack to come along side as soon as she has maneuvering capabilities. Maintain a thousand kilometers separation. Scanning. Were you able to determine the Guardians course?"

"Yes, sir. The visible ship began moving just before we lost visible and scanner contact."

"Communications, send a priority message to Telecoup Mular. Tell him that I am going to need the Landex and Napla to assist in the hunt."

"Message sent and acknowledged, sir."

"Sir! I have helm response," calls out the Helmsman of the Palup!

"Telebisque, the Junnack reports they have helm control," reports Matilosk.

"Helm, as soon as the Junnack is in position, follow the course the Guardians were taking when they engaged their concealment device. Culmit Cudrosia, you have the bridge."

"Yes, sir. Will you be in your quarters?"

"No," answers Teka. "I'll be in my ready room. I want to study the contact reports we have on our friends again."

Within a few minutes, the two Fighting Stars are moving through the void of space much faster than the prey they are seeking.

CHAPTER NINETEEN

"What's Teka doing now that he's lost us?"

"He sent a message to the Junnack once both of us disappeared, sir. He also sent a message to the Landex."

"Maintain course and speed until we're out of their effective scanner range. If Freslof wants to know anything about our destination, send the same message with the same static. I'll inform the High Commander that we're under way. Nuk-Ma, you have the bridge."

As the invited guests arrive at the quarters of the High Commander, they are surprised to see him in his once familiar flight uniform.

"Are you planning a trip that we should know about," asks Lamminta?

"No, sir. I just thought I'd get a little comfortable," says Hops, gesturing for everyone to take a seat. "I hope I haven't inconvenienced anyone, but I think I've found a very unusual pattern concerning Freslof and the Revenge."

"Excuse me, sir," says Captain Seeret as he remains standing, glancing at the senior officers and Council Members. "I think I'm here by mistake."

"You're here because I need your talents, Captain, so if you will take a seat with everyone else, I'll get started," replies Hops. Without waiting he continues. "Before anyone passes judgment I'd like for everyone to hear me out, and I hope I'm wrong. First, since when did we start giving our ships a name that relates to an act or action? I've searched the records and every ship that has been built at the Fleet construction dock has been named either for a person of great respect or for a significant event in our history, that is every ship except the Revenge. Freslof is correct when he said the Revenge was built just prior to the Tirgs attack, but the original name was Gimmerlick, referring to the late Admiral, and was commissioned under that name."

"I don't think that's a good position to take, High Commander," says Lamminta. "As you know, the Hope is not named for a person, or an action. Hope is a feeling."

"That's a little different, sir," argues Hops. "The Hope was built at Seven, not at the Fleet construction docks. We've never had any kind of official commissioning ceremony, but we do have her name on the bow. Where is the Revenge's name? We haven't seen it anywhere. Now forgive me, sir, but when would a ships' captain, hiding inside enemy territory, take the time to stop and take the name of his ship off of the bow?"

"The name may not have been place on the ship prior to its shakedown cruise," says Carol.

"Not likely," answers Hops. "I finally found the records, and for some reason, they were buried in the files under about seventeen tons of garbage. Here, look, at this," says Hops as he activates a small sensor on the wall mounted sensor pad, producing a small holographic image showing the Revenge while it was still in the construction dock. "If you take notice to the bow, Gimmerlick is already on the bow."

"Very interesting," says Williams as he studies the projected image. "I think you just got everyone's attention. What else do you have?"

"A lot," says Hops, "and Orin already knows about this, but every time Freslof engaged the Tirgs, he didn't immediately activate his navigational interrupter. Instead, he runs for about six hours, staying just out of the Tirgs weapons range. If he does this at every engagement, how does he account for taking out twenty-three ships without getting a scratch? Even with the protection of our concealment device we haven't been that lucky."

"If the Revenge was damaged, maybe Commander Freslof has had enough time between engagements to make repairs and get her back into fighting condition," says Jo-Ich.

"If that's the case, where are his maintenance and repair logs? Why didn't he ask for anything that to be used for structural repair? He could've only had a minimal amount of repair parts aboard when he left the docks. All he asked for is basic medical supplies and a couple of spare parts for their secondary systems. If he had any significant structural damage, why didn't he ask for any heavy repair material, parts, or other major components? Maybe I'm wrong, but how do you engage twenty-three Tirg ships, destroy every damned one of them, doesn't get a single trace burn, suffer zero casualties, and never send out a single Dragon? He has to be one hell of a ships' captain and tactician, but I don't think so. Take a gander at his service record.

"The largest thing he ever commanded, before the Revenge, was the Raddington, a supply frigate. He never had a combat command, and now he says that the original skipper suddenly decided to retire and that he was next in line for command. How in the hell do you go from commanding a supply frigate, which has only basic weaponry, and suddenly get promoted to take command of a newly designed and built, top of the line battleship, carrying the latest state of the art weapons, and is armed to the teeth? How does someone with his experience take command of a new ship without receiving the required training? His service record doesn't indicate anything but the basic command courses. There isn't anything that even remotely resembling a senior battle command course on his record." Pausing for a moment, he looks the leaders gathered in front of him before continuing. "Now, and this is according to the official logs he sent over, we should have had contact with the Revenge right after we engaged the Landex the first time. His logs indicate the Revenge was within thirty thousand kilometers of our position at that time. I think our sensors are able to accurately identify anything out to five hundred thousand kilometers with a maximum range almost doubled that. We didn't detect any ships in that entire area except the Landex, Napla, and the Hope. If he was that close, and didn't have a concealment device, how did we miss him?"

"Are you saying that Freslof may not be who he says he is," asks Williams?

"Exactly. He's either a damned good imposter or been real damned lucky, and I personally don't believe in that much luck," answers Hops. "I'm not real sure which one he is, but I intend to find out."

"If he is an imposter, how do we account for the rest of the crew on the Revenge," asks Lamminta?

Pausing slightly, Hops says, "We really didn't see all that many people while we were there. There were only six or seven in the landing bay, another dozen or so we passed on our way to the bridge and maybe five or six more on the bridge. We saw only about two dozen crewmembers the entire time we were there. For a ship the size of the Revenge, where was everyone else?"

"How do you propose we find out the truth," asks Jo-Ich?

"Very carefully."

"Sir," says Seeret. "May I ask a question?"

"That's why you're here."

"All I see so far is speculation, and a lot of unanswered questions. I don't see any hard proof to support what you are saying."

"You're right, Captain," agrees Hops. "And that's where we all come together. This is what I'm going to need from everyone. First, Jo, I want you to set up a frequency scanner in your quarters to monitor the frequency spectrum of the concealment device and navigational interrupter. Compare our frequencies with the ones the Revenge is radiating."

"I should have it operational in about an hour or so, sir."

"Next, Orin, I'm going to need your expertise on the bridge. Between you and Jo, I want confidential updates on everything Freslof wants or does. Use your best judgment. I don't want anyone know what you're doing, and that includes Nuk-Ma. I don't want anything to leak out to give Freslof the slightest hint that we're on to his little game. When you get back to the bridge, tell Nuk-Ma send another signal with the same static. Tell Freslof to move to within eight thousand to improve communications. Once he's there, take some of the static out. Keep just enough interference in all further communication to make it convincing that we're still having trouble with interference from the interrupter, but we're working on it.

"Trilla, I want you to go over the schematics of the interrupter circuit by circuit until you know the entire system configuration forwards, backwards, sideways, upside down, inside out, and in your sleep. I want to know if that thing could be capable of accepting an external signal that could give Freslof any chance of taking over navigational control of the Hope. In addition, if it can, could it compromise the integrity of any of our other systems or circuits? I need you to come up with two homing devices that can be easily hidden, but impossible to detect.

"Carol, I'd like for you in your official capacity as a member of the Council, to visit the Revenge for an inspection tour and a complete detailed briefing. We may not be able to use our standard communications homing signal because Freslof has the same ones and we may not be able to keep a lock on you. Trilla, I want you to change the frequency pattern on a couple of communicators so we can keep track of their movements. If Freslof suspects anything, he could easily jam, or possibly alter the locator frequency signal and we need to keep one-step ahead of him.

"Next, Captain Seeret you will accompany Council Member Quince on the tour, I also want you to analyze the Revenges energy consumption since they left the construction docks. How much fuel did they have? How far have they traveled? How many times have they fired which weapons and at what intensity? What targets have they fired and what were the results? What has their total energy consumption been? Have they ever refueled? If so, where, when and by whom?

"Understood, sir. I'll get Lieutenants Televy and Craig started on that right away."

"Negative, Captain," admonishes Hops. "If I had wanted them to assist you on this, they would be here now. No one outside of this room is to know what we're working on, and I mean no one."

"Aye, sir," says Seeret.

"Don't take it too hard, Captain," says Hops. "I need someone that I can trust working on this. If I didn't think you could handle this on your own, you wouldn't be here now. In addition to piloting her shuttle, you're going to be her official escort. She is not to leave your sight for any reason and make . . ."

"For *any* reason," interrupts Carol?

"Within reason, of course," says Hops with a slight grin as he continues to give his instructions, "and make sure you're carrying your side arm. At the first sign of trouble, you're to get her back here regardless of what you have to do to do it. Nothing is to happen to her, and I emphasize *nothing*. You are authorized to use whatever force is necessary to keep her safe."

"Understood, sir," replies Seeret as he accepts his new responsibilities.

"Now the last thing I'm going to need is for someone to handle Tro-Ja and Pidera. If they get wind of what we're doing before we're ready, this whole thing could blow up in our face."

Lamminta, who had been listening quietly to everything Hops has outlined, asks, "Haven't you forgotten one very critical point, High Commander?"

Thinking quickly about what he has just instructed everyone to do Hops answers, "Nothing that I can think of, sir."

"Then what are you going to do if I disagree with your assessment of the situation?"

"Sir?"

"You have presented what you think is the only possible explanation for Commander Freslofs' actions. You have given orders to everyone, including Council Member Quince and myself. Don't you think a better approach to this situation would have been to inform me about what you were planning? I don't like being kept in the dark about what our High Commander is doing, especially when it involves serious charges not only against a fellow officer, but a ships' captain."

"Sir," begins Hops as he defends his actions. "If I had informed you prior to this meeting, you would have been required to call a formal Council meeting to inform everyone. I don't think that would have been the way to handle this. If Tro-Ja or Pidera knew about this before now, you would not have had any choice except to convene the full Council, but by then it may have been too late for anyone to do anything. You've seen the evidence, and I don't think you would let a fox in the hen house while the hens are roosting. Besides sir, we have a Council majority right here, which makes this a legal vote, unless you disagree with what I've explained."

"No, I don't disagree, I fully support your actions," says Lamminta. "I just wanted to know why you didn't inform the entire Council, and don't worry about Tro-Ja and Pidera. I'll handle any problems you might have with them."

"Thank you, sir," Hops as he again looks about the room. "Does anyone have anything they would like to say, or add?" No one speaks as he ends the meeting saying "Then I suggest we all get started. I want to know what Freslof is up to as soon as possible."

"Captain on the bridge," says Nuk-Ma as Commander Williams steps through the doorway.

"Nuk-Ma," begins Williams, "contact the Revenge and inform Commander Freslof to move to eight thousand separation to improve communications. Tell him we're still experiencing interference with our communication systems since we installed the interrupter. Send it with the same static as before but once he gets within eight thousand clear up seventy percent of the noise."

"Message sent, sir," says Nuk-Ma. "Commander Freslof wants to know if there's anything that he can help with. He said he could send over his chief engineer to give us a hand."

"Just tell him to move to a closer position and that we can handle the problem, but if we need any help we'll be sure to ask."

"Revenge closing to eight thousand. Separation distance in two minutes."

"Maintain a careful watch behind us. Teka may have picked up that signal and could be heading this way," says Williams.

"Aye, sir."

"Helm, how soon before we reach the first course correction?"

"Two hours and forty-six minutes, sir."

"Okay. Maintain speed and steady on course."

"Bridge to Telebisque Teka."

"This is Teka."

"We just intercepted a coded Guardian signal. Coordinates and probable course relayed to the helm, and to the Junnack. Sub-Telecoup Envela has acknowledged. I also informed the Landex of the Guardians location. We should be able to intercept them without very much difficulty."

"Has there been any reply from the Landex?"

"No sir, not yet. It will be about another hour before any signal carrying his reply could reach us."

"Where did the signal originate?"

"Seven three two by one six five, sir. They have slipped past us and are approximately four hours ahead of us."

"Keep me informed and notify me when we are within one hour of that position. Notify fighter command to return to ready alert. Teka, out." After a few minutes of quiet thought as he sit at the main terminal in his ready room he activates the intercom sensor. "Bridge, this is Teka."

"Cudrosia, sir."

"What would their destination be if they maintained that course?"

"Unknown at this time, sir."

"What other Groups are close enough to assist?"

"The Loksija and Gissoc, sir. They could be in a blocking position in two days. The next closest group is the Hidlok. It will take them about four days before they could be in position."

"Relay the Guardians suspected course and speed. All Groups are to move into blocking positions at maximum power immediately. If they have any contact with the Guardians, they are to report directly to me. They are not to engage until we arrive, they are only to detain the Guardians."

"Message sent, sir."

"Commander, Teka just sent a message to the Landex, Loksija, Gissoc, and Hidlok. It's going to take some time to get it decoded."

"Don't worry about that right now," acknowledges Williams. "If we know the Landex and Napla are behind the Palup and Junnack, the other three Groups are ahead of us somewhere. Teka may be trying to trap us. I hope we'll be able to avoid whatever he has in mind before he can get it set. How long to course correction?"

"Thirty-eight minutes, sir," replies Cherrick.

"When we make the course change, make sure the Revenge is still with us. At this distance, we can't afford any wrong moves. Nuk-Ma, send a quick message to the Freslof to increase speed to six point zero."

"Six point zero. Aye, sir," says Cherrick.

"Revenge acknowledges and is following."

CHAPTER TWENTY

Several days pass without anything discovered which could explain the mysterious appearance of the Revenge. Carol has completed her studies of the basic schematic diagrams of the newfound ship. Captain Seeret finally finished the computations work on the fuel and energy consumption analysis. The clandestine operation goes unnoticed by the remainder of the crew, and most importantly, Council Members Tro-Ja and Pidera. The slight changes in the day-to-day operations of the Hope is also undetected by the rest of the crew.

"Commander," calls out Nuk-Ma quietly as he continues to monitor the Hopes scanners. "The Tirgs are definitely planning some sort of surprise party for us. The Landex and Napla just entered scanner range and it looks like they're following our original course."

"Anything out in front of us yet," asks Williams?

"Nothing that I can confirm, but I definitely feel something's out there and its heading this way. I still can't find anything the Loksija, Gissoc, or Hidlok Battle Groups. If the Landex is planning to join the Palup, they're going to be able to cover one heck of a lot of territory. Hopefully we can find a way around them."

"Next course correction in ten minutes, sir," reports Cherrick.

"Execute as planned," orders Williams. "Nuk-Ma, keep a positive lock on the Teka and Mulars' Groups. Coordinate with Novac to determine the most likely place Teka could set up a defensive blockade. Have Lieutenant Germick handle the scanners for a while. Maybe if we can figure out where Teka might try to intercept us we might be able to determine a location on the other Groups."

"Aye, sir."

"I'll let the High Commander know what's going on, then, I'll be in my quarters if anything comes up. Jo, you have the bridge."

As Williams nears the High Commanders quarters, he encounters Lamminta and Carol.

"Excuse me, Council General," begins Williams. "I was just on my way to see the High Commander. I think you might be interested in this new information as well."

"By all means, Commander," says Lamminta. "Lead the way."

As they reach the door leading to the High Commanders quarters, Williams reaches out and activates the door chime, and invited to enter.

"The Landex and Napla just came into scanner range. Mular seems to be following a course that will take him straight to Teka," begins Williams. "We still don't have any idea where the other Groups are, but we believe they are ahead of us and heading towards this sector. What do you suggest?"

"First, I think it's about time we have our little talk with Freslof," says Hops. "If we're going to find out what he's been up to it looks like we're just about to run out of time to do it."

"I believe you're right," says Lamminta.

"Carol, are you ready for your inspection tour," ask Hops as he looks at the woman he once considered as only an unnecessary distraction?

"Yes," calmly replies Carol.

"I'll notify Commander Freslof to prepare for my visit," says Lamminta, knowing that this simple action would set Hops plan in motion.

"The Council General making his own request for an inspection tour," asks Hops cautiously? "I'm not sure that would be such a good idea. It would be better if I made the request in your name. Then I could change the inspecting Council Member a lot easier."

"Agreed," says Lamminta.

"Orin, notify Seeret to get his shuttle ready."

"What about the course change," asks Williams?

"Keep doing what we planned until we can come up with a few more answers," says Hops. "If Freslof hasn't caught on to us by now, maybe he is on the level. Besides, if he is, it will be a lot easier to go up against Teka with the extra firepower. We're going to need all the help we can get to get out of this mess."

"Okay," says Williams. "I'll let Jo know to change course on schedule. When Freslof comes aboard I'll personally escort him to your ready room."

"No," calmly answers Hops. "I want all of us to meet him in the landing bay. If we all greet him together, we might be able to shake his tree and see what falls out. I don't want him to see any more of the Hope than he already has. We'll do this in the landing bay operations ready room."

The short meeting quickly adjourned. On his way back to the bridge Williams stops at a communications panel.

"Williams to Captain Seeret."

"Seeret, sir."

"Get Council Member Quinces' shuttle ready. Full dress uniform at zero nine thirty hours tomorrow to take her to the Revenge."

"Understood, sir. I'll be ready as soon . . ."

"Good luck, Captain," interrupts Williams abruptly. As soon as he enters the bridge, he begins his part of the covert plan. "Nuk-Ma, open a secure channel to the Revenge."

"Channel open, sir."

"Commander Freslof, this is Commander Williams."

"Commander," acknowledges Freslof. "I'm glad you were finally able to clear up the interference. How may I help you?"

"The Council General wants to maintain Council protocol as much as possible. He would like an official inspection tour of the Revenge."

"Do you really think that's a good idea right now?"

"Personally, no," answers Williams. "The High Commander tried to talk him out of it, but Lamminta still wants to see the Revenge. He couldn't have picked a worse time for an inspection but I it looks like we don't have much choice."

"Will the rest of the Council be accompanying him?"

"No, just Council General and a small escort, but that's not the half of it," continues Williams. "Hops wants you to come over here at ten hundred tomorrow so that we can plan our next move together. It looks like Wester will have the honor of showing the Council General the Revenge."

"What," exclaims Freslof! "What in the hell is going on! The Council General wants an inspection tour of my ship and I'm supposed to be on the Hope, meeting with you and Hops at the same time! What in the hell is going on! Let me talk to him!"

"He's meeting with the Council right now."

"How in the hell am I to get my ship and crew ready for an official inspection . . .?"

"I don't know, Vic, but I guess we'll find out what's going on tomorrow. All we can do right now is to follow orders."

After a moment of eerie silence Freslof says, "Okay, I'll be there at ten hundred tomorrow. I still don't like it and Hops had better have one hell of a good explanation for this. Freslof, out."

Slowly the commander of the Revenge turns his attention to a small view screen at the scanner station where he has been standing.

"Sir," quietly asks Wester. "Do you think the High Commander has figured out what we've been doing?"

"I don't know," says Freslof just as quietly. "But you heard the orders, you've got the inspection with Council General while I have a meeting with Hops and Commander Williams at the same time, in two different locations, is more than a little unusual. It seems that he wants to separate us and compare stories."

"That's what I've been thinking, sir. I guess we'll just have to wait until tomorrow to find out what the High Commander actually knows, or suspects. I'll get the crew started on preparations for the Council Generals visit."

"Telebisque," calls the Communications Officer of the Palup. "I just intercepted another coded signal between the Guardian ships."

"Were you able to determine their location," quickly asks Teka?

"Yes, sir. They have changed course and we are within one and a half days of their position."

"Helm, plot an intercept course at full power," orders Teka. "Send a message to the others and inform them of the Guardians heading and suspected position."

The following morning Hops contacts the Revenge personally.

"Vic, I've got some good news and some bad news."

"I'd just like to know what in the hell is going on," replies Freslof angrily. "The Revenge is my ship, so how in the hell am I supposed to conduct an inspection tour for the Council General and attend a meeting with you on the Hope at the same time?"

"Calm down, Vic, this isn't the kind of inspection that you're used to when a Council Member comes aboard. He just wants to follow protocol and try to give what's left of our people some sense of normalcy. He's just trying to follow our traditions as much as possible. This so-called inspection isn't anything but a formality. However, the Council General won't be the inspecting Council Member. It seems that whatever he ate yesterday isn't agreeing with him today."

"The inspection is postponed?"

"Not exactly, he's sending Council Member Quince in his place."

"Why didn't you tell me this yesterday?"

"You really didn't expect the full Council to come aboard for a formal inspection while we're still playing hide and seek in the Tirgs backyard, did your?"

"No, and I guess you're right," says Freslof. "I guess I really wasn't thinking straight."

"Then I'll see you at ten hundred."

"How many people are going to be coming over with Council Member Quince?"

"Just one. Captain Seeret will be her pilot and also act as her official escort and aide."

"Just one Captain," asks Freslof?

"That's all we can spare right now. We don't exactly have the luxury of being able to provide her with a full entourage. Don't worry about it. Vic. This one Captain is more than capable of handling the job."

"Okay. I guess I'll see you in half an hour."

"See you then. Hops, out." Adrenaline is pumping through his veins as he turns and looks squarely at Lamminta. "Phase two complete, time for phase three."

Hops, Lamminta and Williams leave the bridge and head directly to the landing bay. They enter as the shuttle carrying Carol, and piloted by Seeret, receives the final launch clearance. The small ship departs just as a similar craft lands.

"Welcome aboard, Commander Freslof," greets Lamminta as he extends his hand. "You already know everyone here except Lieutenant Commander Jo-Ich, Executive Officer of the Hope."

"It seems that you have made a remarkable recovery, Council General," says Freslof as he courteously accepts Lammintas' hand.

"I think it would be best if we keep the formalities to a minimum and get straight down to business," says Hops as he gestures towards the operations ready room.

Once everyone sits down, Lamminta, still being, cordial, asks, "Would anyone care for some refreshments"?

"No, thank you," says Freslof as he looks towards Jo-Ich. "Excuse me, Council General, but I was told that this meeting was to be between the High Commander, Commander Williams, and myself. What is going on and why am I here when a Council Member is inspecting my ship?"

"I think it would be more appropriate if we would begin with the High Commander," says Lamminta as he takes his seat at the head of the table.

"Thank you, sir," says Hops as he turns his attention directly to Freslof, sitting at the far end off the table. "Commander, I asked you once before, and I'm only going to ask you one more time, how in the hell did you get that ship, and how in the hell did you make it this far?"

"I must protest, Council General," counters Freslof! "If the High Commander has specific charges he would like to levy against me, I have a right to hear them! I haven't hidden anything from anyone! If anyone has any suspicions as to how I became the commander of the Revenge, or how I managed to survive this long, all you have to do is to read my ships logs! Everything I have accomplished as Captain of the Revenge is contained in complete detail in them. I object to what you are insinuating, High Commander! You're accusing me of treason!"

Slowly Hops begins, "First, Commander Freslof, the largest thing you have commanded, prior to the Revenge, was the Raddington, a supply frigate. You never attended the Senior Battle Commander Course. In fact, you barely made it through the Basic Command Course, and now you want us to believe you were next in line to take command of the newest battleship Fleet ever built?

"Secondly, and we had to do some serious digging through your logs, but where did you get you fuel from? Your engines are a standard design and your logs show that you left the docks with the normal initial fuel load that would have been just enough for the standard fifteen day shakedown cruise. You refueled and got a full load of zithium two months ago. Whoever modified your logs did a decent job but left a few fingerprints. Where did you get your fuel? Did you get a Tirg transport to stop and let you fill up, or did you stop at a Tirg supply depot?

"Third, why isn't the name of this ship on the forward hull? And it isn't the Revenge," says Hops as he activates the holographic imager. "It's the Gimmerlick. The name is clearly on the ships' bow while still in the construction dock. Lastly, how in the hell did you manage to take out over twenty Tirg ships without suffering any damage? The Revenge doesn't have a single energy burn mark, and according to your own logs, you never even took a hit. Now, Commander Freslof, or whoever in the hell you are, I think you better start explaining, and it better be good!"

"If I may," asks Freslof as he removes a small device from the waistband of his uniform? This simple action causes Hops, Williams, and Jo-Ich to draw their sidearm. "Hold it! Wait a minute! It's a communicator developed on Uri Two. You can have your communications chief check it out."

"Who are you planning to contact with that thing," asks Hops, still pointing his weapon at Freslof?

"There are more of us that survived the Tirgs initial attack than you think, and the Hope isn't the only ship with the new concealment device," answers Freslof. "When Commander Trilla finished the initial development work on the prototype and turned the plans over to Fleet Research and Development, it was fine-tuned and secretly installed on selected ships. There had been rumors but they had been kept quiet for more than a year. These rumors indicated the Tirgs were planning something, but no one knew just what."

"What in the hell are you talking about," asks Hops harshly?

"I'm getting to that," answers Freslof calmly. "I was given command of the Gimmerlick while she was still in the construction docks. Wester and I went through all the necessary command courses secretly. Except for the instructors, we the only ones in any of the classes. The entries on my records are there to keep anyone who started nosing around from finding out the truth.

"The crew was hand-picked. Once a name selected and that individual passed a complete background check, they received a crash course without knowing anything about what they were going to be doing, where their next assignment was going to be, or why. Once they completed their training, Fleet reassigned the crew to either Pine Tree Five or Uri Two. Once the Gimmerlick was completed, and keeping with standard procedures, all I was given was a skeleton crew and ordered to pick up the remaining crewmembers to begin the shakedown cruise.

"We just cleared the defensive zone around Uri Two when all hell broke loose. As soon as I received the communiqué, I contacted the ships that had been equipped with the new concealment device and told everyone rendezvoused at the edge of the Agreed Zone. We crossed it and began doing the Tirgs what they did to us."

"Commander, your logs indicate that we should have had contact with you several months ago," says Jo-Ich.

"I was under secret orders that came straight from Fleet Security. As you have already discovered, the logs I had sent over are fake. I need to have a talk with Wester about not hiding the truth very well. I'll have the actual logs sent over as soon as I get back to the Revenge. They can only be accessed through verbal recognition, and that can only be done from the bridge."

"That I would like, Vic," says Hops, lowering weapon, but not as much as Jo-Ich. "Now just whom are you planning to contact with that communicator?"

"I'm going to prove to you there are more of us that survived than you may think," says Freslof as he opens the small device and begins speaking into the small voice transmitter. "Delta Five Alpha Seven Zulu."

"Bridge to Commander . . .! High Commander . . .! Anyone! Bogies! We're surrounded," suddenly blares over the Hopes' intercom! "I'm going to need help!"

"Don't worry," quickly answers Freslof. "They're all ours."

"Bridge, this is the High Commander. Transfer everything here." Turning to observe the main view screen Hops immediate identifies several of the ship. "Damn! The Fetting! Dormet! Ghia! Jackson! Ophic! Yatdown! Where in the hell did they come from?"

"They've been escorting us and providing a little extra protection," answers Freslof. "These are the ships that have been fitted with the new concealment device. The Revenge didn't get one because whatever it was that Fleet was planning, they were going to use us as the bait. The Tirg ships listed in my log, as having been destroyed, were, but not by me. You're looking at the ships that have been whittling the Tirgs down to size."

The Guardian leaders now understand what they are looking at and they now have the truth.

"Vic," calmly asks Hops as holsters his weapon, "why didn't you tell us this from the start? It would have saved a lot of work and suspicion."

"You didn't exactly trust me, and I wasn't exactly sure I could trust you. These have been some hard time for everyone. I couldn't get reliable information, or any accurate intelligence that I could use, and there wasn't any way that I could have known about the Hope since its construction as done at Seven instead of Fleet headquarters. Moreover, as far as any other survivors were concerned, and from what I saw that was left of Seven, I had to assume, as you did, that our initial contact had all the earmarks of a Tirg trap. I went along with you in hopes of finding out what you were planning. I notified the other ships Captains and told them that if my locator beacon activated, they were to attack this ship and destroy it."

"We have the same concealment device that the other ships have, but we didn't detect them," says Williams.

"Fleet R and D came to the same conclusion that Commander Trilla did, only sooner. They programmed it with a random frequency oscillation pattern. If someone doesn't have the exact oscillation pattern the only way to find a concealed ship is by sheer luck, and then you'll only have the location for a micro-second."

"One last question, Vic," says Hops. "How would the other captains have known if this meeting started heading south? You would have to have notified them somehow."

"If anyone but me touches this communicator, an emergency signal have immediately been transmitted and they would immediately attack. I don't think the Hope would have lasted very long going against that much firepower."

"Very ingenious, Commander," quietly says Lamminta as he leans back in his chair and studies the view screen. "We now know exactly what you were trying to protect, and because we didn't completely trust each other, so do the Tirgs."

CHAPTER TWENTY-ONE

"Telebisque," reports Cudrosia! "A Guardian fleet has just appeared!"

"What!"

"We have a positive identification on seventeen additional Guardian warships!"

"That's impossible," shouts Teka as he rushes to the scanner station!

"No, sir. Positive identification confirmed."

"Why is there such a large hole in the middle of their formation," hastily questions Teka as he studies the scanner screen? "Why are they not . . . They're protecting the first two ships! Now we need to know what they are planning to do next. First, there was only one ship, there were two, and now there are nineteen. Under-Culmit Matilosk, inform Telecoups Mular, Veskin, Lorakin, and Vandilkor I want an immediate meeting. Secure the channel in my ready room. Cudrosia, you will join me."

Teka and Cudrosia leave the bridge and enter the private domain reserved for the Palups commanding officer. The requested Group Commanders are already ready online and waiting as Teka sits behind his desk and activates the small view screen, motioning for Cudrosia to sit down.

"It appears that we now have a more serious problem facing than we originally thought. Have all of you received our scanner report and the information indicating we are now facing nineteen ships instead of the original one or two?" All four commanders acknowledge they received the information as Teka continues. "Then I do not have to explain that with so many ships remaining, it appears that there are more Guardian survivors, and they are stronger, than we previously believed. We can effectively engage six, or possibly seven of their ships with the forces we currently have, but we cannot successfully engage all of them at once."

Telecoup Veskin is the first to speak saying, "I believe we can engage the entire Guardian fleet with the five Battle Groups you have assembled. The Supreme Commander has ordered additional groups into this sector. The Costic and Tablor Battle Groups will be here within two days. By the time the Guardians could effectively deploy we will have reinforcements converging on their position. Surely seven Battle Groups, with over fifteen hundred Pilinicun fighters, we can end this war here and now."

"I agree with Telecoup Veskin," says Vandilkor, commander of the Loksija Battle Group. "We could close the blockade and attack from all sides. Even with their concealment devices activated, once we hit their defensive shields we will know their exact position. We would have confirmed targets to engage and destroy. Telecoup Mular proved this could be accomplished during his encounters with these Guardian scum."

Mular is not as hasty in the assessment of the situation by his counterparts. "Telebisque Teka, I am not sure I agree with Veskin and Vandilkor in attacking the Guardians at this time would be the wisest thing to do. These Guardians, though passive in the past, have proven themselves as competent warriors. They now possess the skill to elude our traps while snaring us in theirs. I suggest that we wait, but no longer than a day, two at the most. We need to determine their true intentions before we attempt any action against them. If they do not move, this could be an indication they planning a strategy to counter any move we would attempt. If we move too quickly, we would reveal our attack posture and they would surely have time enough to establish an effective counterattack. Losses on both sides would be catastrophic. I suggest we maintain our current blocking position. If we position our Battle Groups around them, we would essentially have them trapped. With the additional Battle Groups we would then be in a better position to block any attempt to escape."

"Telecoup Lorakin? What would your battle plan be," asks Teka?

After a thoughtful moment, the commander of the Gissoc Battle Group says, "An ancient earth style siege could prove very interesting. Telecoup Veskin and Telecoup Mular have both presented valid arguments, but I still believe these Guardians would rather talk than fight. They have had time to re-establish their Council of Elders. If they have indeed accomplished this, then their Council must approve all military actions suggested by their High Commander. They . . ."

"Are you sure they will still debate every military action," asks Teka? "During their last encounter with the Landex I do not believe their Council had sufficient time to debate and then agree with the actions of their High Commander. If they have re-established their Council, as you suggest, I believe that they may have given their High Commander more freedom to take action without their approval. Their tactics have changed so much that this may now be true. I do not believe they will debate all major decisions as they did in the past."

"I still believe they would be more willing to talk than to fight, just as they did during the Empires last confrontation with then," continues Lorakin. "Even thought they were constantly engaged in battle, their Council of Elders continually tried to contact our Supreme Commander and negotiate a peace settlement. If we could occupy their attention with the one thing they do best, we could attack and destroy them when they would least expect it. Whoever they would send as their peace delegation would become our honored guests."

"That idea might have been feasible during the last war," says Teka thoughtfully. "However, at this time I do not think they would be as careless as you would have us believe. If a conference were held, I'm sure they would insist that the talks be conducted on one of their ships to guard against such a move."

"If the negotiations were to be conducted on one of their ships, as you suggest Telebisque, we could use that to our advantage, instead of their," says Vandilkor. "We could, as Telecoup Veskin has stated, wait until the other Groups arrive, then we attack in force. The Empire would be rid of these puny lunatics in one swift blow."

"Do you think they are naïve enough not to understand what we are planning when they discover two additional Battle Groups approaching this sector when there are five Groups here already," asks Teka? "As Veskin has stated, fourteen Fighting Stars would be no match for them. However, I do not believe they will remain here once they realize they are about to be trapped. They may still desire to live in peace, but I am convinced they will continue to fight much harder than before and will not allow themselves to be subdued."

"We have them at our mercy," exclaims Vandilkor! "I say we attack and attack now! Seven Battle Groups certainly have the firepower to destroy them! Look at the size of their ships Telebisque! Scouts! Destroyers! Cruisers! One Star Class Battleship and one Universe Class Battleship! I say we attack!"

"And how would you attack them once they return to the protection of their concealment device," counters Teka? "Fill the entire engagement area with energy fire and hope you achieve a hit on their defensive shields? Do you think they will maintain their course? How do you propose to continue the engagement when you lose your target? They will disperse and we would be required to waste time trying to locate them again. If you can provide me with a proven method of locating them while they are under the protection of their concealment device, I would support such an attack. Until that time, such an attack would be fruitless and waste unnecessary resources."

"If we attack and are able to destroy even a small number of their ships before they could escape, it would still be a victory," argues Lorakin. "Surely you have not forgotten that even a small victory is better than no victory at all."

"I have not forgotten," answers Teka. "I will inform all of you of my decision shortly. For now continue moving into you blockade positions. Palup, out."

Teka remains sitting in front of the now blank screen. Slowly he turns towards Olderin and asks, "What would you do in this situation?"

"It appears as if we have traded places with them, sir," answers Cudrosia. "Now we are the ones who are talking and debating. Maybe we are no as different from these Guardians as we thought."

With the appearance of additional Guardian ships and survivors, Hops realizes that he must now make several changes to his planning and the operational organization of his now larger fleet. He calls a conference of all ship captains and executive officers. He also has all department heads and sections chiefs board the Hope present. As the officers begin to gather in the Council Chamber, he is a little surprised to discover that almost half of the officers present are female.

"Will everyone take a seat," calls out Hops loudly as soon as everyone has gathered. "I know several of you have family and friends here on the Hope and as soon as we get finished here there will be plenty of time for reunions."

The officers begin to find their seats and the noise begins to subside slowly.

"Okay," begins Hops, "everyone needs to find a seat so we can get started." The officers appear to ignore the instructions, causing Hops to give a sharp whistle, then shouts, "Shut up and sit down!" The noise quickly dies out as everyone moves quickly to an empty chair. "Now, that's better. There was so much noise in here that I almost forgot why I called everyone together. First, is that I understand everyone is in agreement with the formation of the current Council and with me as your High Commander? Does anyone here know of any crewmember who might have a severe case of heartburn with this?" No one speaks, allowing Hops to continue. "Good. Then I'm naming the Hope as the Fleet Flagship. All orders will originate from here. Now that that is settled the next thing we need to . . ."

"Excuse me, High Commander," calls a soft subtle voice.

"Yes?"

"If we are in agreement with respect to the configuration of the present Council, and the designation of the Hope as our Flagship, I believe it would be a good idea to disperse the Council among several of the other ships. To have the entire Council, and our High Commander, concentrated on one ship would give the Tirgs a very tempting target that would unnecessarily endanger our leaders."

"I would agree . . . ah . . . Lieutenant Commander?"

"Maggie Hitchcock, commanding the scout Unissis."

"I would agree with you Commander Hitchcock, and your suggestion does sound like a valid point, but for right now I think we need to focus our attention on more urgent problems. Things such the Telebisque Teka, the five additional Battle Groups he has heading this way, just waiting for us to screw up. Do you have any idea that might help us to get the hell out of this mess? And I don't think one of your ancestors ideas of having a buffalo hunt, with us taking the part of the buffalo, would be in our best interest right now."

"Your reputation for observing insignificant details has preceded you, High Commander, and as far as how I think we should move and get the hell out of this mess, I believe we now have a slight advantage over the Tirgs," answers Hitchcock. "They started hunting what they thought to be two separate ships, one a renegade black marketer and the other a bona fide Guardian target. They now have nineteen ships that now pose a greater threat than before. I believe we have captured their undivided attention and I don't think they will be too eager to attack. The last intelligence reports indicate they are trying to consolidate their forces in an attempt to keep us from leaving. They haven't attacked yet and I don't think they will, at least not until the additional reinforcements arrive, or we make a move to leave. Since they're waiting to see what we are going to do next, I suggest we take the initiative. My suggestion is to engage the concealment device and get this damned buffalo herd stampeded before we lose what little we have left,"

"Well said, Commander," replies a stunned High Commander who is not used to someone talking to him in such a manner, but he also knows there was not anything he can do about it. "If they do find us again, which I'm sure they will do eventually, what would you suggest we do then?"

Hitchcock, slowly controlling her anger at the initial words of her superior officer, says, "Since we are now a greater force with which they must now contend with, I believe it would be in our best interest to return to our own territory. We are once again observing our traditional laws and traditions, and if we could deal the Tirgs a major defeat in our own territory, we would be in a better position from which to negotiate a peace settlement."

"Not a bad idea," says Hops as the somewhat attractive, but fiery blonde commander takes her seat. "Does anyone else have any other ideas on how we might be able to use to stay in the frying pan and keep out of the fire?"

"High Commander."

Thinking only one though, Hops quietly recognizes another female officer, indicating her to present her idea.

"Commander Jo-Ann Rickler, captain of the Attack Cruiser Jackson. I agree with Commander Hitchcock. We can conceivably fend off another attack from our own territory better than we could from here, inside the Tirgonian Empire. We could use one of our destroyed outposts as cover and use it as a base from which we could launch our attacks."

"Like I said, it sounds like a good idea, except for one slight drawback," agrees Hops as a smirk creep across his face. "What if we would do as you, and Commander Hitchcock, suggest? Suppose we do find one of our outposts that we could get back into operation relatively easy. What do we do then? Once we start offensive operations, we would be limited in the territory we would be able to control. All of our operations would have the same point of origin, therefore, how long do you think it would take the Tirgs to figure out where to look? It would be like turning on a homing beacon to Teka and the rest of his friends. He would be able to gather one hell of a lot more firepower that we could. I don't think we could survive a full-scale assault against an already heavily damaged, stationary outpost. We wouldn't be able to withstand the onslaught. Personally, I think we should remain as mobile as possible."

"High Commander," calls out yet another female voice.

"Yes?"

"Commander Samantha Triheadly, captain of the Cruiser Osage. As I see it, the only problem before you, and the rest of us, is academic. Do we fight here and now, or do we run and fight another day when we can pick the time and place. Personally, I'm in favor of running today and fighting tomorrow."

"Thank you, Commander. I guess that sums up the situation in a nutshell. Does anyone else have any suggestions," asks Hops? No one volunteers any additional suggestions, allowing him to continue. "I'll let you know what we're going to do as soon as I get a better handle on whom, and what, we now have. Now, I'd like to turn this Fleet into an organized Task Force of our own. Right now, we have one Star Class Battleship, three Cruisers, six Destroyers, and eight scouts to protect one Universe Class Battleship. I'm going to break everyone down into three Divisions, under the control of a central Fleet Headquarters that will here on the Hope. One of the scouts will provide close support for the Hope with everyone else broken down as evenly as possible after that. As soon as I have everything figured out, I'll let everyone know his, or her, specific Division assignments.

"Next, I'm going to need is the correct concealment device modulation frequency so that the Hope isn't blind, and we can see each other. Commander Freslof, I want you to have your chief engineer to coordinate with Commander Trilla and get everything aligned. Now, to the personnel problem. Several of you have ships appear to be suffering from overcrowding, and a couple of you are severely under manned. I would like everyone to get with Commander Tu, our Chief of Personnel, and give her a complete ships' roster. She'll handle any personnel reassignments based on current organizational requirements. We have, for lack of a better term, a Fleet Training Academy, and I would like all the kids of academy age, and anyone else who now has a desire to attend the academy, assigned here. Classes should be able to begin as soon as we can get a firm count on the number of cadets we'll have. In addition, to your extra personnel, I want all single parents and parentless kids transferred here. That should give the ships that are overcrowded some extra room.

"Up here with me are the main Department heads, now Chief of their respective sections. First is Commander Wallop, our Chief of Supply and Logistical Support. He's going to need a complete list of everything that you currently have, or need. Medical records, assets, and requirements will go to Commander Wicks, our Fleet Surgeon. Give your list of your Dragons and drivers to Commander Jo-Ich. He's my Director of Fleet Flight Operations. The operational status of your Dragons and general maintenance requirements will go to Commander Gallaski, Chief of Maintenance Operations. Some of your Dragons are probably in need of some heavy repairs. If any of your Dragons need major maintenance, or can't fly, get it over here for repairs, or salvaged for parts. Also, send over your extra Dragons that are taking up space, but keep the best ones you have. We have a few extra birds that we can swap out for the ones that are in bad shape, but that will be on an as needed basis.

"I guess that's all for now. Does anyone have anything to add for the betterment of all," says Hops as he surveys that faces of the men and women in front of him, hoping that no one will have any further questions? "I'll let everyone know about their Division assignments within the next day or two, so for now all of us need to get things organized and see if we can't find a way out of this mess. Dismissed."

As Hops leaves the Council Chamber, he is already working on the task of assigning which ships to which Division as he walks towards the bridge with Williams. As soon as they enter the Hopes main nerve center, they are informed that all officers have returned to the safely of their respective ships.

"Commander Trilla, have you received the correct frequency modulation for the Fleets concealment device," asks Williams.

"Yes, sir. I've already changed the frequency modulation for our device to match everyone else."

"Good. Nuk-Ma, inform the Fleet to get back into hiding."

"Signal sent and the Fleet is in hiding."

"Do you have all ships on the concealment screen?"

"Yes, sir. All transponder signatures are identified."

Hops, acknowledges the information with a nod of his head as he quietly turns, and leaves the bridge.

"Telebisque! The Guardians have activated their concealment device. I no longer have a positive lock on their position."

"Did they appear to be moving," immediately asks Teka?

"No, sir. All ships were stationary."

"Then they haven't yet left the sector. Maintain course and speed. I want a complete scan of the entire area. With so many ships concentrated in such a small area, they will leave a spatial distortion when they begin moving. I want constant computer enhancement of all scans," says Teka. Gazing at the scanner monitor, he asks himself quietly, what are they trying to do? Are they still here, waiting for me to make the first move? On the other hand, have they already slipped away, leaving me to guard an empty trap? Returning his attention to Under-Culmit Dramek he asks, "Have you detected anything yet?"

"No, sir," reports Dramek. "All scans are negative."

"This Guardian commander must like to play games," says Teka as he leaves the bridge of the Palup without giving any further instructions.

The Eleventh Battle Group continues racing towards the last suspected position of the now larger Guardian Fleet as Teka enters the bridge several hours later.

"Have the Guardians been found yet."

"No, sir, still nothing to indicate they are still stationary, or they have left the area."

"Send a signal to all commanders. They are to return to their previous assignments. They are to immediately contact me if they discover anything to indicate they may have found these devil rats," orders Teka.

"Message sent and acknowledged, sir. All Groups returning to their previous assignments."

"Commander," calls out Nuk-Ma. "It looks like Teka just gave up looking for us. The Battle Groups that were heading this way have turned around."

"Let's just hope he doesn't decide to turn back by himself any time soon," says Williams. "I'll inform the High Commander that Teka has just given us a little more breathing room."

Williams departs the bridge and heads directly for his ready room where he knows he'll find Hops.

"Sir," begins Williams as soon as he enters the room that was once his private domain "Teka and his friends have just left."

"Damn," says Hops. "Finally got something to go right. Tu just finished with the personnel assignments and I just completed the Division assignments. It looks like we're about ready to get all ships captains over here so we can get this Fleet organized into some sort of effective fighting force of our own."

"What time do you want everyone here," asks Williams?

"Thirteen hundred today. Has Ski received the extra Dragons yet?"

"Last one from the Revenge came in about an hour ago. All department chiefs report they've received all reports and logs that they need. Wallop is working on the commissary and supply inventory. Wicks has finished compiling the medical files. All cadets who need to begin academy training are aboard, or should be aboard within the next hour or so. Tu was able to find several more instructors with the proper qualifications for the academy. All that's needed to get everything started is for you to sign the orders."

"I know the first thing I'm going to do is to give Tu a little more authority so that she can sign personnel assignment orders for me. I just need her to keep me informed on what she is doing, or what she needs to do. How soon before the academy classes will be able to begin?"

"I should be able to give an orientation briefing in three or four days. That should be enough time to get them properly quartered and everything they're going to need issued."

"Sounds good, Orin. I guess we'd better grab a bit to eat before we brief the captains and have some of them jumping all over me with their broomsticks because they don't like where they're assigned."

"They aren't all that bad, Hops," says Williams with a grin. "They did manage to help Freslof take out how many ships. How many have we managed to destroy? They seem to have been able to rack up a better score than we did."

"Yeah, I know. And that's what scares me," replies Hops as he pushes his chair away from the console station. "I'll see you in the Council Chamber at thirteen hundred."

"Eat light," calls Williams as Hops steps into the outside corridor. "You know it's a bad idea to eat a heavy meal right before you get into a fight."

"Thanks," calls Hops as the ready room door closes behind him.

At one o'clock, all ships Captains are talking quietly in the Council Chamber, waiting for the arrival of the High Commander.

"A-a-a-T-T-T-T-E-E-E-E-N-N-N-N-N-t-t-t-t-i-i-i-i-o-o-o-n-n-n-n," barks Williams as Hops enters and walks down the center aisle! Immediately the talking ceases as everyone rises and looks straight ahead. "High Commander on deck."

As Hops approaches Williams, he pauses long enough to say quietly, "That's enough of that. We're not going to stand on that much ceremony." Taking his proper place, he again pauses, this time looking out upon his new command before ordering, "Take your seats.

"First things first. Everyone should have a complete Fleet roster. Your crews should be able to find family and friends that made it this far. Division and ship assignments have broken down with the names of all personnel listed in order. The names at the bottom of the roster are the extra personnel that I want transferred to the Hope. If anyone has any problems with any of the names, or would like to make any personnel changes, coordinate your requests with Commander Tu. Whatever she decides will be final.

"Now to the actual Division assignments. First Division will be our heavy one. I've decided to put the Revenge out front with Commander Freslof as Division Commander with the following ships. The cruiser Epat, attack destroyers Dormet and Ophic, scouts Vinsoke, Fedasu, and Isonosi. Second Division will be under the commander of Commander Triheadly. Her ships will be the cruiser Osage, destroyers Ghia and Papike, and the scouts Allekia and Rubisk. Third Division will be commander by Commander Cutler with the Yatdown. Destroyers are the Jackson and Fetting along with the scouts Puzi and Yick-Smu. Commander Hitchcock and the Unissis will remain in close support of the Hope. Any questions?" Hops pauses as he again looks at the officers seated in front of him. "Good. Division Commanders and Hitchcock remain seated. Everyone else will return to your ships and start getting your personnel realigned or transferred as necessary."

The chamber quickly empties, allowing the remaining personnel to gather in a smaller and, more manageable group.

"I think we could get more accomplished if we moved to your ready room," says Hops as he looks towards Williams.

The battle leaders move quietly from the Council Chamber to Commander Williams' ready room. Once there Hops activates a small holographic image projector, revealing the formation he wants the Fleet to assume.

"Okay," begins Hops as, "Here's what I want. When we move we'll be using the 'Flying V' formation. Vic, as I said, you're going to be on point. Maintain standard Fleet speed and keep your scans concentrated in front of you. The rest of us will take care of the flanks and rear. Don't hesitate to give a yell if you see something that doesn't look right. I want your scouts a thousand kilometers in front of the Revenge with the Epat halfway between the Revenge and the scouts. Put your Destroyers a thousand behind and to your flanks The Hope will be twenty thousand behind them." Looking towards Triheadly and Cutler, Hops continues, saying, "Second Division will be on the left flank, Third Division will cover the right. Cruisers will lead. Put your scouts twenty thousand out and your Destroyers inside them at ten thousand. Hitchcock. I want you five thousand behind the Hope to maintain a good watch behind us. Next is the problem of where do we go from here? Commander Cutler?"

"Any direction that we take we stand the chance of running into the Tirgs," begins one of the three female Commanders present. "However, we are in a better position to defend ourselves than before. Personally, I think we should keep heading across Tirgonia. As you have said High Commander, there's nothing left for us on what used to be our side of the Agreed Zone, so why don't we find out what the Tirgs have been hiding from us all these years since the last war and see if we can't use that against them?"

Nodding his understanding Hops continues, saying, "Commander Triheadly?"

"Sounds like a plan to me. Go where we haven't been and see if we can make it across their far border, wherever that is."

"Commander Hitchcock?"

"I agree with them, and since Commander Freslof has been able to keep us supplied with fuel, and everything else we needed so far, why don't we keep going across Tirgonia and let the Tirgs keep supplying us?"

"Which remind me, Vic," says Hops as he turns towards his old friend "How come we've never heard about you and the others before this? Every motherless Tirg has been chasing us and it seems that you've been able to stay one step ahead of them while the only thing we've been able to do is to barely stay out of weapons range."

"The first ship we took out, which by the way is credited to Commander Hitchcock, was a Hunter," begins Freslof. "First, we targeted its' communications antenna. Secondary target was the propulsion port. We convinced the commander that it would be in his best interest to surrender. He, and his two sidekicks, are still enjoying the brig accommodations on the Osage. We made just enough repairs to keep it operational and used it as bait. That's how we managed to take out several of our initial kills."

"Where is it now," asks Hops?

"Finally broke down beyond repair and had to scuttle it."

"Where do you think we should go?"

"I'm in agreement with Commander Cutler," says Freslof as he reaches for the holographic sensor. "May I?"

"Go ahead."

"I think we should keep going heading across Tirgonia towards this planet called Paporia Two," points Freslof. "Along the way we try to avoid any contact with the Tirgs because it seems that they've changed their tactics." Again, touching the control panel he changes the display. "Here's every encounter we've had with them since this thing started. Add in your fights and this is what we have. So far, no one in our Intelligence or Combat Analysis, Section has been able to come up with a method to their current madness."

"From the contact that we've had," says Cutler as she observes the displayed images "it seems that they're operating with a helleva lot of a larger area for their Battle Groups than we know about."

"I know," agrees Hops. "And that's what scares me. So far, the only thing the Hope has encountered has been Fighting Stars. Where are their cruisers and destroyers? And we haven't seen anything of their war hawks or hunters."

"If I remember right one of their Battle Groups has a standard two Stars and a Battle Armada has three Groups," says Williams as he again changes the holographic display, adding the last known configuration of a Tirgonian Group, "two heavy cruisers, four light cruisers, two attack destroyers, seven Hunters and fourteen War Hawks. Thirty-five ships with the slowest one being able to hit light seven. If they haven't changed their configuration, maybe we can find a hole we can sneak through."

"Aren't you forgetting a few of their other ships like their supply and transport barges," asks Hops as he adjusts the displayed image, adding several more Tirgonian ships? "Damn, imager isn't big enough. Right now, we're looking at an area that's at least four sectors square and we still don't have enough room. Looks like we're going to need to use the imager in fighter ops. I want a few more people to take a look at all the information we have. I want the best pair of eyes from each Division, not currently assigned to the Intelligence Section, temporarily assigned to the Hope. They're going to work on finding out where their supply bases and repair facilities are located and possibly, where we can expect the Tirgs to be looking for us. I hope that they'll be able to come up with a tactical scenario that we can implement and still be able to stay in one piece a little while longer. Orin, I'm going to need . . ."

"I know," interrupts Williams. "You want Lieutenant Germick."

"Right," says Hops. "I guess it looks like we keep heading across the Empire and try to make it to Paporia Two. Everyone get back to your ships and be ready to move out at fifteen hundred. Any questions?"

"High Commander?"

"Commander Cutler?"

"Why do you want . . .?"

"Why do I want the best pair of eyes, not assigned to your Intel Section," asks Hops? "It's quite simple. Intelligence personnel receive specific training to look for specific patterns and make their observations and deductions based on what they assume to be true, or standard, assumptions. Someone who hasn't received that kind of training will look at the same information from a different prospective and hopefully come up with a different conclusion. That's what we need right now, a different solution to our current problem as to what in the hell do the Tirgs want this time?"

"Understand, sir."

"Now, if there are no further questions I suggest that we all get back to work."

CHAPTER TWENTY-TWO

It has been several days since Telebisque Teka has had any contact with the enemy he seeks. He knows his adversary cannot continue indefinitely without replenishing their expendable supplies. Wanting to be the first Tirgonian Battle Group to locate this elusive foe, he contemplates the options available to him while taking a rest period in his private quarters when he receives a sudden call from the bridge.

"Telebisque Teka, this is Under-Culmit Dramek. I have found a weakness in the Guardians concealment device."

"Bring everything to my ready room and inform Culmit Cudrosia to join us," immediately replies Teka.

A few minutes later Teka enters his ready room and indicates for the junior officer to start.

"Telebisque," begins Under-Culmit Dramek, "the Guardians are using randomly selected frequencies for their concealment device. I was able to isolate one of these frequencies and scanned for this single frequency. I have found three more frequencies in the same random pattern. Since there are only a specific number of frequencies that can be used, I went back to every encounter and scanned for these four frequencies."

"You are telling me that you were able to locate the Guardians using only four out of thousands of known frequencies," questions Teka?

"Yes, sir. I have found these same four frequencies in the same random pattern during every encounter every Group has had with them. All information has been confirmed."

"Have you been able to locate their present position," asks Teka?

"Not yet, but now that we know what to look for we will find them soon enough, sir," answers Dramek. "I will inform the other Group commanders of the frequencies to scan for. We will then . . ."

"No," warns Teka harshly! "We will keep this information to ourselves for the moment. I will let you know when to release the information to the other Groups. Culmit Cudrosia, inform the helm to set a course back their last known location. Maximum speed. That will be all."

The Guardian fleet has left the area of the attempted Tirgonian blockade, but only a day before the return of the Palup and Junnack.

"Commander Williams, we have a problem," reports Nuk-Ma as he monitors the arrival of the Eleventh Battle Group. "It looks like Teka is back at the blockade position and appears to be scanning for us, but I can't be sure."

"Keep me informed," acknowledges Williams heads towards the bridge exit.

"Aye, sir."

"Cherrick, increase speed to light six."

"Increasing speed to light six," responds Lieutenant Brooks.

"Our problem just got a lot bigger," says Nuk-Ma causing Williams to suddenly stop and turn as he reached the bridge door. "The Palup and Junnack are following our course and are on an exact heading after us. Speed is light seven. Weapons off line. Horses still in the barn. Forward scanners are the only ones active. Flank and aft scanners appear to be off line. It looks Teka has found a way to find us."

"Damn! Inform the Fleet to increase speed to light seven, and ship-to-ship distance another five thousand. Maintain our current distance in front of the Palup," orders Williams as he returns to the scanner station. "High Commander, report to the bridge. We have company heading this way."

Within a few minutes Hops rushes through the bridge door and heads directly to the scanner station asking, "What's up?"

"Teka's found us," reports Williams without looking up. "He's following our exact course with all scans concentrated to his front. Fleet speed is light seven and we're maintaining our current distance in front of him and I already spread the Fleet out another five thousand."

"Where are the rest of his friends?"

"Nothing is showing up except the Palup and Junnack so far, sir."

"What in the hell is he up to this time," asks Hops quietly? "Has he notified anyone else?"

"We haven't intercepted up any communication signal."

"Then if it's just Palup and Junnack following us, he might have something else in mind other than getting into another fight. He has to know that two stars wouldn't have snowballs chance in hell of taking us on and winning. Let's see what he has up his sleeve. Bring the fleet full about."

"But sir, even though we haven't picked up any communications signal between Teka and the other Battle Groups, that doesn't mean that this couldn't be another trap," says Williams.

"If it is a trap and I'd rather be able to head straight into a fight instead of wasting time turning around later. Inform all Division Commanders to be prepared to launch their cavalry at a moment's notice. Tell Fab ring all weapons on line," orders Hops. "If Teka wants a fight we'll give him one he won't soon forget."

"Telebisque! The Guardians have turned around and are heading straight towards us," reports Cudrosia.

"Maintain course and speed. How soon before we are within maximum fighter range?"

"Approximately six hours, sir."

"What is their current weapons status?"

"I can't be sure, but from the frequency modulation, I would guess their weapons have been activated and are on line."

"Be assured, Culmit, their weapons are definitely activate and on line," calmly replies Teka. "If I were in their place my weapons would be at the ready and my fighters would be prepared for immediate launch. Their commander is not taking any chances. Open a secure channel and contact their flagship."

"Telebisque," asks Cudrosia?

"Send a message and contact their flagship, Culmit," again orders Teka. "Once contact is established, secure the frequency and transfer the channel to my ready room. I will make the necessary log entries from there."

"Understood, Telebisque," acknowledges Cudrosia as he watches his commander leave the bridge.

"Commander! I'm receiving a general message from the Palup," reports Nuk-Ma. "Telebisque Teka wants to speak to our High Commander."

"What," exclaims Williams as he looks at Hops who is standing behind Germick at the main scanner station! "Don't answer! I think we're going to need a meeting of the minds on this one.

"Nuk-Ma, if Teka sends another message, secure the channel and relay it to Commander Williams' ready room," immediately orders Hops. "Notify the Council General that I would like to see him on a . . . on a . . ."

"On a personal matter, sir?"

"Yeah," answers Hops with a wide grin. "On a personal matter."

Hops and Williams, not wanting any unnecessary rumors to spread among the crew, depart the bridge and immediately enter the main ready room of the Hope. As soon as the door closes behind them, Nuk-Ma voice comes in over the intercom.

"High Commander, another message coming in from the Palup. Channel is secure and transferred."

"Understood," acknowledges Hops as he activates the small blinking communications sensor at the workstation. "This is High Commander Hoppinzorinski of the Guardian Flagship Hope."

"You have indeed survived, my old friend. I am Telebisque Teka of the Tirgonian Fighting Star Palup."

"Damn it, Serligh! What in the hell is going," openly challenges Hops? "Why in the hell you cross the Agreed Zone and destroy our outposts. Why did . . ."

"Patience my friend," begins Teka. "I was not a participant in the initial attacks along the Agreed Zone. I have only recently received my orders to join . . . I only desire to find a peaceful solution to this madness."

"That worked once," replies Hops as he begins remembering the first encounter with this particular Tirgonian officer. "What makes you so sure your Supreme Commander would be willing to go along with your idea of peace a second time?"

"That my friend, I cannot answer. I can only try."

"Then why should I trust you? I think we did that once only to be at each other's throats again."

"As I have said my friend, I can only try. Fighting a force such as the one you now have surrounding you, with just two Fighting Stars, would not be beneficial for me, nor would it benefit either of our people."

"So exactly what are you proposing Serligh?"

"I think you already know the answer to your question my friend."

"I doubt that I will be able to accommodate your request under the current circumstances."

"I understand," says Teka. "You must first present this proposal to your Council of Elders. I will not precede any closer as I wait for your answer. Should you choose a different location, I will follow without allowing anyone else know of your presence."

"That won't be necessary," replies Hops. "Since you're apparently out on this limb by yourself, I think we should maintain our current positions. However, if I even smell another Star, I'll be obliged to cut that limb and blow you to hell on the way down."

"You have my word that we should not be bothered. The other Groups have been ordered to return to their previous assignments."

"For your sake, I hope you're right."

"Then it appears that we may be written into the history book twice in one lifetime, High Commander."

"I wouldn't go so far as to say that just yet, Serligh. I'll get back to you once I figure this out."

"Don't take too long my friend. I don't know how long it will be before someone notices that I am not following the normal patrol procedures. Palup, out."

"Commander Nuk-Ma, bring the fleet to a full stop and maintain this position." Turning around, Hops sees Council General Lamminta standing just inside the doorway.

"I'm sorry, sir, I didn't know you were already here."

"You were a little busy at the moment, so I thought it would be best not to announce my presence. I think we need to sit down and go over what we have before presenting it to the full Council."

The three leaders move silently to the conference table before anyone speaks.

"Sir," begins Williams as he takes his seat. "Do you actually believe Teka is on the level?"

"I really don't know. He talks like the same man I met before, only a little older, and hopefully a lot wiser. For our sake I hope he is."

"What about the people you have working on the Battle Group configuration," asks Lamminta? "Have they been able to come up with any answers yet?"

"Nothing yet," answers Hops. "Every scenario they come up with doesn't seem to fit any known Tirg battle formation. There never seems to be enough room or there's too much room for the number of ships normally assigned to a standard Group. Nothing seems to fit."

"So what do we have that we can use from Tekas' message," says Lamminta thoughtfully. "Your analysis?"

"First, I definitely believe he's out on his own limb. Why, after finding a way of detecting us, didn't he contact any of the other Battle Groups for support? He may actually think he'll be able to convince their Supreme Commander to end this war just as he did the last time."

"Do you actually believe that he has a way of detecting us," asks Williams? "Or could he have just gotten lucky playing a hunch?"

"Oh, he can find us alright," confirms Hops. "You heard him ask if we wanted him to follow."

"It could still be a bluff," observes Williams. "He could be trying to keep us within close communications range. Once he has a lock on the stationary origin of our signal he would have something to lock on that would definitely enable him to locate us."

"Good point," agrees Lamminta. "Just to be on the safe side, why don't we back the fleet off a few kilometers and actually find out if we have his complete and undivided attention."

"Not a bad idea," agrees Hops. "Let's see just how much he does know about finding us. Commander, inform Nuk-Ma to move the fleet back five thousand meters at dead slow speed. Keep a constant scan going and look for the slightest movement out of Teka, and for any unexpected visitors."

Commander Williams presses the small intercom sensor and relays the orders to Nuk-Ma. As soon as the fleet begins to move Hops receives an immediate response from Teka.

"This is the Hope," answers Hops.

"Why are you attempting to deceive me! You said that you would remain and now you withdraw! Are you attempting to deploy so you can destroy my Group? I gave you my word that I have not informed anyone else of the method I have used to discover to locate your ships. You can see that I have come to you under a flag of truce. However, if you desire to continue this fight, I will not disappoint you! If you have a desire to attack, then do so! Our destruction will not be as easy as you may think! I have spoken the truth only to discover that you have not! Teka out!"

"Full stop," immediately orders Hops!

"That was enough for me," says Lamminta in his usual calm voice. "I believe we can safely assume Teka has definitely found a way to track out movements. High Commander, what do you suggest?"

"Teka must really think we're a bunch of stupid jerks right about now," says Hops. "He made an offer and we counter with what appeared to him to be complete deception. The first thing we need to do is to reestablish contact and try to take the edge off this situation. If we're going to try to talk peace the last thing we need is distrust."

"A very reasonable observation," says Lamminta. "See if he is still willing to talk and if he will accept our explanation. If not, we fight."

Hops activates the secure communications channel, saying, "Palup Command, this is the Guardian ship Hope."

"Telebisque Teka here," is the terse response. "What are your wishes? Talk or fight?"

"We only wanted to know for certain that you had the capability to detect us. Our desires are the same as they have always been. We wish only to live in peace and let others do the same. As you can see, Telebisque, we have returned to a dead stop. If you still want to pursue a path to peace, allow me time to present your proposal to our full Council. I should have an answer for you in no more than," pausing to look at Lamminta sees the Council General hold up two fingers, "two hours."

"Do not take any longer," warns Teka. "I can wait only so long for your answer."

"One more question, Serligh?"

"Ask, and I will answer, if I can."

"How are you going to explain your situation if one of your Groups decides to stumble on to you? Two Fighting Stars, with all systems functioning, dead in space. This could be a little embarrassing for you."

"That, as you would say, is one that I will have to play by ear," answers Teka. "I am sure I will think of something that will be convincing."

"Good luck. Hope, out," says Hops. "Turning to the others in the room he asks, "Since we already have a secure channel here I think we need to get the others in here."

Reaching out Lamminta activates the intercom sensor, initiating the automated Council call. "The Council General requests the presence of the Council in the bridge ready room. Hotel One."

Within a few minutes, the remaining Council members enter the ready room immediately sit down. Lamminta wastes no time in explaining the situation.

"As you may know by now, Telebisque Teka, commanding the Fighting Star Palup, has contacted us. He comes with an offer of possible peace, alone. We must now decide what our answer will be. How do we proceed if we are to accept his offer? High Commander, as our military leader, what is your suggestion and recommendation?"

"I'm not sure, sir," begins Hops. "All we know for certain is that Teka definitely has the capability to locate us. Trilla has already started on reconfiguring the concealment device frequency modulation. That's the only way he could have found us. My guess is that he was able to isolate a few of the frequencies and scanned for them. Once he found the pattern, he used that information to find our trail. Therefore, until we can figure out what his actual intentions are, I suggest that we establish a negotiating team and meet with him face to face. That should give us a little more time to plan our next move."

"Who do you suggest as members of the negotiating team," asks Pidera?

"Just me," replies Hops. "Under the present circumstances, the team should be kept as small as possible. Since I'm a member of the Council, and a qualified pilot, I don't think there is any need to endanger anyone else. To me, this is the only practical solution."

"High Commander, I disagree," says Council Member Quince. "I don't believe your solution is practical, or completely legal. If memory serves me correctly, it is not, and has never been, the policy of the Council to allow a single Council Member to conduct any negotiations alone. Besides, how do you plan to effectively pilot a shuttle and still be able to conduct the talks? Or had you planned to take your Dragon to the negotiations?"

"So who do you suggest accompany me," asks Hops? "Or do I get to thank you for volunteering?"

"I do believe that I am the only other Council Member who is just as qualified as you to pilot any ship that you can," answers Carol with a hint of sarcasm in her voice. "And since you have already stated that you want to keep the negotiating team as small as possible my recommendation is that the Council agree the negotiation team should just the two of us."

"Not so fast, Council Member," counters Hops as he turns and looks towards Lamminta. "I think that either Council Member Pidera or Council Member Tro-Ja should accompany me on this mission. Council General I don't think it would be a good idea for the Council to allow the only two Council Members with combat experience to be together for these talks. If something should go wrong, Council Member Quince would be the one I would recommend to replace me as High Commander. I also believe it would be a better idea for one of the Probe Leaders were to pilot the shuttle if I can't pilot it myself."

This move catches almost everyone off guard.

Pausing for a moment, Lamminta makes his decision. Looking directly at Hops as if daring him to object, he says, "I think that it would be in the best interest of our people if Carol . . . Council Member Quince would accompany you as a member of your negotiating team. She understands and knows as much about Tirgonian tactics and procedures as you do. For that reason, I do not believe Council Member Pidera or Council Member Tro-Ja would be as effective in the negotiations as she would be."

Tro-Ja, recovering from the surprise suggestion of Hops, says, "High Commander, I must agree with the Council General. You, and Council Member Quince, are more far more knowledgeable about the Tirgonian tendencies and abilities of than I am. It would be better for our people if you had as much expert help as possible beside when you meet with Telebisque Teka. With only limited knowledge of this man, I would prove to be more harmful than useful on this mission. Therefore, I request to be removed from consideration for this mission."

"High Commander," says Pidera before Hops has a chance to respond to Tro-Jas' concerns. "Should these talks actually take place, you are going to need knowledge and wisdom by your side, not ignorance, or possible foolishness. I have yet to prove my abilities as an effective negotiator. You have already proven that you can achieve peace for our people under the most difficult of circumstances. Council Member Quince has also proven that she is capable of handling herself quite skillfully against any adversary. For the good of our people, I also remove my name from consideration."

Knowing that it would again be useless to oppose the decision of the two Council Members, Hops quietly concedes, saying, "I would still like to have one of the Probe Leaders to pilot the shuttle."

"I see nothing wrong with that," says Lamminta with a slight grin. "However, I think it would be a good idea to also have a copilot assigned. My choice for your pilot would be Major Cherrick as your pilot, and the copilot to be Lieutenant Televy. Major Cherrick because he has already landed, though covertly, on a Fighting Star and has that limited knowledge. Lieutenant Televy because she has proven to be a very capable shuttle pilot and has shown that she is quite capable of working under the most difficult of circumstances." Without waiting for Hops to challenge the suggestion, he continues. "Now that we have the negotiating team settled at four individuals, I believe the next question we must answer is where are these negotiations are to be held, and then notify Teka of the location. High Commander?"

"If I may have a moment to consider a few options, sir?"

"Of course," agrees Lamminta.

Slowly rising from his chair, Hops moves to stare out of one of the large glass portals. As he gazes out the window into the emptiness surrounding the Hope, he begins to remember the first encounter he had with this same enemy so many years ago. Would they actually be able to achieve the same results as they once did? Where would the best location to meet the man he knew so long ago? Slowly he turns to face the rest of the Council and Commander Williams.

"Halfway," begins Hops slowly. "We increase the distance to half a day travel by a shuttlecraft at quarter light speed. A full escort will launch and accompany each shuttle, but will move no closer than a thousand kilometers from the center point. Three Probes will continue following us but will hold a position five hundred kilometers from meeting coordinates. We tell Teka that his will have an equal number accompanying Horses they will hold the same positions on his side of the center point. Since he initiated the first contact, I suggest this first negotiation take place on our shuttle. If he's sincere about finding a way out of this mess, he has to prove he trusts us as much as he's asking us to trust him."

"If he insists that the meeting is to be held on the Palup, what then High Commander," asks Pidera? "If you cannot convince him to join you aboard your shuttle, what will you do? Do we abandon this chance for ending this war and finding possible peace? I think we should pursue all available options. If one solution doesn't work, we look for another. How many times have you yourself, High Commander, stated, 'What if . . .'?"

"I believe your concerns have already been addressed, Council Member," says Hops. "Major Cherrick has already landed on a Fighting Star once before, and if necessary, he may have to do it again. Only this time the Trigs will know about it ahead of time. I just don't like the idea of having two Council Members on the Palup at the same time, even if it is under a flag of truce. If that does happens, Teka just got a better hand than we're going to be playing with. Beside, Major Cherrick will have to land on the Palup, and if these talks actually work out just as Teka will eventually need to land on the Hope. Either way, we're going to have to trust each other."

Lamminta, remaining quiet through these last exchanges of cautious ideas and suggestions, says, "Then we are decided. High Commander, would please notify Telebisque Teka that we accept his offer to talk and the conditions under which these first talks will take place?"

"Of course, sir."

CHAPTER TWENTY-THREE

Teka agrees to the conditions presented by Hops, with the meeting scheduled for thirteen hundred hours the following day. Throughout the preparations, Commander Williams notices that Hops appears irritated by something and goes to the quarters of the High Commander.

"Listen, Hops," begins Williams as he hands Hops a small device, "you don't really know what you're getting into on this one. Here's something that might come in handy if things start to get a little sticky."

"I don't think I'm going to need a concealed weapon. Everyone will be carrying side arms."

"It's not a weapon," says Williams. "It's a communicator. Do you remember the one Freslof had when he first came aboard the Hope? He let Trilla borrow it, and all senior personnel have received one, so here's yours. The security protocol has you DNA code, and once you touch it, the alert sequence activates. If anyone but you touches it, all hell is going to break loose."

"Thanks," says Hops as he accepts the tiny device and tucks it under his tunic. "I just hope I don't have to use it. By the way, who's going to lead Black Bravo since Televy is going to be my copilot?"

"Black Bravo has been assigned to the thousand kilometer security line," is Williams only answer.

"Has the rest of the fleet closed on the Hope yet? If we end up in a fight I'm going to need some help getting my butt out of the fire."

"All ships are in position. I've never heard of an entire fleet moving into a Beta One Alpha before."

"There are still quite a few Battle Groups out there that we can't account for. I don't think ending up getting ambush by one of them would be a good idea. If anyone decides to show up, I want the Fleet to be ready for a fight and give us decent a chance of winning. One last thing, I don't want any of your drivers to get trigger-happy. At the first sign of trouble, I want the fleet to remain concealed and if need be, fight that way. The old man won't disperse the fleet unless the situation turns sour. If the Fleet dose have to disperse, make sure you give everyone enough time to reach the rendezvous point before the Fleet, or what's left of it, moves out."

"You still have that feeling, don't you?"

"Yeah, something just doesn't feel right," says Hops as he turns to leave his quarters. "I guess it's about time to get this show on the road. If everything goes our way I'll see you when I get back."

"Good luck," says Williams as he extends his hand, which Hops accepts.

As they leave the quarters, Hops turns towards transport tube, heading for the shuttle bay. Williams turns and heads in the opposite direction. As soon as Hops is out of sight Williams stops at a communications panel.

"Williams to the Bridge."

"Bridge, sir" responds Nuk-Ma.

"I'll be there in a little while. There's something that I need to check on."

"Understood, Commander. Bridge, out."

After agreeing to the conditions for the meeting from the Guardians, Teka carefully studies the details. He does not have much time to make any changes and knows that he must once again trust the man he knew so many years ago. Finally, it is time to leave the Palup. After seven hours of uneventful flight, the scanner of his shuttlecraft displays the image of the Guardian shuttlecraft and the formation of escorting Dragons.

"Tirgonian shuttle, this is the Guardian shuttle Tiberian, over," calls Hops as he initiates the first contact.

"Shuttle Tiberian, this is the Oplig," answers Teka. "May we join in peace?"

"That is all we have ever wanted," answers Hops. "You're welcome to come aboard the Tiberian."

"Your invitation is accepted, my friend," says Teka. "I see that you are still a man of your word. Your escort is holding position. My escort will also permit me to proceed alone. I thank you for your trust."

"Let's see just how far our trust goes before you thank me. Tiberian, out." Hops immediately changes the communications channel to the one used by the protecting Dragons. "All Probes, maintain your position as ordered. Stay out of the way, but be prepared to pull my butt out of the fire if this meeting falls apart. Acknowledge."

"Red, roger."

"Gold, roger."

"Orange, roger."

"Blue, roger."

"Purple, roger."

"Green, roger."

"Indigo, roger."

"Yellow, roger."

"Black Alpha, roger."

"Black Bravo, roger."

"Black Charlie, roger."

Hops realizes who was to replace the leader of Probe Black Bravo.

"Black Bravo One, this is the Lost One."

"This is Black Bravo One. What's the problem, Lost One," replies the familiar voice?

"I don't know what you think you're doing but you ass back to the Hope, and take Black Bravo with you. That's an order, and I mean now, Commander!"

"Sorry, Lost One, but I can't do that. If I leave now Teka, will see the Probe leave and is going want to know what's going on. How are you going to explain to him that you brought one too many Probes only to end up one short? The agreed number of Probes was eleven, not ten. We have forty-four Dragons and they have forty-four Horses. If your bacon starts to fry it would be a good idea to have the extra help to put out the fire. Like I said, I can't leave right now."

"Okay," agrees Hops as he tries to control his anger. "But as soon as we get back, I want to see you in my ready room! And I do mean as soon as we get back! Tiberian, out."

Carol seeing the irritation Hops face along with the emotional stress quietly asks, "High Commander, may I speak freely?"

"What," snaps Hops before he realizes the harshness in his voice? "I'm sorry, sure."

"I don't believe it would be wise to be too hard on Commander Williams right now. Both sides agreed the exact number of escort ships. If you show up with the wrong number, it could have an unwanted effect on this meeting. Orin and Jo are the only two remaining qualified pilots who could have replaced Lieutenant Televy. It's only natural that he replaced her ship with his. Besides, Hops, if the situation were reversed, wouldn't you have done the same thing?"

The use of his nickname causes him to glance at the woman sitting next to him in the passenger compartment of the shuttle.

"I guess you're right," slowly agrees Hops. "But he could have asked for permission before he did something as stupid as this."

"And you would have given him permission," asks Carol?

"Hell no I wouldn't have! A ship's captain ain't supposed to leave his ship when he's about to get into a fight he may not win," answers Hops. "I'm still going to have that talk with him when we get back, if we make it back in one piece."

"You're still having that feeling aren't you?"

"How can you tell?"

"Just by the way you're acting. What's bothering you?"

"I don't know. I just have a feeling that something's about to happen and we're not going to like it when it does."

"I know, I having the same feeling."

"Shuttle Tiberian, this is the Oplig," calls a female voice over the vehi-com. "Are you prepared for docking?"

"This is the Tiberian," answers Cherrick. "Affirmative. Slowing to one quarter light."

"Acknowledge. One quarter light."

The two small ships continue moving towards each other at reduced power. Any miscalculation by either pilot would spell disaster. If either ship nudged the other by the slightest bit, both vessels would spin wildly out of control, or possibly destroyed.

"Oplig, this is Tiberian. Reducing power, going to inertia. Power off."

"Understood Tiberian. Power off, going to inertia. Contact in ten seconds."

"Affirmative, Oplig. Contact in five. Four. Three. Two. One. Contact." The two alien ships gently touch as Cherrick and Televy move their finger rapidly over the control panel input sensors. "Docking pins engaged. Green light on the docking seal. Oplig, your status?"

"Tiberian, I also have a green light. Commence pressurizing the seal."

"Understood, Oplig. Pressurization complete."

"I have a green light on full pressurization," acknowledges the Oplig pilot.

"Roger, Oplig," replies Cherrick as he turns and gives the thumbs-up sign to the two passengers sitting behind him. "Opening our hatch."

Hops, standing with Carol who has already moved to the hatch opening, nods his approval. With a whisper of escaping air, the hatch slides open, exposing the open outer hatch of the Oplig.

Telebisque Teka, dressed in the formal uniform of the Tirgonian Space Defense Fleet and standing in the open hatchway, calmly says, "My old friend Captain Hoppinzorinski is now High Commander Hoppinzorinski."

"And Sub-Culmit Teka is now a Telebisque," returns Hops, though not as gently as his guest does.

"High Commander, I request permission to come aboard,"

"Permission granted, Telebisque," says Hops as he steps aside, allowing Teka to step across the threshold of the two shuttles. "May I present Council Member Quince, Telebisque Serligh Teka."

"My pleasure, Council Member," says Teka as he bows slightly and extends his hand in greeting. Turning his head slightly to look over at Hops he adds, "It seems that your Council has greatly improved its appearance since the last time I had the pleasure of meeting with its members."

"Thank you," says Carol as she smiles politely and accepts the outstretched hand. "There are several very important issues that need to be discussed, beside the current appearance of our Council. I think we should begin."

"Of course, Council Member," agrees Teka.

Hops, following Carol and Teka, moves towards the small table in the corner of the passenger compartment. As he stops, he indicates that they should seat themselves.

"Thank you," says Teka allowing Carol to the sit first. "If I may make a small request, High Commander?"

"Which is," asks Hops?

"Since I am here in good faith, I believe that we should continue to extend our trust to the others who have accompanied us in our journey."

"And you request is," asks Hops cautiously?

"Just a small gesture of trust between our junior officers," says Teka. "I believe your pilot might be interested in seeing the inside of one of his enemies' ships, even if it is a lowly shuttlecraft."

"I think we should stick to the agreed agenda, Telebisque," replies Hops in a formal, yet stern tone.

"Perhaps it would be a wise precaution. But what harm could such an offer do at this point in our common history," counters Teka?

"I think we should accept his offer," says Carol carefully. "An opportunity to demonstrate trust, regardless at what level, is always a welcomed push in the proper direction, however gentle the thrust."

"One speaks with caution, the other speaks with wisdom," observes Teka. "An admirable combination. However, High Commander, if you do not think this would be the time for such a small gesture I will not be offended and will honor your judgment."

Glancing briefly at Carol, Hops slowly says, "If Council Member Quince believes this would be a good idea I'll go along with her recommendation. And since my pilot will be touring the Oplig, I guess it would only be fitting to allow your pilot to have a tour of the Tiberian."

"I'm sure she would like that," accepts Teka as he stands and moves towards the open hatch.

Watching Teka as he summons his pilot, Hops calls out, "Major Cherrick, would you report back here."

"You need something, sir," asks Cherrick as he enters the small compartment?

"How would you like to take a tour of the Oplig?"

"Sir?"

"Would you like to see the inside of the Oplig," again asks Hops?

"That I would sir! I'd like to see what those bast . . ." suddenly realizing what he was saying and in whose presence he is standing, he quickly adds, "My apologizes, Telebisque."

Teka, seemingly unmoved by the slip of the tongue made by the young officer, dismisses this breech of protocol with a gently nod, saying, "I believe I have heard worse from your High Commander many years ago, and I might add regretfully, he has heard similar words from me during the same encounter. Under the circumstances, I understand your mistrust and your feelings against the Tirgonian Empire. Please announce yourself to Under-Culmit Sevnik. She is awaiting your arrival."

"Thank you, Telebisque," says Cherrick as he steps towards the hatch. As he starts to step through a Tirgonian female suddenly appears. "Under-Culmit Sevnik?"

"No, I am Sub-Culmit Zon," answers the officer as a second female appears beside her. "This is Under-Culmit Sevnik."

Cherrick steps back slightly as he looks at the two women in Tirgonian combat uniform. Both women, though his enemy, are strikingly attractive.

"Please, allow me," says Cherrick as he extends his hand to help the pilot of the Oplig step across the threshold.

"Excuse me, sir," says Zon without accepting the assistance and steps past Cherrick. "A Tirgonian officer does not need . . ."

"Zon! It is a Guardian custom for a man to offer assistance to a woman," snaps Teka! "You will show respect since you are entering their ship."

Looking harshly as Cherrick, Zon answers coarsely as she accepts his hand with a firm grasp, "Thank you, Major."

Taken by surprise, and by her strength, Cherrick reacts by squeezing Zons' hand just as roughly. The two officers, now standing face to face, grimacing at the increasing pressure exerted by the other, try to smile as if nothing were wrong. This momentary amusement brings a smile to the faces of the three senior officers.

"It seems that the exchange of officers was not such a bad idea," comments Teka.

"Looks that way," agrees Hops. "It appears like our two pilots are going to get along just fine."

The young officers, realizing that their attempt to insult the other was failing, reluctantly release their grasp, trying not to show any sign of the discomfort.

"Isn't it a good to see such young officers get along so well," asks Teka?

"Yes, it is," agrees Carol.

Once Cherrick disappears aboard the Oplig and Sub-Culmit Zon joins Televy in the cockpit of the Tiberian, Hops begins, "Now, down to business. What are you offering that will let us believe you have the authority to agree to a truce that will stop this war?"

"I see you have not changed," says Teka as he smiles and looks directly at the man sitting across the table from him, "always impatient, and straight to the point. As you may have already surmised, I am here without any authority from the Supreme Senate. Whoever would find us here at this time, without the expressed authority of the Supreme Commander, would arrest me, take me before the Senate and would be certainly sentence to death. My only hope is that somehow we find a way to end this bloodshed as we did once before. And if you remember correctly, that was not an easy time for either of us."

"Yeah," agrees Hops. "I remember that we were both almost hung for treason, and if this is going to be a repeat we did before, I think we're going to need to move very carefully."

"An astute observation," says Teka. "Now, as far as what I can offer at this time, what are your needs?"

"I don't think you'll be able to provide us with what we want."

"Please, ask and let me be the judge of what I can, or cannot, provide."

"Okay," say Hops without any hesitation, knowing that his request would be impossible to fulfill. "How about providing complete information of your Battle Groups and Armadas, supply lines, lines of communications and battle tactics for starters."

"You ask a great deal, my friend," says Teka. "Perhaps Council Member Quince could suggest a simpler need? Perhaps one that I could to give that would be within reason at this time?"

"Telebisque," begins Carol. "We both desire peace, at least that's the appearance of what we have before us. That is the one simple reason why I believe we are here. I don't believe we're going to agree to any specific requests made here today except one that we have already granted to each other. The two of you once trusted each other enough to at least be able to sit down, face to face, at the same table, without trying to kill each other. That in itself, just as this meeting today is a remarkable feat that was unthinkable just a few days ago. We should be content with this one small step for the moment. Peace shall come to those who wait, not to those who choose to fight. This war will end at some point in the future, not here, not now, and definitely not today. This is only the first step in a process, which as we all know, will not be an easy one. It is enough for now just to be able to sit and talk, without any promises made that might be broken later. I for one would like to hear the actual detail of the first encounter between the two of you."

"You have already learned of that time, Council Member," says Teka.

"Only what is recorded in the historical library and what is taught to young cadets," counters Carol. "Not everything is saved on memory circuits."

Smiling, Teka looks at Hops and says, "A very intelligent, and quite lovely, addition to your Council. Maybe it is just as well that we are able to sit and talk. It has been a long time since I have been able to enjoy this simple pleasure."

"Yeah," agrees Hops, "it does feel good to be able to . . ."

Suddenly Under-Culmit Sevniks' voice explodes over the shuttles communication system, "Telebisque Teka! Two Battle Groups approaching and are attempting to contact the Palup!"

"You dirty son of a bitch," exclaims Hops as he rushes towards the cockpit!

"Understood," yells Teka as he jumps to his feet, rushing after Hops!

"This hasn't been anything but a damned trap from the start," bellows Hops as he peers down at the small scanner screen and begins giving orders over the vehi-com! "Cherrick! Get back here! Seal that hatch and blow the damn pins! We need to get out of here! All Probes! Close on my position! I'm about to get my bacon fried!" Turning towards Teka he shouts, "Get your ass off my ship!"

"I assure you that I had nothing to do with this. My last orders to all Group commanders were for them to return to their original mission assignments. There are not to be any groups in this entire sector except mine," explains Teka.

"I'll see you in hell before I believe a damn word that comes out of your mouth," roars Hops! "Now get off my ship before I throw you out an air lock myself!"

"Too late, sir. The Battle Groups just entered scanner range. We have to move, and we have to move now, sir," reports Televy. "The Oplig has closed and sealed the hatch. Major Cherrick is still on board her."

"Blow the damn pins, Lieutenant! Carol! Keep an eye on our two guests. If either one of them tries to make a move, shoot both of them," orders Hops! "Come on, Lieutenant! Let's get this tub moving!"

Televy begins moving her fingers rapidly over the sensor-input panel as he jumps into the pilots' seat. "Major Cherrick has already completed the undocking procedures. Retracting the docking pins."

Council Member Quince, standing in the doorway of the cockpit, motions for the two Tirgonian officers to remain in the small passenger compartment. Sub-Culmit Zon immediately obeys. Teka however, too shocked to move, remains standing, still watching the approaching Fighting Stars on the scanner display screen.

"Damn it, Serligh! Get strapped in," bitterly snaps Hops. "This is going to be a rough ride and I don't need any interference from you or your damn bitch back there! When we get back to the Hope I'm going to personally see that both your asses are thrown in the brig and key is flushes out with the garbage waste!"

"Then you do believe me," asks Teka?

"Look! I don't have time to discuss whether or not if I believe you right now. I just want to get out of here in one piece and you're not helping by standing there in the way! Just shut up and get yourself strapped in! Now!"

Teka, under the watchful stare of Council Member Quince, does as ordered and returns to the passenger compartment. Noticing that his junior officer is about to speak, he gives her a stern look, shaking his head ever so slightly. Zon, glaring harshly, first towards Hops and then at Carol, remains silent as she adjusts her safety restraints.

"Engines on line with full power," says Televy. "Locking pins disengaged. Docking collar retracted and stowed. Concealment device engaged. Deflectors and shields at full strength. Course to the Hope plotted and locked in."

"Then let's get moving, Lieutenant," says Hops in a slightly calmer voice as he touches the main engine control sensor.

"Full inertia," reports Televy as she monitors the power indicator. "Half-light, increasing to three-quarters light. Light one, two. Holding steady at two point five."

"I need more power," says Hops. "Divert one quarter power from the forwards deflectors to the engines."

"One quarter power diverted from forward deflectors to the engines," acknowledges Televy. "Speed increasing to three point three five! The Oplig is following us!"

"What," shouts Teka!

"The Oplig is following, sir."

"You're about to have a real short trip Serligh," yells hops over his shoulder!

"I assure you again, I had nothing to do with this," replies Teka. "You must believe me!"

"Just shut up and keep your mouth shut!" orders Hops harshly. "I'll deal with the two of you when we get back to the Hope!"

"Receiving a signal from the Oplig, sir," reports Televy. "Major Cherrick is trying to contact us."

"What in the hell is he doing," asks Carol?

"I believe he's trying to get his ass back to the Hope just like we are, and he's bringing his girlfriend with him," says Hops.

"He's stealing my ship," bellows Teka!

"Right now I don't think he's too worried about being called a thief," says Hops as he answers the incoming vehi-come message. "Oplig, this is the Tiberian. What's going on back there? Do you think you can make it?"

"I don't know yet, Tiberian," answers the nervous voice of Cherrick. "It seems that Sub-Culmit Sevnik didn't want to leave her boss and have to face the music that's about to be played back on the Palup. If this piece of obsolete space junk can move as fast as it's supposed to we should be able to make it back to the Hope without any problems."

"Don't forget that the Tirgs can see you."

"That's why I want to make it back to the Hope before you do. If things get any worse, I'm going to need a little more help that you will. I couldn't get the frequency set. Let the Probes know that I'm on their side. I don't think I'm going to be able to dodge them at the same time I'm trying to outrun those bastards behind us."

"Roger," acknowledges Hops as he nods for Televy to switch communications frequencies. "All Probes. This is the Tiberian. The Oplig is coming back with us. Major Cherrick is at the helm. You should be picking us up right about now. Acknowledge."

"This is Red One. We have both shuttles on screen. The Fighting Stars are still coming in and should reach the Palup in about three hours. We should be able to link you with in a lot less time than that time. No sign of any Horses outside the barn. Everyone should be able to make it back to the Hope in one piece."

"I hope you're right. If those Stars decide to head this way they might be able to cut us off before we make it back to the Fleet."

"Tiberian, this is the Hope, over."

"Go ahead Hope," answers Hops.

"Don't worry about keeping your butt covered," says Lamminta. "The Fleet is closing on you as we speak. When you come in head straight for the landing bay. You take Alpha and the Oplig will come in on Bravo. If those Stars get too close they're going to have a little surprise they won't like."

"Roger, Hope. We're coming in hot."

"Don't burn out your injector coils. You still have six hours before you can put that fire out," says Lamminta.

"All you have to do is to pull the welcome mat in as soon as we get there," answers Hops.

"Understood, Tiberian. Just get back here in one piece. Hope, out."

CHAPTER TWENTY-FOUR

The unexpected arrival of the two Battle Groups causes alarm not only for the negotiators, but also for Cudrosia, the temporary commander of the Palup.

"Culmit Cudrosia," reports Under-Culmit Matilosk. "Telecoup Veskin is demanding to know why we are not searching for the Guardians. He wants to speak to Telebisque Teka."

"Inform Telecoup Veskin that I am in command of the Palup. I will speak with him."

"Understood," replies the Palups communications officer as he relays the message. "Sir, Telecoup Veskin is requesting an explanation as to why we are not obeying orders and actively searching for the Guardians."

"Secure the channel and transfer it to the ready room," orders Cudrosia as he departs the bridge. As soon as the door to the ready room closes behind him, he activates the communications panel view screen. "This is Culmit Cudrosia. Why are you in this sector, Telecoup? Your assigned sector is three one seven."

"I follow orders, Culmit, and go where I am directed. I do not answer to you," answers Veskin with clear disdain in his voice. "Now where is Telebisque Teka?"

"I am in command of the Palup, and of this Battle Group, Telecoup. Again, I want to know why you are in this sector."

"As you wish, Culmit, this is you sector," snarls Veskin. "I have been ordered here, along with the Battle Group Loksija, to join your Group. The Supreme Senate received information that has led the Supreme Commander to believe the Guardians are in this sector. He wants them found and destroyed. Have you had any contact with them?"

"No," answers Cudrosia, "we have not had any contact with any of the Guardian ships."

"Then why have I been ordered here," demands Veskin! "You will answer me! I want to know where the Guardians are hiding!"

"I do not know where the information reported to the Supreme Commander came from. I have not had received any information indicating the Guardians are in this sector, and I assure you that the information, whether true or not, did not come from this Battle Group."

"The Guardians are hiding somewhere in this sector and I want to know where they are," again demands Veskin!

"The Guardians are . . ."

"Lock all batteries," hastily orders Veskin! "One last time, Culmit! Where are the Guardians! What contact have you had with the Guardians and where are they!"

Countering the move by the commander of the Hidlok, Cudrosia gives his own orders. "All batteries! Target the Hidlok! Engage the deflectors and defensive shield! Now, Telecoup, fire if you so desire. As I have said, I have not had any contact with the Guardian fleet!"

"Then explain the absence of Telebisque Teka! The Supreme Commander knows that he had direct contact with them two and a half days ago!"

"I do not have any direct knowledge that Telebisque Teka has made any direct contact with them," answers Cudrosia. "Thirteen hours ago he departed the Palup on a personal matter. He did not disclose the nature of this matter to me. Nor did he disclose his destination or his time of return. My orders are to remain in here until his finished whatever personal business required his attention. At this time, I am unaware of his location, or his intentions."

"If you are indeed in command of your Battle Group, then why haven't you confirmed the location of you absent commander? Or are you as incompetent as your commander," asks Veskin sarcastically? "A true commander would confirm the location of an absent crewmember."

"I was ordered not to attempt any unauthorized scanning of his shuttle, nor was I to attempt to contact him. As you yourself have stated, Telecoup, I am following orders."

"Very commendable, under other circumstances, Culmit," says Veskin with open contempt showing in his voice. "What about the Junnack? I see that Sub-Telecoup Envela has not questioned the absence of his Group Commander. Has he received orders not to inquire about the absence of his commander? His communications logs indicate that on several occasions he requested to know what is going on, without any response from you."

“I am following my last orders, Telecoup. You will leave this sector and I will return to my mission orders,” thwarts Cudrosia.

“One last time, Culmit, if you are indeed in command of your Battle Group, it is you direct responsibility, as the current commander, to assume full responsibility for your actions, not to hide behind the authority of your absent Telebisque. You have a lot to learn about command and the responsibilities of command. Culmit Cudrosia, you are relieved of command! I am assuming command of you Group and you will report to the Hidlok as my Fourth Officer! Sub-Telecoup Isk will take command of your Battle Group! Here, you will again learn the duties of command! Veskin, out!”

Cudrosia storms out of the ready room and immediately begins to issue his orders. “Helm! Plot and execute the same course as the Oplig! Full power! Now!”

“Sir, message coming in from the Hidlok. Telecoup Veskin demands that you obey your orders and report to the Hidlok,” reports the Communications Officer.

“I have not received any such orders,” says Cudrosia as he reclaims his composure. “I am still in command of this Fighting Star. You will follow my orders or you will find yourself charged with treason and placed in confinement. Disregard all communications except those from Telebisque Teka. What you are hearing is the beginning of a trap designed by Telecoup Veskin to lure the Guardians into attempting to lure Telebisque Teka revealing his true reason for leaving his post and telling anyone why.”

“Understood, sir.”

“Course and speed established,” reports the helmsman. “Engaging power transfer. Helm responding.”

“I don’t know what your first officer is trying to do,” says Hops as he monitors the progress of the approaching Fighting Star, “but it looks like he’s trying to follow us.”

“The fool,” exclaims Teka! “There is nothing that he could possible gain by disobeying his orders!”

“Sorry, Serligh, but I once heard someone say that just because someone happens to be a Tirg, doesn’t mean they’re stupid. He may have figured out what you’re trying to do and he may be thinking the same thing,” says Hops. “If that’s true, it looks like he’s trying to accomplish one of two options. Either he’s trying to save your bacon or he’s trying to get out of a bad situation himself. Either way, he’s going to have his hands full when he gets within range of our fleet. I don’t think one Fighting Star is going to have much of a chance of survival going up against the firepower we can put out.”

"He understands what you have said, my friend," agrees Teka. "And if he understands that he does not have any chance of surviving an attack against your fleet, why does he persist in trying to find me? He must know that my life is now worthless. Why would he risk the Palup in such a foolish attempt?"

"I ain't an answer for that," says Hops. "Whatever he's trying to accomplish we're not helping our chances with the Oplig following us and showing up like a beacon on the scanners.

"Junnack," screams Veskin as the Palup races away! "Join the Hidlok! Take your position opposite the Quiger. Loksija Group! Maintain rear guard. All Groups will follow the Palup. If Cudrosia refuses to relinquish command of the Palup, then that ship will be destroyed."

"What about Teka," asks Telecoup Vandilkor?

"What can he hope to gain without his ship," replies Veskin? "Once he is found he will die, as he should have that last time. We leave now!"

"Oplig, this is the Tiberian."

"Go ahead, sir. If you have a plan to get us out of this mess, Sev and I are all ears."

"Sev," questions Teka?

"I'll explain later," says Hops as he begins maneuvering the Tiberian closer to the Tirgonian shuttle. "Oplig, we're going to try to hook up without slowing down. You with me?"

"Your theory sounds fine sir. When will your test results ready?"

"I'll let you know if this works just as soon as we get these two pieces of junk together," replies Hops. "Coming out of hiding. Match your speed to three-quarters light."

"There's not enough time to program the computers for this, sir."

"Damn it, Cherrick, stop calling me 'sir', and forget about the computers. We're going to do this on manual. Now get beside me at three-quarters light."

"Okay" says Cherrick hurriedly. "If you're calling the shots I guess that makes the target."

"Just be careful and close to one hundred meters."

"Are you mad? Do you really believe two shuttles have the capability to dock at this speed," asks Teka as he stares at the Hops? "I know this meeting hasn't turned out exactly the way we originally planned, but this maneuver you are about to attempt is suicidal. If you are trying to prove a point, I think you might consider the lives of the others."

"Telebisque," quietly says Carol "I'm sure he is thinking about all of us, here and on the Oplig. He realizes the only way we can safely return to our fleet is to shed our excess baggage. If we don't leave the Oplig behind, the Hope will have to disengage the concealment device for Major Cherrick to land. That would give everyone in this, and the neighboring, sectors the exact location of our fleet. Docking at this speed, though never tried before, don't mean it won't actually work? The only thing we can do at the moment is to be patient and allow Hops to do the one thing he does best."

Hops is shocked at hearing the words of Carol as he has a fleeting thought. "What in the hell am I doing?"

"Tiberian, this is Oplig. Three quarters light and one hundred meters separation."

"Roger," acknowledges Hops as the distance between the two ships slowly decreases. "Close to fifty, watch your angle of approach."

"Closing to fifty. Holding approach angle at three degrees down. And by the way boss, who's ordering the shovels if this doesn't work?"

"Don't worry about the shovels, Cherrick, just keep the Oplig steady. Close to twenty-five and decrease your angle to one degree."

"Sorry boss, but you confused me on that last one. Do you want one degree decrease or decrease by one degree to a two-degree down angle?"

"Set you angle of approach to one degree down," clarifies Hops.

"Roger. Holding steady at twenty-five and two degrees angle of approach."

"Looks good on screen," says Hops as he activates sensor to extend the docking collar. "Close to five meters and hold steady. I'll do the rest."

"Closing to five and holding steady. It's all yours boss."

Without acknowledging Hops continues the unorthodox procedure, calling out, "Carol! Check the hatch. Make sure the collars are going to line up. We may only get one shot at this."

Council Member Quince immediately releases he safety restraint. Moving to the hatch portal she reports, "Docking collars appear to be in line."

"Closing to four meters," is Hops only response.

"Four meters," acknowledges Cherrick.

"Collars still lined up."

"Three meters," says Hops as he his voice begins to show a slight sign of stress as he maneuvers the Tiberian closer.

"Three meters," calls Hops. "Two meters."

"Collars off line," yells Carol! "We're half a meter in front!"

"Damn it! Hold steady, Cherrick," yells Hops! "I'm going to try it again. Moving out to five meters."

"Roger," says Cherrick. "Holding steady."

"Closing to three meters."

"Three meters," answers Cherrick.

"Collars lined up," reports Carol.

"Two meters," calls out Hops.

"Roger on two meters," says Cherrick.

"I can't see the docking pins" calls out Carol.

"Just stay with the collars. It they're lined up the pins will be in line."

"Collars still in line."

"Closing to half a meter. Pins should be engaging," reports Hops.

"No pin light," calls out Cherrick.

"I have a yellow light on the docking collars. No pin light," warns Televy.

"Damn it," yells Cherrick! "Where's the docking pin release!"

"Here," replies Sevnik as she activates the appropriate sensor.

"Yellow light on docking collar and pins," reports Cherrick. "Pressurizing."

"Collars pressurized," confirms Televy. "Green light on collars and pins."

"Major," calls out Hops. "I suggest you and your girlfriend get your asses over here. The Palup is about five hours out and that's not much of a margin for us to get back to the Hope in one piece."

"We're on our way! Open the hatch!"

"Hatch open," calmly replies Televy.

Even before the Tiberians' hatch is fully open, Under-Culmit Sevnik steps through the partial opening and, as tradition requires, asks, "Permission to come aboard, sir?"

"Just get your ass in here! Take a seat and get strapped in," snaps Hops! "Seal that hatch! How soon before the pins disengage?"

"Hatch sealed and depressurizing," reports Televy.

"I set the auto release to close the hatch and disengage the pins two seconds after decompression," says Cherrick as he remains next to the closed and sealed. "That should shove the Oplig clear."

No sooner than the words are spoken when everyone aboard hears the escaping air and feels a severe jolt as the docking pins of the Oplig tear away from their hold on the Tiberian.

"How secure is that hatch seal," yells Hops as he banks the Tiberian sharply to starboard as he avoids direct contact with the errant Oplig.

"Sealed and holding," reports Cherrick who has not left the hatch since stepping across only a few moments ago. "From what I can see, we're going need some fancy repairs when we get back to the Hope. And speaking of the Hope, where are our Dragons?"

"Let's find out," says Hops as he activates the communications sensor. "And by the way Cherrick, I think you got the release sequence backwards."

"Sorry, boss," says Cherrick as he relieves Televy as the shuttle copilot. "Tirgs have been known to do a lot of things that way just to confuse us."

"Just as long as we can stay together for a little while longer we should be okay," says Hops as he contacts Commander Jo-Ich. "Red One, this is Lost One, over."

"Roger, Lost One," answers Jo-Ich. "I'm charging hard and the cavalry is right behind me. You should have visual contact shortly. You're clear so far."

"Thanks, Jo. I hope we don't end at the Little Big Horn. I'm beginning to understand how Custer felt."

"Affirmative, Tiberian. Where are Major Cherrick and the Oplig? I only have you on screen."

"He's right here. Make sure to open a hole so I can sneak through. Watch the flanks for a blitzing linebacker. I don't want this quarterback betting sacked for a loss."

"There's nothing to worry about. I've a double tight end set, wide receivers on the flanks and full backfield. If they blitz the corners we'll pick them up."

"Roger, Red One. See you in a few minutes. Lost One, out."

The five others aboard the Tiberian glance at each other in confusion as Cherrick quietly asks, "Sir, what code file did that come from? What's a blitzing linebacker?"

"I would like to know what is a quarterback," asks Teka?

"Why wouldn't you want to put it in a sack to keep from losing it," asks Carol?

"Don't worry about the code," replies Hops with a grin. "Jo understood and will handle his end of this fight. All we have to do is to get through that hole and hope like hell he gets it closed before any damned Tirgs make it through."

"What about Under-Culmit Sevnik, Zon, and myself," asks Teka?

"Present company excluded, Serligh," answers Hops jokingly.

"Tiberian, this is Lamminta. We still have the Palup heading towards our position. The Junnack has joined the Hidlok and Loksija Groups. All are heading this way. If

Telebisque Teka has any idea what his Executive Officer is planning, I believe this would be a good time to let us know what might be going on."

"Guardian ship Hope, this is Telebisque Teka. I do not know why my Executive Officer is attempting to follow me at this time. With you superior numbers and capabilities matched against a single Fighting Star, we both would undoubtedly suffer losses that could be ill afforded. He is fully aware that a lone Fighting Star could not possibly hope to engage and defeat a force such as the one currently under your command. Other than that, I have no idea as to what he believes he can to gain by this tactic."

"Could you Culmit be acting completely on his own," asks Hops?

"It is a definite possibility," replies Teka, "but for what purpose, I do not know."

"Hope, this is Lost One. How soon before the Palup will be within range to launch her Horses?"

"Four and a half hours at the most."

"We should coming through Jos' offensive hole in less than ten minutes. You're still too far out to give us any effective cover. It looks like my original idea of talking with Serligh wasn't such a good one after all."

"Don't worry about that right now," says Jo-Ich. "Increase power and duck in between that pulling guard and right tackle before that sack happens."

"I'm flat out now. I can't divert any more power from the deflectors or shields."

"Just stay in one piece. I don't feel like scheduling another Council vote to replace a Council Member, as well as a High Commander," says Lamminta.

"I appreciate your concern, sir," says Hops with a slight grin as he turns to look back at the Council Member. "We'd prefer you didn't schedule that vote just yet either. Besides, do you actually think you could find someone to replace Council Member Quince?"

"That would be the more difficult choice," agrees Lamminta. "It will be a lot easier to find your replacement than a qualified replacement for Council Member Quince. Just get back here in one piece."

"Thanks," says Hops with a chuckle. "Tiberian, out."

"The Palup just reached effective scanner range," reports Cherrick.

"Scan for anything Cudrosia lets out of the barn," orders Hops. "I'm not getting anything to indicate he's opened the barn door yet."

"Barn door," questions Teka?

"He hasn't opened his launch bay blast doors yet," answers Hops. "It would be kind of hard to launch any Horses with the doors closed."

"Of course," acknowledges Teka as he removes his safety restraint and moves to stand behind Hops. "May I have an open channel to the Palup? Maybe I can find out what Cudrosias' intentions are."

"Sure."

"Palup Command, this is Telebisque Teka, over."

"Guardian shuttle Tiberian, this is the Fighting Star Palup. We have recovered the Oplig, which has sustained damage to the entire docking system. What is your status, Telebisque? We shall overtake that puny shuttle within the hour."

"Why are you attempting to interrupt me at this time," immediately demands Teka? "I did not request your presence, nor your assistance. I am not in any danger from the Guardians at this time. If you persist in following, you will only cause the Palup to either be severely damaged, or entirely destroyed, nothing more."

"My intentions are not to initiate any hostile action, Telebisque. My only concern is for your safety."

"Then why did you not remain as ordered? What is the reason for the arrival of the Battle Groups Hidlok and Loksija?"

"The Supreme Commander received information that the Guardians were in this sector and ordered the Hidlok and Loksija to assist in your search of this sector. Telecoup Veskin requested to speak directly with you."

"A simple communiqué would have been quicker, and easier. What did he say to you? I want to know the exactly what he said."

"After informing him that you were not aboard the Palup and, that I was unaware of you exact location, he ordered me to report to the Junnack as Fourth Officer. Sub-Telecoup Isk was to take command of the Palup."

"Then I have been officially recalled and no longer in command of my Battle Group," slowly says Teka as he stares out the forward view portal of the Tiberian. "It appears that I am not one to be associated with. If I return to Tirgonia now, the Supreme Senate would summons me to appear before it. I would be courts martialed for treason, and sentenced for execution. If you return now, the most that will happen to you would be a reduction in rank to Under-Culmit. I will never be able to return to Tirgonia, but you still have a chance to return and regain you honor. You must know my destination, and realize that with the number of Guardian ships you will undoubtedly encounter, the Palup will not survive. To win glory, one must first win the battle. As commander of the Palup, you prepared to be responsible for the loss of the five thousand lives under your command?"

"I will not return with you, Telebisque," replies Cudrosia. "If I return, I will be ordered to find you, and destroy any ship you attempt to board. That, I will not do."

Hops can only stare at the reflection of the empty face in the forward portal of the man who once had saved his life.

"It seems that Cudrosia is determined to have me return to the Palup," says Teka quietly. "I do not believe he is fully prepared to engage your forces, and that places him in a very difficult position."

"What will he do when he does realize he's about to be engaged not only by our Dragons, but our entire Fleet," asks Council Member Quince?

"Your Dragons do not pose the greater threat, Council Member. I do not believe he will initiate any engagement with your fleet. His only wish is for my safe return to the Palup."

"He must know that we will not allow him to proceed much closer," continues Quince. "We cannot permit the Palup to continue and penetrate our defenses. Even if he does not initiate a fight, we will. If he continues on course, we will not have any other choice."

"He does understand, Council Member, but I do not see any other alternative at this point."

"There's always an alternative," says Hops, "and as far as I can see, there are three. First, we can start another fight. Secondly we could return Serligh to the Palup, or third, we could try to get the Palup to join us."

As if one person spoke, the others exclaimed in unison, "What!"

"Well," says Hops with a shrug of his shoulders, "it is an option."

"There isn't anything that would convince Cudrosia to surrender the Palup," answers Teka. "He would rather die fighting a losing battle than surrender."

"I didn't say surrender," says Hops. "I said 'to join us'."

"You are proposing that he turn sides, sir," asks Televy?

"It worked once before," calmly replies Hops.

"Yes," agrees Teka, "but that was with me."

"And hasn't Cudrosia been trained by the same man I once knew not so long ago," counters Hops? "And if he was trained by this same individual, what would his training tell him to do? Continue to fight and, at best, hope to break even? Or, would he try to find a way to end the fighting and return to peace?"

"He is a Tirgonian officer," says Teka. There is pride in his voice as he spoke of the honor possessed by every member of Tirgonian Defense Force. "He would never dishonor his allegiance or his duty."

"Doesn't that sound just like something someone once told me about a certain Tirgonian officer a little while back?"

"That was during a forgotten time, my old friend," says Teka. "Beside Telecoup Incisch was old and tired."

"The same way we are right now, my friend, but it is worth a try."

"Shuttle Tiberian, this is Red One. Visual contact. We have a whole open, so come on through."

The sudden call startles Hops and he does not immediately respond.

"Shuttle Tiberian, this is Red One, over."

"Roger, Red One," replies Hops. "Close that hole and maintain position. Get ready for a second and ten."

"What," exclaims Jo-Ich! "You've got five Fighting Stars chasing the Palup, who just happens to be breathing down your exhaust ports, and you're telling me to maintain and hold position! What in the hell are you planning this time, boss?"

"I'll explain later, Jo! Just do it!"

Cherrick, anticipating Hops next order begins maneuvering the shuttle saying, "Slowing to half-light and coming about. Palup dead ahead. Fifteen minutes to intercept."

The sudden maneuver of the Tiberian causes several of the protecting Dragons to react radically, barely able to avoid being hit by the larger craft.

"Maintain half-light," calmly orders Hops as he activates the communications sensor. "Fighting Star Palup, this is the Tiberian, over."

"Shuttle Tiberian, this is Culmit Cudrosia. To whom am I speaking?"

"This is High Commander Hoppinzorinski. I understand that you may have a slight problem and I think I have a solution that may benefit both of us."

"The infamous Guardian called Hops," replies Cudrosia. "Under different circumstances I would say this is an honor, but now I am forced to destroy you and your ship."

"Before you try to stop me from breathing, I'd like to request permission to come aboard under a flag of truce to discuss a few things."

"This is nothing but a Guardian trick."

"Culmit! You will accept a flag of truce from this man," orders Teka! "I will be returning to the Palup with him! Now, do you question me, or my authority?"

"I apologize, Telebisque. I did not understand that High Commander Hoppinzorinski was speaking on your behalf. Permission granted to come aboard,

High Commander. Your flag of truce will be honored guests. You, and the others accompanying you, will be honored guests aboard the Palup. Again, High Commander, I apologize for the misunderstanding."

"Thank you, Culmit Cudrosia," accepts Hops. "Just maintain course and speed. Our concealment device will be disengaged when we reach the final approach point."

"That will not be necessary, High Commander, unless you wish it to be so. We are able to track you ship with your device engaged. We await your arrival."

"Again, Culmit Cudrosia, thank you. Tiberian, out," says Hops as he switches communications frequencies to the one used by the Hope. "Hope, this is the Tiberian. Don't wait up for us. We're going to be a little late and will probably miss midnight curfew."

"Negative, Tiberian," exclaims a very irritated Council General! "Return to the Hope! Immediately!"

"Could you say that again, Hope? Your transmission is starting to get garbled."

"Don't give me that damn excuse," shouts Lamminta! "There isn't . . ."

"Damn," mutters Hops as he turns off the communication sensor. "Just lost contact with the Hope. Did anyone catch what Lamminta was trying to say?"

CHAPTER TWENTY-FIVE

"Tiberian! This is Lamminta! You are ordered to return immediately," yells the Council General as he turns towards Nuk-Ma! "Do you still a lock on the shuttle?"

"Yes, sir," answers Nuk-Ma. "But I can't raise the High Commander. He's still heading towards the Palup."

"If he gets out of this in one piece, I'm going to have him drawn, quartered, castrated, beheaded, and then I'm going to kill him," mutters Lamminta. "Let me know as soon as contact has been reestablished."

"Aye, sir."

Time drags by as Nuk-Ma continually repeats the call in an attempt to get a reply form the shuttle.

"I have the contact with the High Commander, sir. Channel open."

"High Commander," quickly snaps Lamminta, "I am ordering you to return to the Hope! Now!"

"I'm afraid I can't do that right at the moment, sir," answers Hops. "I have an idea that just might swing things in our favor."

"Damn it, Hops! We have six Fighting Stars closing on the Fleet! There isn't any way you can possible accomplish whatever it is you're trying to do without endangering the lives of everyone on the Tiberian! I'm ordering you back here now!"

"I'm going to have to put that request on the back burner, sir. Cudrosia just gave me clearance to land on the Palup. Right now, we'd be a lot safer there than trying to get back to the Fleet. I'll let you know how things work out just as soon as I find out myself. Tiberian, out."

"Damn it! Get back here," again yells Lamminta as the communications channel again goes silent!

"Shuttle Tiberian," calls Cudrosia, "Telecoup Veskin will be within weapons range shortly after you arrive. I may be required to engage several Fighting Stars that have the same capabilities, and maneuverability, as the Palup. It appears that you will not be able to return to your Fleet unless you do so now."

"Listen, Culmit, I'm a hell of a lot closer to the Palup than I am to my own ship. The only chance I have right now is to land on the Palup. I don't have time to turn back."

"If you are discovered aboard the Palup, you, and the other members of you crew will be immediately taken prisoner, and very possibly put to death. I can only protect you under the flag of truce to which I alone have agreed. Telecoup Veskin will not honor the protection I have promised. For the safety of the others, you must return to your fleet."

"I told you that I can't do that, Culmit! I'm coming in so get ready for my final approach and landing sequence! I'm heading for Alpha Ramp like a bat out of hell! Tiberian, out!"

"Initiating landing sequence," reports Cherrick "Slowing to . . ."

"Negative," orders Hops! "We're going in hot. Maintain full power. Be ready to hit the reverse thrusters and maneuvering jets when I tell you. We don't have time to slow down."

Cherrick, glancing towards Hops with a worried look upon his face answers nervously "Sir, I don't think it would be such a good idea to land on a strange ship under full power. If we were landing on the Hope it might be a little easier."

"Just do it. You've landed on a Star once already so this shouldn't be any different."

"I must agree with you, Major," says Teka. "This procedure is not recommended for our own shuttles under ideal conditions, and definitely not recommended for a Guardian vessel under these circumstances. A shuttle cannot withstand the strain. Your engineers did not plan for any Guardian ship to undergo this degree of structural stress."

"This isn't one of you antiquated shuttles, Serligh. Just hang on. It might get a little rough."

The Tiberian is now within a thousand kilometers of the Palup and closing fast. Five hundred kilometers and the landing bay opening looms directly in front of the Guardian ship.

"Forty-five hundred. Forty. Thirty-five. Thirty," calls out Cherrick at the rapidly diminishing distances as he again glances nervously at Hops.

Appearing calm, as if this landing procedure is nothing other than a normal occurrence, continues with the landing procedure checklist.

"Begin reducing power. Get ready on reverse thrusters and maneuvering jets. Keep all power levels steady."

"Twenty thousand. Speed steady at fifteen hundred."

"Shut down concealment device and defensive systems," calmly orders Hops.

"Fifteen hundred," calls out the nervous copilot. "Still too hot. Speed down to one thousand."

"Settle down, Major. Divert all available power to maneuvering."

Cherricks' fingers begin moving rapidly over the control input panel. The shuttle begins slowing down, but not enough to please the passengers aboard the Tiberian. Their strained looks reveal only part of their fear.

"One thousand meters. Speed seven hundred."

"Ease two degrees to port," orders Hops.

Amazingly, the shuttle responds to the control adjustments.

"Two degrees and holding steady," says a much calmer reply from Cherrick. "Five hundred. Still holding hot. Speed one hundred."

In the blinking of an eye the Tiberian zooms past the entrance of the landing bay as Hops immediately begins giving rapid orders.

"Reverse thrusters! Watch the attitude! Five degrees positive pitch! Keep the nose up! Hit the brakes! Maximum bow thrusters!"

The shuttle continues towards the protective force field barrier at the far end of the ramp. The bow thrusters' continue firing, rapidly slowing the Tiberian. The force of the reverse thrusters throws everyone aboard violently against their safety restraints. The Tiberian, stopping only inches from the force field barricade, begins slowly moving backwards.

"Disengage bow thrusters. Maintain minimum forward thrust. Continue normal landing procedures," quietly orders Hops as he turns to look towards the cramped passenger compartment. "Is everyone still with me back there?"

"I believe we're all okay," answers Carol, trying not to sound as shaken as she actually is.

Teka, only slightly calmer than the Council Member, says, "If that was a demonstration of your normal landing procedures, it is a miracle that you survived this long. I think I need a stiff drink to settle my nerves, once I find them again."

"That doesn't sound like a bad idea, Serligh," says Hops with a slight chuckle as he contacts the Landing Bay Control Officer. "Palup Landing Bay, this is the Tiberian. Request permission to come aboard."

"Permission granted, Tiberian," grants the officer. "The force field has been lowered. Please follow the guidance markers to your docking pad. An escort will be waiting for you when you disembark."

"Understood," acknowledges Hops.

"And if you would, High Commander, you must teach me that maneuver."

"I don't think your commander would appreciate you trying that one just yet," answers Hops as Cherrick completes the docking sequence.

"Contact. Shuttle docked. Securing all systems," reports Cherrick. "One hell of a flight, sir."

"Just take care of her, Cherrick," says Hops as he loosens his safety restraints. "We're going to need her to get back to the Hope," continues Hops as he climbs out of the pilots' seat. "Televy, I want you to stay with Major Cherrick. We need to be ready to leave at a moment's notice. I don't think we're going to be here very long." The others, after releasing their safety restraints, are waiting for Hops in the passenger compartment. Entering the already cramped aft cabin and reaching for the hatch sensor, he says, "We're not going to get anything accomplished standing here with our thumbs up . . ."

"Shall we go," interrupts Teka as he steps through open hatch. As soon as he steps onto the deck, he turns and salutes the flag of the Tirgonian Empire. His two junior officers, showing the same respect for their homeland, follow the example of their commander. Teka, turning, introduces the Guardians under his protection to the awaiting escort. "I would like to presence High Commander Hoppinzorinski and Council Member Quince from the Guardian Council of Elders."

"Your flag of truce will be honored by all aboard the Palup," acknowledges the Tirgonian officer in charge of the official escort. "I am Under-Culmit Tomdoc. If you will follow me, Culmit Cudrosia is waiting for you in his ready room."

This last comment causes Teka to glare sharply Tomdoc. However, the Under-Culmit does not respond to the look from his commander as he leads the way towards the landing bay exit.

The Tirgonian escort employs strict security measures as everyone moves quietly along the corridors and passageways of the Fighting Star. Finally, they arrive in front of an unmarked door. It appears no different from the uncounted number of entranceway they already passed. Tomdoc pressed the door sensor on the bulkhead, producing a gently sound.

"Enter," calls a female voice from the other side of the door as it silently opens.

Teka, stepping aside, allows his guests to enter first. As he follows them into the room, he motions for Tomdoc to remain outside the still open door. Hops does not waste any time, or words, as he enters.

"I thought we were to meet with Culmit Cudrosia?"

"High Commander Hoppinzorinski, I am Culmit Flexia Raccesia, Aide to Telebisque Teka. Please, be seated," returns the Tirgonian officer with an equal amount of disdain in her voice as she dismisses the security detail with a nod of her head. "Telebisque, it is good to have you back aboard."

"That remains to be seen, Flexia," says Teka as he indicates for everyone to be seated. "Telecoup Veskin will be here soon."

Hops, though visibly irritated by the delay, sits in the chair opposite Raccesia.

"High Commander," begins Tekas' Aide as she again looks directly at the Guardian officer, "it is common knowledge that you disapprove of women in such positions of authority as mine and, possibly even you own Council Member who has accompanied you today. However sir, I suggest that you put your personal feelings aside while you are here aboard the Palup."

"My personal feelings are not the issue, Culmit Raccesia," says Hops with controlled anger. He does not like someone he has just met, to speak to him in such a manner, especially a woman. "I really need to speak with Cudrosia."

"This is not your ship, High Commander, nor is it under your control," calmly replies Raccesia. "Here, aboard the Palup, we have the virtue of patience. Normal ships business has detained Culmit Cudrosia. He shall be here as quickly as possible."

"Look," loudly complains Hops, "we don't have time to waste! If I can't talk with Cudrosia right now, we may not have a chance to do it later!"

"Please, Hops," says Carol softly as she places a hand on Hops arm. "Unexpected things happen, even on the Hope."

Hops, still inflamed by the delay, stares harshly at the woman sitting across the table from him, remaining quiet. Within a few minutes, the door of the ready room opens as a tall, muscular Tirgonian officer enters.

"I apologize, sir," begins the officer as he bows slightly towards Teka before turning his attention to the guests, extending his hand towards Hops. "I am Culmit Cudrosia, Temporary Commander of the Fighting Star Palup."

"High Commander Hoppinzorinski," says Hops as he stands and accepts the outstretched hand. "May I present Council Member Quince?"

"It is an honor to finally meet you High Commander, and Council Member," says Cudrosia as he greets the second of the two guests, his hand cautiously accepted. "Do not believe all that you have heard about us. We are not all as anxious to continue this war as others may be," continues Cudrosia as he again turns towards Teka. "I return command of the Palup to you, sir." Returning his attention to Hops he says, "High Commander, it is with Telebisque Teka to whom you should present your offer of peace."

"First, may be all please be seated and you are correct, Culmit," says Teka. "We are indeed searching for any option to end these current hostilities. And it seems that I must now decide between two options." Turning, he looks directly at Hops. "First, I could continue the fight against your current fleet, which I now have the ability to detect, even while it is concealed. The second option, I could fight beside you and against the Empire. There is a third option, but returning to Tirgonia at this point would only result in my certain death, which the Supreme Commander, and the Senate, would surely recommend.

"The crew must make a decision between the first two options. I cannot order them to desert their way of life just because their commander has become old, and tired of the constant fighting. If enough of the crew decides to join me, we would be only in a slightly better position to convince the Supreme Commander that a continuation of this war would be ill advised. How would your people react to their enemy suddenly appearing, and fighting beside them instead of against them?"

"That I can't answer," says Hops. "It would be difficult at best. We'll only know the answer to that question when we try."

"It is time for the killing to stop on both sides," says Teka as he looks directly into the eyes of the High Commander. "Once the crew learns of my intentions, we may no longer be safe aboard the Palup. I do not know how many, if any, of the crew will follow me." Turning towards his aide, standing next to the outside bulkhead, he asks, "Flexia, what is your opinion?"

"It is my duty to obey. I will follow you wherever you go, sir."

"I did not ask for your loyalty, Flexia. I asked for your personal opinion."

Looking first at Hops, then Carol, and finally at Teka, she says, "I am also getting tired of the fighting. I want to return home, I want to live as I have seen others live. I want to live in peace, sir. In addition, I believe I speak for most, if not all of the crew.

I have heard rumblings they are also getting tired to the constant fighting that the Supreme Commander seems to enjoy. I have heard several speak of wanting this war to end. However, as you have just suggested, there may be some who wish to continue fighting until there are no longer any Guardians to spread the ideas of a peaceful existence."

"Where would you say the greater number would be?"

"With peace, sir."

"Culmit Cudrosia, what do you think of this?"

"I am in complete agreement with Flexia, sir. I have also heard these same quiet sentiments from a majority of the crew, privately, and off the record of course."

"Of course," agrees Teka with an understanding smile. "Then I will offer peace to those who wish to join me. For the others, if they desire to continue fighting, they shall have the opportunity to do. I will allow them to leave the Palup to join Telecoup Veskin. Culmit Cudrosia, if you will inform the crew I will address them on all view screens in five minutes. The choice will then be theirs."

"Telebisque," says Cudrosia, "what do you plan to do with the Palup? If the Guardians do allow us to join their fleet, I do not believe that they will permit us to have access to their concealment technology. Telecoup Veskin will be within weapons range shortly and will attack. We cannot hide and the Guardian fleet will be discovered the moment we are found."

"It seems that we are rapidly running out of time. Please inform the bridge . . ."

"Telebisque Teka," suddenly explodes over the Palups' intercom! "Guardian Dragons approaching in attack formation. The entire Guardian fleet is close behind them. Battle Groups Hidlok and Loksija are closing from the opposite direction. The Junnack is with them."

"Understand," acknowledged Teka as he turns his attention back to the others. Noticing a small device on the table in front of Hops, he asks "A weapon?"

"No," answers Hops. "A touch activated communicator. Just want to let our folks know that we're still safe."

Teka, not quite satisfied with the explanation, returns to his previous conversation. "It seems that we have run out of time and the decision has been made for me. High Commander, Council Member, I formally request political asylum for myself and as many of my crew who wish to follow me."

"I believe your request will be granted, Telebisque," says the Council Member. "Now I think you need to inform your crew of the situation, and your decision."

"Thank you, Council Member," accepts Teka as he bows his head slightly. "High Commander, will accompany me to the bridge?

"It would be my pleasure, Serligh."

"I'll use a secure channel on the Tiberian to inform the Council General. I'll also tell Major Cherrick to be prepared for an immediate departure," says Quince as she rises and moves towards the door.

"Culmit Raccesia will accompany you to the shuttle bay," says Teka.

"Thank you, Telebisque."

"Nuk-Ma," says Lamminta as he stands looking over the shoulder of the officer. "Inform all ships to engage their concealment devices. I don't want . . ."

"Too late sir, we've been spotted."

"Damn" mutters Lamminta. "Bring the fleet to attack formation. It looks like we may end up fighting our way out of this mess."

"Aye, sir. All ships acknowledge."

"Any idea what Hops is up to this time," quietly asks Lamminta?

"No, sir, not a clue. Still nothing from the Tiberian, or the Palup."

"Keep that secure channel open and the frequency clear. If he, or Council Member Quince, decide to let me know what they are doing, I don't want any interference."

"Channel open, secure, and clear."

Telecoup Veskin is not as patient as his counterpart is.

"Increase speed! I want to overtake the Palup before the Guardians have a chance to capture her!"

"Maintaining maximum allowable speed," reports the helmsman. "Any additional increase could possibly damage the engines as well as put extreme stress on the primary external hull."

"You are relieved! Security! Place him in detention! Now," screams Veskin as the subordinate helmsman moves to occupy the vacated position of the primary helmsman! "Reduce aft deflector strength by fifty percent! Slowly increase the energy flow rate to the engines. I want Teka and his Guardian friends destroyed!"

"Reducing aft deflector strength," reports the Weapons officer.

"Engine circuits are accepting the power flow increase," says the secondary, now primary helmsman. "Current flow rate holding steady at fifteen percent above maximum designed safety capacity."

"Maintain current flow rate," orders Veskin as the Hidlok races forward. "All ships. Increase speed. Battle formation Echo Three. Arm and lock all weapons on the exhaust ports of the Palup. Prepare all fighters for immediate launch. Do not allow the Palup to escape."

"Sir," calls Nuk-Ma as he monitors the change in the Battle Groups configuration. "All Stars moving into attack formation. Weapons armed and on line."

"Inform the scouts to pull back," orders Lamminta. "All ships are to accelerate to attack speed. Cruisers and destroyers are to assume attack formation X-Ray. Have all of the Dragons been recovered yet?"

"Just secured the last bird, sir," reports Dunlipee.

"Have them refueled and prepared for launch. When Veskin sends out his Horses, I want to be able to counter with our Dragons. Notify the rest of the fleet to make sure their fighters are ready to go. I don't think Veskin realizes our exact strength so we should be able to surprise him and gain the initial advantage."

"What about the others, sir," questions Fab? "They're still aboard the Palup."

"I realize they are, Commander," acknowledges Lamminta. "I don't know of anything that we can do for them right now."

"What about the concealment device?"

"If Teka found a way to find us, I'm sure Veskin already knows about it. The High Commander will find a way to return to us as soon as possible. For right now, I think we need to concentrate our efforts of saving the fleet. He will take care of himself and the others. Just maintain your station, Fab. Nuk-Ma, as soon as Commander Williams has the Dragons prepared to be launched, he is to report here immediately."

"Aye, sir . . . message coming in from the Tiberian. It's Council Member Quince."

"This is Lamminta. What is your status?"

"Right now, we're safe," reports Carol. "Hops is on the bridge with Teka. The others are here in the shuttle with me."

"Do you have any idea what Hops is up to?"

"Teka has requested asylum for himself and anyone else who wants to join him. I indicated that there shouldn't be any problem granting his appeal. Before you ask, we know about the other Stars closing on our position. It doesn't look like we're going to be able to make it back to the Hope.

"Just stay where you are for the moment. Do not attempt to leave the Palup. We'll get you back here just as soon as it is safe. Lamminta, out."

Teka and Hops listen to the exchange between Lamminta and Council Member Quince. Teka, knowing that he must now inform the crew of his decision to defect, begins his ship-wide broadcast.

"All personnel, this is Telebisque Teka. As you must know by now, there are two members of the Guardian Council of Elders aboard the Palup under a flag of truce. The Supreme Senate and the Supreme Commander will regard their presence aboard this ship as an act of treason. I cannot endanger the lives of those who may disagree with my recent actions of granting this flag of truce to the sworn enemy of the Empire. I have also made a personal decision that I must stop fighting against a race of beings just because they believe in peace instead of constant war. I have asked for asylum and their protection in an attempt to end these hostilities. The Palup will no longer participate in any further aggression against the Guardians. I will guarantee safe passage for any member of this crew who does not agree with my decision and still has a desire to continue fighting against them. Anyone who desires to leave the Palup to join Telecoup Veskin may to do so. All shuttles shall prepare for immediate launch to carry out these orders. For those who wish to join me in seeking peace, I only ask that you remain at your duty station and continue to perform your duties with honor. All sections report." As he ends his message, he quietly slumps back in his command chair. He has nothing else to say and can only wait for the reaction, and decision, of his crew. He slowly looks at the face of the man he first encountered so many years ago, managing only a slight smile saying, "That is all I can do. I can no longer accept the senseless waste of the Empire. I only want to stop this needless fighting, and to grow old in peace."

"You can only do what you think is right, Serligh," says Hops softly as he stands next to Teka, gently grasps the shoulder of his friend. "I just hope we can both grow old together."

The two leaders as quietly interrupted by Cudrosia. "Sir, all sections have reported. The entire crew, down to the lowest raking Sidlico, praises your decision and desires to remain aboard."

"The entire crew," asks an unbelieving Teka?

"Yes, sir. Everyone understands that we are now considered as traitors and will never be allowed to return to Tirgonia."

Hops, grasping Tekas shoulder as he receives the news, feels a surprisingly strong hand grasp his. He again looks into the face of his former enemy as sees a lone tear slides silently down the cheek of the man for which he has newfound respect.

"High Commander Hoppinzorinski," begins Teka as he rises, relinquishing command of the Palup, gesturing for Hops to sit in his captains' chair. "Would you please inform your Council General of our decision? Also, inform him that the Palup is now the property of the Guardian Defense Fleet. You are in full command."

"Sorry, Serligh, but I can't do that," replies Hops. "You're still in command of the Palup. But I will inform the Council General of your decision."

Both men, now facing each other, grasp the hand of the other in mutual respect. Both men look at each other in muted silence as they nod their heads in understanding.

CHAPTER TWENTY-SIX

The five Fighting Stars, under the command of Telecoup Veskin, continue moving dangerously close to the Palup.

"Helm, come to course three four seven by six eight three," orders Veskin. "Communications, inform the Quiger and Junnack to course five nine seven by four two one and engage their concealment device. The Loksija will attack on course seven one seven by six two one."

"Sir," asks Culmit Harlinkin, Veskins' Executive Officer. "Telebisque Teka will still be able to monitor our movements with or without engaging our concealment device. Why should we use the additional power needlessly? Shouldn't we maintain all available energy in reserve for our defensive batteries?"

"That is exactly what Teka will be waiting for," calmly answers Veskin. "What will he be forced to do once we are concealed and attack?"

"To fight under the protection of his concealment device. Detection of your enemy is always easier when both are using the same tactics."

"Exactly, and that will also weaken his power reserves. We have numbers in our favor. As soon as he goes into hiding to neutralize our assumed advantage, we will disengage our concealment device and have all the power we will need to fire a stronger volley against his weaker defenses. There isn't any way a single Star can withstand the force that five Stars will be able to unleash against him."

"The Guardians are still closing in. How can we defend ourselves against them if they decide to attack while we are engaging the Palup?"

"That is the purpose of dividing our forces," explains Veskin. "With our forces divided they will also be forced to divide their ships to counter our move. They will be too busy defending themselves to protect the traitor. Once the Palup is rendered useless as an effective force we will be able to join in the destruction of these inferior pests."

"We still have not found a way to penetrate their new concealment technology."

"They will not be using their device. They will be required to be visible in order to help Teka. If they use their concealment device and attempt to fight from hiding, how would he be able to find them, or have any hope of escaping," replies Veskin? "Now Culmit, insure all fighters are prepared to launch. They will launch at ten thousand instead of the normal battle distance they are accustomed. That will allow them to remain in close contact longer before being required to refuel and rearm. We must keep Teka, and his new friends, off balance for as long as possible so that it will be easier to destroy them."

"Understood, sir."

"Sensing, has there been any change in the position of the Palup?"

"No change, sir. The Palup is still maintaining the same stationary position."

"Then either Teka realizes that it would be foolhardy to clash with our forces, or he is planning a useless trap of his own. Increase scanner range."

"Telecoup," hastily call Culmit Sprahvic! "The Guardian fleet is proceeding on a direct intercept course for the Palup! I was able to detect the leading edge of their attack formation just before they engaged their concealment device. I have determined their speed and course. They should be . . . sir! The Palup has disappeared! I no longer have any trace of its presence! I have lost all contact!"

"What," screams Veskin as he shoves two crewmembers out of his way as he rushes towards the scanner station? "That's impossible! I will not let this traitor slip through my fingers! Find the Palup!"

"The Palup is not visible on any known concealment frequency, sir."

"Impossible! There was not time for the Guardians to convert their technology to be compatible with our systems," yells Veskin! "Sub-Culmit Sojon! Were there any communications between Teak and the Guardians before you lost them?"

"A communications signal was intercepted but has not yet been decoded sir," answers the communications officer.

"I want the Palup found! Now," again screams Veskin! "A Fighting Star does not just disappear! There has to be a malfunction with the sensors! I want a complete diagnostic analysis of all systems. Inform the Frema and Junnack that we have lost the Palup and that they are to relay their scanner information to us. I want all information and I want it now!"

"The Frema and Junnack report the same thing," reports Sojon. "They lost contact at the same time we did."

"Fire all batteries along the projected course of the Guardians! Engage the Palup! Concentrate on the intercept coordinates! Once they are found I want the Palup destroyed!"

As soon as the order is given, five of the most feared fighting platforms in the Tirgonian arsenal unleash their combined deadly firepower. That barrage lasts for almost fifteen minutes.

"Cease fire," hotly orders Veskin! "Scanning! Location of debris field!"

"No debris located, sir. We did not hit the Palup."

"This cannot be happening! The Palup cannot have just disappeared! The Guardians must have withdrawn and have taken the Palup with them! Follow their reciprocal course and inform Telecoup Vandilkor that his group will remain in support of the Hidlok. Relay all reports to the Supreme Commander," screams Veskin as he storms off the bridge. "I'll be in my ready room!"

Lamminta allows several hours to pass as he waits for the Tirgonian Battle Groups leave the immediate area and begin searching for the Palup, and the Guardian fleet. Finally, even though the Battle Groups are still searching the adjoining sectors, he feels it is safe enough to contact the newest, and unexpected, addition to the Guardian fleet.

"Palup command, this is the Hope."

"This is the Palup," answers Hops. "It looks like it worked because we're still in one piece."

"We got lucky this time," says Lamminta. "Were you able to monitor the departure of the Hidlok and Loksija?"

"Yes, sir. Tell Trilla that I owe him."

"Let's not worry about whom owes whom just yet. Right now, I think it would be in our best interest to get out of here before Veskin discovers what we did and heads back here to finish what he started. I want you and Council Member Quince to bring Teka back here to the Hope. Leave Televy and Cherrick aboard the Palup as friendly observers. They are not to interfere with any of the crew without provocation."

"Understood, and we'll be back there just as soon as practical. Teka has a few housekeeping chores to finish."

"Just be safe."

"That's what we plan to do. We should be back there shortly. Palup, out."

"Nuk-Ma," continues Lamminta as the frequency with the Palup goes silent, "notify the fleet to establish protective defensive positions around the Palup. No hostile action is to be taken against that ship, or her crew."

"Aye, sir," responds Nuk-Ma as he transmits the fleet wide message. "All ships acknowledge."

"Now notify Pidera, Tro-Ja, and all Division Commanders that I want to meet with them in the Landing Bay Operations ready room in thirty minutes. That's where we'll greet Telebisque Teka. I don't want him to see too much of the Hope until we decide what we are actually going to do."

As soon as the Tiberian is back aboard the Hope, Hops, accompanied by Carol, immediately escort the two Tirgonian officers to the Operations ready room. As the doors silently close Hops introduces the two enemy defectors.

"Council General, Council Members Pidera, and Tro-Ja, may I present Telebisque Serligh Teka and his aide, Culmit Flexia Raccesia, of the Fighting Star Palup."

"We welcome you, and your aide, Telebisque Teka," says Lamminta as he steps forward and extends his hand. "Would you care for some refreshments while we wait for the others to arrive?"

"The others," asks Hops?

"The Division Commanders, High Commander"

"Oh," answers Hops.

"Thank you, Council General," says Teka as he accepts Lammintas hand. "I would like a cup of your coffee. It has been a long time since I have had the pleasure of sipping such a delightful beverage."

"And for you, Culmit Raccesia," asks Lamminta?

"I will also try a cup of your coffee. I have heard Telebisque Teka speak of it many times and have always wondered about his fascination with it."

After Lamminta places the coffee, cream, sugar, and several different pastries, on a small side table he asks, "Telebisque, what do you plan to do now that you and your crew have defected?"

"I believe I should wait to answer your questions until the others arrive. Unnecessary advantages at a time such as this could cause more harm than the intended goodwill."

"I understand, Telebisque," say Lamminta as he sits at the head of the main conference table, indicating for the others to sit.

The wait for the Division Commanders is not a long one. As each commander enters the ready room, they cast belligerent, glaring glances towards the Tirgonian officers. Teka, sitting quietly next to Hops, knows there isn't anything that can be done except to endure the intense, hostile feelings generated by the presence of him and his aide.

"As leader of this Council," begins Lamminta as the last commander arrives and takes her seat at the table "I will formally inform everyone that asylum has been granted to Telebisque Teka, and his entire crew. There will not be any hostile action taken, nor committed, against them, or the Palup. To this, the Council has given its collective agreement.

"Now, Telecoup, I will introduce everyone so that you may know the names of those who may speak against you, and your crew. First, you have already met the Council. Next to Council Member Quince is Commander Williams, Captain of this ship, the Battleship Hope. Next is Commander Freslof, commanding the Battleship Revenge and First Division Commander. Next to him is Commander Triheadly from the Cruiser Osage and commanding the Second Division. Finally, Commander Cutler commands the Yatdown and is our Third Division Commander."

The officers give a polite, yet hostile nod of his or her head in acknowledgement, the only respect shown towards Teka as Lamminta continues.

"Telebisque, how can we be assured that some members of your crew are not following your decision in an attempt to deceive you and may actually attempt to disclose our location to forces still loyal to Tirgonia and the Supreme Commander? Once they gain such vital information as to our capabilities and technologies, they could return to Tirgonia with this information and be welcomed as heroes with our mutual destruction. I'm sure the Supreme Commander would be delighted to receive such information."

Under different circumstances, Teka would have exploded under such accusations. Now, he can only quietly answer saying, "Council General, as a Tirgonian officer, just as your own officers, I am ultimately responsible for the actions of all under my command. I offered every member of my crew the opportunity to remain with his, or her, families and friends. All chose to accompany me in this attempt to end this war. They each have given up any chance of ever returning to Tirgonia and their loved ones. Anyone who would now attempt to return home, regardless of what vital information they would be able to provide to the Supreme Commander, would face charges of treason. If the Supreme Commander found the information creditable, he would definitely use it, but only after the individual were sentenced to death and executed. Then, according to Tirgonian law, their families would be disgraced and be forces to live a life of internal exile. The only dishonor my crew must currently endure is their own. For now, they are still alive. I do not believe any crewmember of the Palup is willing to return to Tirgonia and force their families to live with unforgivable shame."

After a slight pause to allow Tekas' words to have the desired effect upon the others, Lamminta says, "Then the main question would now to be what are we going to do with you, your crew, and what do we do with your Fighting Star? You must understand why it will be unacceptable for us to allow your crew to remain intact aboard the Palup. We must divide your crew among the ships of our fleet while at the same time providing enough support personnel to maintain all primary sections. I'm not quite sure how to accomplish this.

"The second option would be to completely evacuate the Palup and disperse you entire crew among our ships. We would then salvage all essential equipment and information before scuttling her. These are the only two options that I can see at this time and I'm open for suggestions."

The Guardian leaders sit in silence for several minutes as they consider the two alternatives presented by Lamminta.

"Council General," says Teka just as quietly as before. "I believe I may be able to offer a third option that would permit your fleet to remain intact, without destroying the Palup. If I may be permitted to present my idea?"

"This is outrageous," screams Triheadly! "We're trying to decide what to do with over five thousand Tirg defectors, a Fighting Star that's more of a liability than an asset, and Telebisque Teka says he has an idea that could save the Palup and help us get our asses out of this mess! I'm sorry, Council General, but I don't believe what I'm hearing!"

"Please, Commander," says Lamminta as he tries to calm the angry officer. "I did open this meeting to all present, including Telebisque Teka. He has abandoned his entire way of life in his attempt to stop the fighting and allow us to survive. If he can offer another solution, we should at least have the courtesy to hear what he has to say."

"I think Commander Triheadly is correct," says Cutler in only a slightly calmer voice than her counterpart did. "How do we know that we can actually accept his solution regardless of how enticing it may sound? This could be nothing more than another elaborate Tirg trap and I seriously doubt that he can offer any viable solution."

"That we will not know until we hear what he has to offer," answers Lamminta. "Telebisque? What do you propose?"

Hops, being amazingly quiet during this exchange, leans forward with his elbows on the table, his chin resting on clenched fists.

"Thank you, Council General," says Teka in the same calm voice. "What I propose is that instead of abandoning the Palup, why not combine your forces, and use her to continue your journey across the Empire? You landed on the Landex to avoid detection, so why not hide your entire fleet in the same manner? There is enough room on the Palup for many of your ships to be stored there. You could then have your own personnel take command of the primary functions and operational control of her. My crew will be available to assist with all normal operations until your personnel becomes familiar with the different functions and can handle the Palup without further assistance from my crew. If anyone from my crew is purposely misleading your, or any of your crewmembers, I would be able to immediately deal with the individual and the situation, under the control of High Commander Hoppinzorinski, of course.

"Secondly, should you become engaged with other forces, not only would you have the ability to launch your own fleet for protection but you would also have the additional support of the Palups' Horseheads, I believe that is what you call our Pilinicun Fighters, as well as the Palups' defensive batteries. Besides, you have already proven that you have the ability to hide the Palup. So I ask why do you not use what you have to your advantage, instead of destroying a real, and possibly the only, chance you have for complete survival so that you may continue your quest for peace?"

By now Hops is grinning broadly. His old friend has again presented a viable solution to an otherwise bleak set of circumstances. He has taken a completely dark and hopeless situation and turned it around with a radical idea that has the earmarks of reckless abandon.

"Sounds like a plan to me," says the Hops as he leans back. "We certainly could use the extra firepower. Of course, the Palup isn't as maneuverable as the Hope, but neither is the Revenge. It would be a hell of a lot easier to hide one ship instead of, what do we have now, twenty? I'm in favor of Telebisque Tekas' idea."

"Now just wait a minute," counters Freslof! "You may be in agreement with this crazy idea but I'm not so all fired sure that this is the best way to go. I have the same reservations as Commander Triheadly. How do we know for sure that we can trust Telebisque Teka, or his crew for that matter? I say we forget his suggestion and concentrate of the two proposals presented by the Council General."

"Okay," rebuts Hops. "Suppose we consider only the options presented by the Council General. First is to keep the Palup intact. That would mean that we would have to provide at least a complete skeleton crew to operate and maintain the basic systems and we spread the entire crew among our own fleet. We definitely don't have enough detention space to keep over five thousand crewmembers under lock and key, so what do we do with the ones we can't confine? How do we determine which ones we lock up and which ones we don't? Then, what do we do if, or when we get into another fight? We won't have enough people to operate all of the required defensive systems on every ship so what do we do then?

"The second proposal is to destroy the Palup. Again, what do we do with the crewmembers we don't have jail space for in the detention cells? Every ship we have is going to be over crowded. Sorry, Commander, but if you look at the alternatives, we have to go with the one that gives us that best chance of survival. The only chance we have to survive is to try to make it across Tirgonia, hopefully in one piece, is to keep the Palup and her crew intact. The only option that makes any sense is the one presented by Telebisque Teka and transfer everything we can to the Palup."

After listening to Hops analysis, Teka gives him an almost unnoticeable nod and a gently smile. Lamminta, also listening thoughtfully throughout the discussion, again takes control of the meeting.

"We have heard the arguments for and against the proposals presented and now it's time for the Council to decide upon which option we will follow. Council Member Pidera, your vote?"

"Council General, in light of the fact that our population has just grown by more than five thousand and the fact that without the Palup to provide the additional space and facilities we would be hard pressed for space, not to mention privacy. We could definitely use the additional firepower if we do become engaged in another battle. I reluctantly vote in favor of the proposal presented by Telebisque Teka. I just hope and pray that it is the right decision."

"Council Member Tro-Ja?"

"I must agree with Council Member Tro-Ja and vote in favor of the option presented by Telebisque Teka."

"Council Member Quince?"

Looking directly at Hops she begins by saying, "I don't know how you do it Hop . . . High Commander, but it looks like you and Telebisque Teka are bound and determined to once again find a peaceful solution single-handedly. I also vote in favor of your proposal, Telebisque."

"Then by a unanimous vote the Council has agreed to accept the proposal of Telebisque Teka. Commanders, you will inform your respective commands of the decision made here today. I suggest that we finish our planning and have everyone aboard within the next three days. Will that be enough time to complete your planning?"

"More than enough time sir. I should have the details worked out by tomorrow morning."

"Then if you will prepare the necessary orders," says Lamminta as he glances at the leaders seated around the conference table. "If there is no further business, this meeting is adjourned."

"All commanders will be notified as to their boarding order and time. This train is boarding on track Two. Next stop Peaceful Junction, Safety Hollow, Serenity Ridge, and Catfish Bottoms," says Hops as he raises his hand and imitates the motion of pulling the whistle rope handle of an ancient nineteenth century railroad engine, ending with a loud, "Toot! Toot!"

With these final words, everyone rises and departs the Landing Bay Operations ready room. Commander Williams motions towards the High Commander, indicating that he would like to have a private word with him. Only after the others have departed, except Teka and Raccesia, does he speak.

"That was some trick with the Palup. How in the hell did you pull that disappearing act?"

"Easy enough, Orin. Do you remember the communicator you gave me right before I left?"

"Yeah?"

"I stopped in to see Trilla and had him add a few modifications. He coded the concealment frequencies and added them to the secondary backup program. It was hunch that thankfully paid off. When Veskin began to deploy, I convinces Serligh that we had to scramble his concealment frequencies. Both systems use the same basic theory, but instead of using just one frequency pattern, the Palup would be using two separate patterns at the same time. The only problem with confusing the concealment computer was that you wouldn't be able to see the Palup either. Also, I wasn't exactly sure the computers would accept the command to shut down."

"Now you tell me this," says Teka with a smile.

"I'll be damned," says Williams. "I always heard you were a little on the crazy, sir, but to pull a stunt like that has to be one of the craziest ideas I've ever heard of. I would have liked to have seen the look on Lammintas' face when you vanished."

"That would have been good," agrees Hops, "however I would have rather seen the look on Veskins face when he couldn't find one of his own Stars."

"Yeah" says Williams, "but where did you go?"

"We were a lot closer than he knew," answers Teka. "I was convinced that the only way Telecoup Veskin could have reached our position so quickly was to have diverted power from somewhere. The only logical system that could have supplied the additional power was the aft defensive shields. The High Commander convinced me that the sudden disappearance of the Palup would cause some momentary confusion and these few extra seconds allowed us to move the Palup behind the Hidlok. I knew Telecoup Veskin would concentrate all of his firepower forward and in the confusion, might temporarily forget about his weakened aft shields. If they had fired behind the Hidlok, we would have been able to destroy it with a few well-placed energy bursts. The only compromise would have been that our position would have been revealed."

"And I thought I knew a lot about Tirg tactics. Telebisque. Maybe later you could . . ."

"Bridge to Commander Williams."

"Williams here," acknowledges the Hopes commander as he activates the nearby communications panel.

"The Hidlok has stopped and is holding a stationary position. The Quiger and Junnack are taking up defensive positions around her."

"Understood, I'm on my way to the bridge," says Williams as he looks back at Hops and Teka. "It looks like I need to get back to work. Thank you, Telebisque, and good luck."

Williams leaves Hops, Teka, and Culmit Raccesia standing outside the door to the ready room. Teka is now able to speak to Hops without interruption.

"And I would like to thank you, my friend. Your words to the Council, and the other commanders, convinced them that there are members of the Tirgonian Empire who can be trusted. I only hope my offer has not come too late to be useful to your quest."

"Nothing is ever too late, Serligh. I just hope it is enough. You sacrificed your entire way of life, your ship, and your crew, to help your enemy. Now I'm going to need something else."

"Anything, Hops. Everything I have, or can get, is yours for the asking."

"I'm going to need a complete diagram of the Palup. I need to know where everything is located so that I'll be able to put the right people in the right place. Next, I'm going to need a complete tactical analysis on the capabilities and the last known location of all Battle Groups and Armadas. I still can't get my people to figure how your Groups or Armadas are deployed."

"That is because you are working on a theory that is twenty years. I am correct in assuming that you still believe that a single Battle Armada operates within the confines of a single cubic light year."

"Yeah," agrees Hops.

"That theory would now require too many ships to operate within an area that would be too constrictive to properly function within their full capabilities," explains Teka. "We have added three additional cruisers and two battle destroyers to each Battle Group. We then added three Battle Groups to each Armada. A single Armada now contains six Battle Groups, thus requiring the operational area of each Armada to be expanded."

"Then that's the whole reason behind this war? The Empire just ran out of room."

"Again, you are correct," says Teka. "Now we both have a great deal of work ahead of us. All the information you require will be provided and relayed to your computers as soon as I contact the Palup."

"Then I suggest we go to my ready room."

The two men, still accompanied by Culmit Raccesia, begin walking towards the High Commanders private domain. Teka, as well as Raccesia, show no emotion towards the obvious distasteful looks directed at them as they walk along the corridors and passageways. They hold their heads high with self-pride, one of the few things that no one can ever take from anyone else. They would rather give their life before they would surrender either their dignity, or their honor.

CHAPTER TWENTY-SEVEN

The following afternoon, Hops, still accompanied by Teka and Raccesia, calls a meeting for the Division Commanders aboard the Palup.

"Okay," begins Hops as Commander Triheadly, the last to arrive, takes her seat. "First thing we need to do is to get every ship we can aboard the Palup. The Hope and Revenge are going to have to stay outside. There just isn't enough room for those two inside. I've broken everyone down by landing bay. As soon as we're finished here and everyone knows where he, or she, is going, we need everyone aboard as quick as possible. Staying here any longer than necessary isn't exactly my idea of playing it safe. So listen up for your assignments.

"First Division will be going in to Alpha Bay, Second Division will take Bravo, and Third Division will occupy Charley. I want to use Delta used for the Dragons and Horses. I want all fighters from all ships, except the Hope and Revenge, transferred there. The landing sequence for all bays will be the same for each Division. The scouts will go in first, followed by the cruisers, then the destroyers. That way the Hope and Revenge, already outside in case of trouble, will have our heaviest firepower coming out first for support."

"High Commander," says Cutler. "There are still a few other areas, besides on how we are going to defend ourselves, which we need to know about. Security, standard operations, maintenance, living quarters, and what do we do with the Tirgs? I . . ."

"I'm getting to that Commander. First, does anyone have any questions about where their Division is going to be housed," interrupts Hops as he looks about the room? "Good. Now I want to cover . . ." the door chime stops him from continuing. "Yeah?"

"Culmit Cudrosia and Culmit Tomdoc are requesting permission to enter," states the voice of the security officer stationed outside the door.

"Let them pass, Lieutenant" orders Hops.

"Why are they . . ." begins Triheadly.

"They're here because the Palup is their ship and they know how it operates. If we're going to use that flying bucket of bolts, then we're going to need their help. Culmit Cudrosia is the Palups' Executive Officer and Culmit Tomdoc is their Security and Operations Chief," explains Hops as the two Tirgonian officers enter. "Have a seat Culmits. Once we start getting all of our ships aboard, where is everything, that isn't going to be needed to remain aboard our ships, be stored?"

After taking their place at the far end of the conference table, Cudrosia begins slowly. "High Commander, Commanders. The ships you have referred to, as your scouts will be the first to board, this is correct?

"Yes," answers Hops.

"Then as soon as they have cleared the landing ramp they will be transferred to the hanger deck through the use of the, I believe you would call it a transfer lift."

"Okay," agrees Hops.

"Once the scouts have cleared the landing bay and moved to the lower hanger deck, the destroyers will come aboard and be moved to the upper maintenance deck. The cruisers will then be able to remain in the main hanger deck. Once the Dragons begin their begin recovery operations, they will be maintained with our fighters on the primary and secondary Ready Flight Decks on the Delta arm."

"A Star has that much room," asks Freslof?

"Yes," answers Cudrosia. "Every Fighting Star has the capacity to recover and store twice its standard compliment of fighters. With the additional hanger space, if a Star needs to fulfill another mission, but its Pilinicuns will not needed to support the mission they will be transferred to another Star. Being stored in a separate area, they will not interfere with the normal operation of that Star. However, instead of storing additional fighters we will be using the space to house all but two ships of your fleet."

"That just explained a few things," comments Williams.

"Now that we have the first problem of the ships taken care of, the next problem is the primary and secondary location for all sections." Looking at Teka, Hops asks, "Where in the hell is everything on this ship? We haven't been able to figure out what you have, or where you have it."

Teka, along with the other three Tirgs, smiles as he says, "You have been able to find the one thing that we tried to keep as a closely guarded secret. You did manage to discover the location of our concealment array."

"That's about the only thing that we have been able to confirm," says Hops. "Except we were also able to learn how the Empire is able to refit a Star without any fixed based."

"That was a grave mistake on my part," says Teka as he looks at Hops with a slight grin. "An un-coded message on a frequency that is monitored by the enemy should have never been sent. However, Culmit Tomdoc will be able to answer your questions concerning the location of specific areas, High Commander."

"Okay," says Hops as he leans back in his chair. "Culmit Tomdoc?"

"High Commander," says Tomdoc as he activates a small holographic image displaying the basic outline of a Fighting Star. Using a small laser pointer, he begins explaining, "As you can see, here is the Main Bridge, Emergency Combat Bridge, Engineering Section, Scanning and Security Section, Communications, Weapons and Defensive Fire Battery Control, Science Sections, Medical Facilities, Maintenance, and the Defensive Deflector and Shield Generators. Your personnel should not have any problem locating or learning these areas. For you relaxation and recreational needs, quarters for single enlisted and officers are located here, here, here, and here. For you married personnel, their quarters are located here, here, here, and here. Holographic and Recreational Lounges are here, here, here . . ."

"Just how many Recreational Lounges are there on the Palup," asks Hops?

"A total of twenty. Along with the ones you have aboard you own ships I do not believe anyone will have the opportunity to get bored."

"I guess not. Please, continue."

"A problem that I have not yet been able to solve concerns the education you may require for you children. The additional training for you older, young adults, who may wish become members of our now combined forces also needs consideration. They will undoubtedly be moved to the Palup?"

"Are you sure that you have enough room for all of the extra personnel that will be coming aboard," asks Hops?

"With the facilities offered by your ships, and the reassignment of nonessential personnel, I believe there will be more than enough room for everyone. As you can see sir, here are the decks reserved for living quarters. The areas depicted in green indicate the quarters currently occupied. The red areas indicate quarters that are currently available. Even with a ship wide population of just over five thousand, the Palup has enough room for at least an additional two thousand personnel. We are not the complete demons that you may believe us to be. We take care of our own, just as you do, sir."

"Exactly how many personnel do you have on duty at any given time?"

"Only one fifth of the normal compliment, sir," says Cudrosia. "We also enjoy our leisure time, and the time we can spend enjoying the company of our families and friends. As you can see High Commander, there is more than enough room for everyone not only to work, but to also enjoy their free time."

"Okay that takes care of where we're going to live, work and play, which leaves the question raised by Culmit Tomdoc. What do we do with the personnel ready for academy training and the kids still in school? Let's take the younger children first. Where do you suggest that we set up their classroom education?"

"Depending on the actual number of children, and their ages, their classrooms could be located on the decks already reserved for our primary and secondary education courses. The Education Deck is here," points Tomdoc.

"That's just a few decks under the main bridge," remarks Hops.

"Yes," agrees Tomdoc. "And the reason for locating families so close to the main bridge is that this is the strongest section of any Fighting Star."

"That explains why we had such a hard time hitting anything when we attacked the Landex," says Williams.

"Right," says Hops as he studies the holographic image in front of him. "Okay, the plan sound good. After we get our ships aboard and secured, I'll get Ski to coordinate with your Maintenance Chief and see if we can't get a few more classrooms built, if you don't mind, Telebisque?"

"Not at all, High Commander. I have heard of the talents possessed by this man some have called 'Merlin the Magician'. I'm sure our maintenance personnel would be more than willing to help with something as important as the peaceful education of our children. There are quite a few families aboard the Palup and they understand the importance of a good education"

"Now, about the cadets," asks Hops? Their training could be better accomplished here than aboard the Hope. It looks like there might be some spare compartments and bays right here under the lower hanger deck."

"That area is reserved for quartering the single crewmembers of your fleet, sir," says Tomdoc.

"Then what about these areas just above the upper maintenance deck?"

"That area will be needed to store the extra fighters you wish to bring aboard, sir."

"Excuse me, sir," says Williams. "Why don't we keep the cadets on the Hope? Why interrupt their training any more than it already has? They could use the Palup as a training target and could shuttle over whenever they would be required to learn a specific system, or area, of a Fighting Star. I've already integrated the basic capabilities of a Fighting Star into their regular training scenario."

"Commander Cutler? What do you think about keeping the cadets on the Hope?"

"Sounds like a reasonable idea to me, sir. It would separate the cadets from their families and give them more of a sense of what it will be like to be separated from their families once they graduate."

"Commander Triheadly?"

"I agree."

"Vic?"

"Make it a go from me."

"Then I think we've covered just about everything we needed to talk about for the time being. Get the scouts, cruisers, and destroyers secured aboard the Palup. As soon as everyone is aboard, all personnel are to receive a full briefing. That will be the responsibility of all Division Commanders. I want everything secured and ready to begin moving within the next four hours. I just hope Veskin doesn't return before we're ready to get the hell out of here. That's it, let's get to work."

Hops follows the four former enemy officers and his commanders out of the room. Once in the corridor, Tomdoc asks, "High Commander? Has Commander Trilla been able to reconfigure the scanners of your ships yet?"

"Not yet. He's not exactly sure how long it's going to take to get all ships on the same frequency modulation. He wants to keep the configuration that we used to hide from Veskin and that's going to take a few days to get everything worked out. He's still having trouble getting the systems on our ship to accept the modifications and, still hasn't been able to come up with anything that will completely hide your Horses."

"With his knowledge, and the expertise that we can now provide, I'm sure we will be able to design a system that will be effective."

"I hope so, Culmit, I sure do hope so."

Within a few minutes, the small groups of senior officers enter the bridge and receive a briefing on the location, and possible intentions, of Veskin and the five Fighting Stars he is commanding.

"High Commander," reports Cherrick as he occupied the primary helm chair. "The Hidlok is leaving. Telecoup Veskin is taking the Quiger and Junnack with him. His course appears to be towards Tirgonia. The Loksija Battle Group left fifteen minutes ago but I can't determine any specific destinations. I already informed the

Hope and Revenge. The Fleet is coming board as we speak. The scouts are secure and the destroyers are boarding now. The cruisers are holding defensive positions. A following course for the Hidlok has been locked into the navigational computer, I think."

"Do not worry, Major Cherrick," says Teka as he steps behind the former helmsman of the Hope, inspecting the station display. "The course you have entered is correct and properly placed into the navigational computer. You have learned our helm operations very quickly. Sub-Culmit Glispik has not misled you on your duties."

"I wish I could accept that as easily as you say it, sir. I never thought that I would be at the helm of a Fighting Star."

"Will you stop your worrying, Cherrick," asks Hops? "The crew is on our side. Just get used to the idea that your copilot is a Tirg and you are not having a nightmare."

"Aye, sir."

"Telebisque," quietly says Council Member Quince who has been on the bridge since earlier in the day?

"Yes, Council Member?"

"We've followed one of your Battle Groups and barely escaped the trap Telecoup Mular set for us."

"I have read the reports."

"I don't think we should play that same game again. What lies between Tirgonia and us?"

"There should be only a few small patrols. We should be able to detect them without much difficulty."

"What about the Groups patrolling around Tirgonia?"

"There should not be any Groups closer than half a light year to Tirgonia," says Teka as he activates the communications panel on the left arm of the command chair. "Sub-Culmit Sherrom, what groups are assigned to the Tirgonia Defensive Sector?"

The bridge intercom remains silent.

"Sub-Culmit Sherrom! This is Telebisque Teka! Report!"

Again, silence.

"Lieutenant Carr, this is High Commander Hoppinzorinski. Report!"

Again, only silence.

"Lieutenant Carr, this is . . ."

"Sorry, sir," calls the junior officer over the intercom. "The intercom sensor isn't where I am used to having it."

A slight giggling sound causes Teka to become very agitated.

"Sub-Culmit Sherrom," explodes Teka! "You are there to assist Lieutenant Carr! Your duties do not include embarrassing her in front of the High Commander! If you cannot assist her properly you will be relieved!"

"Telebisque, it was not her fault, it was mine," says Carr. "She wanted to help but I stopped her. If I'm going to learn this station, I will have to do it my way, and on my terms. I have to do it, not her. She showed me what to do and now it is up to me to do it."

"As you wish, Lieutenant," answers Teka. "What Battle Groups are currently patrolling the Tirgonian Defensive Sector?"

"Four as of right now sir," replies Carr. "Landex, Costic, Tablor, and Gissoc. All Groups reported to be a full strength. Relaying scanner information to the bridge."

"That doesn't sound good, Telebisque," says Hops as he studies the small display screen on the arm of the command chair.

"This is not normal procedure," says Teka as he also studies the images displayed on the small screen. "Normally, only two Groups are assigned to the Tirgonia Defensive Sector, not four."

"Take notice to the groups assigned," says Hops. "Every damned one of them has had contact with either the Hope or the Revenge. It looks like the Supreme Commander wants to throw a welcoming party for us once we get close enough to get an invitation. I think we need to look for another vacation spot."

"I agree," says Teka. "Under-Culmit Matilosk, inform the Hope and Revenge of the situation. The High Commander will inform them of our course and destination shortly." Teka looks up at Hops and asks "Your decision, my friend?"

"What would you do if the situation was reversed?"

"A good question," answers Teka. "If we proceed towards Tirgonia we enter their trap. If we do not, the Supreme Commander will know where we are not and order all Battle Groups, and Armadas, to start looking elsewhere. He will eliminate the obvious and will look in the sectors that remain. My friend, it looks like we have found another very curious cat."

"That leaves us with the same question as before, where do we go," asks Hops? "Personally, I'm think a course towards Tirgonia just might be the best way to go."

"That would be sheer madness," says Teka. "What are you thinking of this time?"

"Not really madness, Serligh, it might be the one thing that could give us a slight advantage. The Supreme Commander thinks that he knows that we're heading that way, but we know we are heading that way. How long would it take for reinforcements to arrive once the shooting starts?"

"From the way the Groups are deployed, approximately twelve to fourteen hours, but no longer than that."

"Then we have to make a short fight out of it. If they haven't found a way to penetrate our combined concealment device, we just keep moving as if nothing happened. If they do discover us, we fight and end this war. We either survive, or we die trying."

"As you wish, my friend," says Teka. "Under-Culmit Matilosk, inform the Hope and Revenge that we are going to maintain a course towards Tirgonia."

"Understood, Telebisque. Message sent and acknowledged."

"Major Cherrick, as soon as all ships are secure let's get out of here. Follow the Hidlok but don't get too close or interfere with Veskins navigation."

"Course locked in, sir."

The crews of the Guardian ships could do, except to wait until the remaining ships land on the Palup. Finally, the last cruiser is aboard and secure.

"Cherrick, full power," orders Hops. "Let's get this show on the road."

With a touch of a single sensor, the Palup, accompanied by the Hope and Revenge, begin moving forward, towards possibly the final confrontation with the Tirgonian Empire.

"How long will it take for us to reach Tirgonia," asks Hops after receiving the normal movement reports.

"At our present speed, and if we do not encounter any difficulties sir, eight weeks," replies the Under-Culmit Tinlika, the Palups' navigation officer.

"Two months flying straight into the heart of the Empire without difficulties," says Hops as he sits next to Teka. "Why don't I believe this is going to be a smooth trip?"

"That, my friend, I cannot answer."

CHAPTER TWENTY-EIGHT

The trek across Tirgonia begins with most of the former adversaries finding ways to cooperate. There are nonetheless, crewmembers from both sides that are not as willing to forget the past. Arguments are frequent. If an incident is severe enough, the participants appear before the Disciplinary Board, a duty normally reserved for a separate board of officers, but currently a responsibility of the Council of Elders, with Telebisque Teka representing the Tirgonians, to review the more severe incidents for a final decision.

"Sub-Culmit Zexlon," begins Teka as one of the many discipline hearings, "these charges against you are very serious. Do you agree with the accusations?"

"The accusations are correct, Telebisque," responds Zexlon, "but I should not be the one who is too named first. I was the one who was attacked."

"Ensign Verright," says Lamminta, "how do you answer to the charges against you?"

"Council General, the charges against me do not reveal the complete truth. I wish to speak in my own defense."

"You will have that opportunity, Ensign," says Lamminta, "but in accordance with the agreement with Telebisque Teka, Sub-Culmit Zexlon, by being named first, shall be first to present his case to the Council."

"Telebisque," begins the Tirgonian junior officer with complete disdain in his voice. "I do not believe this Guardian Council of Elders has the authority, nor the knowledge of our laws, to decide who was attacked first, or of the punishments required for this Guardian coward!"

"Silence," warns Teka harshly, immediately silencing the young officer! "I have given my word, and have accepted theirs, for the good of all!"

"I have also given my word sir, but only to you, not to them," argues Zexlon. "I have followed your orders with willingness during this entire fiasco, and I will continue to do so, once this cursed dog ceases to exist!"

"Enough," orders Teka! "Before anyone is dealt with I will caution you this one last time. You will conduct yourself as an officer, Sub-Culmit! If you fail to do so, I will forgo these proceedings and deal with you strictly according to our laws! Is that understood?"

"Yes, sir," replies Zexlon, but still without showing any sign of respect towards the leaders seated in front of him.

"I apologize to you, Council General, and to all Council Members," says the lone Tirgonian representative on the Council. His tone indicates that he is not at all satisfied with the conduct of the officer in front of them. "It seems that there are still a few among us who do not understand that we are both in search of the same aspiration."

"I fully understand, Telebisque," says Lamminta as he accepts the apology. "Please, continue."

"Sub-Culmit Zexlon, what duties were you and Ensign Verright assigned just prior to the reported attack upon Ensign Verright," asks Teka?

"Telebisque, we were to perform a third level analytical diagnosis on the Number Four Hydro-processor, when this piece of Guardian trash . . ."

"Sub-Culmit! I warned you for the last time! You will conduct yourself as an officer! I will not tolerate any further disobedience from you! Do you understand?"

"Yes, sir," says Zexlon without any show of remorse. "Ensign Verright deliberately hit the tool chest, causing the inter-gravitational polarization coupling to short circuit the primary magnetic coil. This caused a flash fire in the access way. I managed to extinguish the fire, which caused severe damage to the processor, without any help from this female."

"Was this a just cause to strike Ensign Verright?"

"Sir, I struck her only after she placed her hands on me."

"Could she have been trying to help you in this situation?"

"How could a Guardian female help repair one of our processors? She is constantly in the way and has never been of any help during any procedure required to maintain the processors. If she had assigned elsewhere and might not be a constant menace, or such a disruptive force within my section. Without her constant incompetence or interference, I would not have been burned, nor would I be experiencing the suffering I must now endure."

This last comment strikes a raw nerve with one of the Council Members, but she remains quiet.

"Sub-Culmit Zexlon, even though the actual designs of the hydro-processors here are only different in design from the ones Ensign Verright was initially trained on, we maintain similar pieces of equipment on all of our ships," interjects Council Member Quince. "She was assigned to your section because her specialty is water manufacturing and processing. I believe you may have a bigger problem with her than you might like to admit."

"The only problem I have with this incompetent Guardian whore . . ."

"Enough! Sub-Culmit Zexlon! You will respect the rank and position of all aboard this ship, or any other ship under our control, regardless of origin or nationality," screams Teka as he slams his fist down on the dais! "Council General, I would like to request a brief adjournment so that I may have a word with Sub-Culmit Zexlon. I shall require no more than a few minutes."

"Of course, Telebisque. A brief recess is granted."

The Council silently departs one of the recently transformed a recreation lounge that now serves as the Council Chamber. After the entranceway closes behind the last Council Member, Teka, still sitting in front of the lone remaining officer, begins speaking in an amazingly calm voice.

"What are your feelings towards Ensign Verright?"

"Sir?"

"What are your feelings towards Ensign Verright," repeats Teka as he leans back in his chair?

"I do not understand what you mean, sir."

"I believe the question is simple enough to answer, Sub-Culmit. What are your feelings towards this Guardian female?"

Zexlon begins slowly, saying, "At times she seems to be a competent officer, but if she had been assigned to a lowly Tirgonian transport ship, I believe that she would have been relieved of duty several weeks ago for sheer stupidity."

"Because she is trying to learn and understand a different of water production, on unfamiliar equipment to accomplish her assigned duties, does not make her stupid. I will ask you again, Sub-Culmit, what are your feelings towards Ensign Verright?"

"She is knowledgeable about the processor, sir, and at times," Zexlon hesitates momentarily before continuing, "at times she appears to be a competent officer. With her limited knowledge of our hydro-processors, she has shown that she can perform better than most others of her rank can. At other times, the she things does which are completely incomprehensible. It is as if she has forgotten everything I have tried to teach her."

"Then you feel that she has the potential to become a good officer?"

"Yes sir, but at other times I . . ."

"Now you yourself are acting as you would desire others to act," says Teka as he looks directly at Zexlon. "We will continue with these proceedings. You will maintain your composure as you are doing now. If you fail, I believe you understand the consequences."

"I understand, sir. I will apologize to the Guardian Council," and with a stern look from his commanding officer adds, "and to Ensign Verright."

Teka satisfied that his youthful officer would now control his emotions, informs the Council that they are prepared to continue.

"Council General, Council Members," begins Zexlon in a tone that does not indicate anything relating to his former outburst, "I apologize to you, and to Ensign Verright. I was wrong in my behavior and actions. I withdraw my request for having my name mentioned second in this action against me. I also submit that I was wrong to have assaulted Ensign Verright when she was only trying to help. I will accept any punishment this Council may impose."

"Your apology and admission of you fault is accepted, Sub-Culmit," replies Lamminta. "Ensign Verright, do you have anything that you wish to add?"

Ensign Verright, unprepared for her Tirgonian superior to accept full responsibility, looks at Zexlon as she begins to speak, "Council General, may I speak on behalf of Sub-Culmit Zexlon?"

"Of course, Ensign"

"I do not believe the accident was entirely his fault. I wasn't satisfied with his diagnostic findings on the processor and tried to move around him in the crawl space. I missed a handhold and hit the tool tray. It was my fault. The inter-gravitational polarization coupling caused the primary magnetic coil to short circuit, which caused the fire that resulted with Sub-Culmit Zexlon sustaining his burns. He does not deserve to receive any punishment since the accident was my fault alone. Sub-Culmit Zexlon was only acting on instinct when he struck me. I accept full responsibility and should be the only one punished."

This is the first time both a Guardian and a Tirgonian officer accepted complete responsibility for any wrongdoing brought before the Disciplinary Board. Lamminta, looking at the two officers standing in front of him cannot help to feel a small amount of pride for both as he turns towards Teka saying, "There just may be hope for us after all."

"It does appear that way, Council General."

"Telebisque, according to our agreement, you may proceed with your decision concerning Sub-Culmit Zexlon."

"Thank you, Council General," says Teka as he looks at Zexlon. "You have admitted your guilt in assaulting Ensign Verright. However, for your honesty I will not impost the full punishment as required by our laws. You will only be reduced in rank to Coident."

Lamminta now looks directly at Verright, causing her to assume a more rigid position of attention, as he hands down her punishment.

"Ensign Verright, for admitting you were responsible for the damage caused to the Number Four Hydro-processor, and for the injuries suffered by Sub-Culmit Zexlon due to the resulting fire, you are directed to conduct a complete level three analytical diagnostic on the remaining three Hydro-processors. Once the damaged processor is operational, you will conduct a complete level three analytical diagnostic on that processor as well. The only help you are will receive will be the minimum assistance for those procedures that require more than one person to complete."

"I understand, sir," says Verright as she continues to look straight ahead.

"If there is not any further business that needs our attention at this time, this session of the Disciplinary Board is adjourned."

As everyone departs the Council Chamber, Verright pauses, reaching out to touch Zexlons shoulder.

"You wish to speak with me, Ensign?"

"Yes, if I may have a moment of your time, sir."

"Of course."

"Well, sir, I'm not quite sure about your laws, but I don't think the punishment you received from Telebisque Teka was fair."

"Ensign, now that we are of the same rank, you are no longer required to address me as 'Sir'. Besides, you are correct, you do not understand Tirgonian law. The full punishment for striking a junior officer is a full reduction in rank and confinement for a minimum of five years. I am fortunate to have lost so little.

"Isn't that a little harsh," asks Verright as the two officers continue walking down the corridor. "We both admitted our guilt in what happened so we both should have been punished equally."

"That may be the way of the Guardians, but it is not our way."

"Well it should be, and I'm going to do something about it."

"What can you do," asks Zexlon as Verright continues walking, not realizing that he has stopped? "The punishments have already been imposed. Nothing else can be accomplished at this time except to comply with our punishment and the orders that we have been given."

Verright stops and looks back at Zexlon with a determined look upon her face, saying, "You may not be able to do anything, but by our laws, I can. I'll see you later."

Zexlon, wondering what she was talking about, watches Verright as she disappears around a corner and heads down an adjacent corridor.

Several days later Verright finds the information for which she had been searching. As soon as the information is in her hands, she requests an audience before the Council of Elders, and specifically requests the presence of Telebisque Teka.

"Ensign," begins Lamminta after all normal business was completed, "what do you have to present to the Council?"

"I would like to know if Telebisque Teka realizes that he is in violation of his, or shall I say Tirgonian law?"

"Now just hold on a minute, Ensign," challenges Hops. "You're not going to accuse Telebisque Teka of acting illegally, are you?"

"In a manner of speaking, sir, you could conclude that is exactly what I am saying," answers the young ensign in a sure and steady voice.

"You're beginning to take a walk very close to a very steep cliff. Be careful you don't a wrong step and fall off."

"I know what I'm doing, sir, I hope," answers Verright carefully. "However, before I continue, may I request the presence of Coident Zexlon?"

"For what purpose," asks Teka? "The incident between you and him has been dealt with, and according to our laws, the incident is closed."

"Then, according to your laws, Telebisque, I challenge your authority according to the Ka-no-Lé," says Verright. "I hope I pronounced that correctly."

"Not quite, Ensign," says Teka with a confused look on his face. "However, I do understand, and I accept your challenge."

"What the . . ." begins Hops. "What's going on?"

"It is an ancient custom, High Commander," explains Teka as he activates the intercom sensor in front of him. "Coident Zexlon, report to the Council Chamber immediately."

"What do you mean by 'ancient custom'?"

"Patience, my friend, you will see."

Within a few minutes, Zexlon enters the Council Chamber, still dirty from crawling through several access ways in the performance of his normal duties.

"You requested my presence, Telebisque?"

"Yes," says Teka as he takes a deep breath, letting it out slowly. "It seems that Ensign Verright has challenged me with the Kâ-ño-Lé on your behalf."

"That is not possible, sir," says a bewildered Tirgonian Ensign. "Only a Tirgonian may challenge a punishment under the Kâ-ño-Lé."

"No," immediately replies Verright. "Your laws do not specify that only a Tirgonian citizen has the legal right present the challenge. The law states that, and I quote, '. . . anyone may challenge a punishment under the Kâ-ño-Lé if they were involved in the accusations and received punishment at the same time from the same body of judges . . .' end quote."

"No," shouts Zexlon! "These laws do apply to non-Tirgonians."

"Then you are the outsider," calmly states Verright. "Look at who we are standing in front of, and would you please answer my question with either a 'yes' or 'no'."

"Okay," says Zexlon.

"Is Telebisque Teka an officer of the Tirgonian Space Defense Fleet?"

"Yes."

"Is he sitting with the Guardian Council of Elders?"

"Yes."

"Are we aboard the Fighting Star Palup?"

"Yes."

"Is the Fighting Star Palup currently on any assignment, or directive, from the Supreme Commander of the Tirgonian Space Defense Fleet, or the Supreme Senate?"

"No."

"Is the Fighting Star Palup the current property of the Tirgonian Space Defense Fleet?"

"No."

"Who currently has control of the Fighting Star Palup?"

"The Guardians."

"When we were punished for our recent actions were we punished equally?"

"No."

"Ensign," interrupts Hops, "exactly what are you getting at?"

"High Commander," begins Verright as she now addresses Hops directly and, disregarding the question, asks, "did Telebisque Teka, and the entire crew of the Fighting Star Palup, defect from the Tirgonian Empire?"

"Yes."

"And did he present the Fighting Star Palup to you, and this Council of Elders, in an attempt to end the current war between the Tirgonian Empire and us?"

"Yes, and again I will ask, you where are you going with this."

Again ignoring the question, she turns her attention to Teka, asking, "Telebisque, did a duly appointed officer of the Tirgonian Space Defense Fleet relieve you of your command for your recent actions?"

"Yes, Ensign. Technically, I was relieved of duty by an officer of the Tirgonian Space Defense Fleet."

"Then I challenge your authority under the Kâ-ño-Lé."

"What is she talking about," again asks Hops?

"She has challenged my authority to lead the Tirgonians aboard this, or any ship, and believes that I do not have the authority to dispense punishment for any crime that may have been committed," explains Teka with a slight grin.

"She what," exclaims Pidera!

"Impossible," comes an equally loud response from Tro-Ja!

"Not really," says Teka, who seems to be the only one, besides Verright, who is able to control their shock. "She has challenged my authority, and to put it quite simply, she believes that I no longer have, nor can I ever again hold, any position of authority."

"Ensign," says Lamminta, "do you understand what you are . . ."

"She fully understands her actions, Council General," interrupts Teka as he continues to smile at the young woman in front of him, "and she is correct."

"What," exclaims Hops!

"She is correct," again says Teka in the same calm voice as before. "It seems that Ensign Verright has researched Tirgonian law and understands it better than anyone else aboard this ship. I was relieved of command by a duly authorized officer of the Tirgonian Space Defense Fleet. My entire crew and I defected, and I surrendered my ship to the enemy of the Empire while it was still intact, and in perfect fighting condition. According to Tirgonian law, under which I have been administering justice to the Tirgonians aboard this ship, I no longer have any authority to conduct any Tirgonian business or affairs. A common street beggar has more authority than I currently do."

"This is preposterous," exclaims Tro-Ja!

"I must agree," screams Pidera!

"Council Members, please," continues Teka. "Ensign Verright is correct. It is, or was, Tirgonian law that gave me my authority. Since we are no longer under the rule of the Tirgonia Empire, I no longer have the authority as an officer of the Tirgonian Space Defense Fleet. It appears that I am, as you would say, out of a job. She has proven her case by requesting the presence of her 'accomplice' and requiring all of us to answer her questions in the manner that she did. Therefore, since I do not have the authority to impose any judgment, or punishment, Coident Zexlon shall have the rank of Sub-Culmit reinstated and I must remove myself from our agreement. Council General, I place my crew and myself under the complete legal authority of this Council of Elders and High Commander Hoppinzorinski."

"I'm not sure I understand," says Hops.

"It is quite simple," says Teka. "Since I cannot punish Sub-Culmit Zexlon and he has admitted his guilt in striking another officer, his punishment lies before this Council."

"I understand," says Lamminta who has been amazingly quiet during this entire time. "And since I ordered Ensign Verright to . . ."

"Excuse me, sir, but I don't think that you can do that," suddenly interrupts the young woman standing in front of the Council.

"Now just hold on for a minute, Ensign," says Hops. "I don't think you realize exactly to whom you are talking to."

"I fully understand whom I am addressing, sir, and I also understand that Council General Lamminta, with all due respect, cannot punish Sub-Culmit Zexlon."

"Now what are you talking about," asks Hops?

"Sub-Culmit Zexlon has already been punished," explains Verright in her still steady and calm voice. "Telebisque Teka, with the permission of the Council, has technically become a member of the Council. This Council, in its present form, deferred Sub-Culmit Zexlons' punishment to Telebisque Teka, who has already judged him. The same person who imposed the punishment has now revoked that punishment. Does our legal system allow a person, accused and then punished, then has their punishment changed, now allows the Council to impose a different punishment without regard to our own laws? When a Council, or Council Member, revokes any portion of a punishment, the Council must revoke the entire punishment. The incident is to be, in its entirety corrected, and that correction placed in the record of that individual. Telebisque Teka only reduced Sub-Culmit Zexlon in rank and he has since rescinded that punishment. According to our laws, no further punishment can be imposed."

"It looks like we've all just been fired," says Hops jokingly.

Smiling, Lamminta says, "Well done, Ensign. Therefore, since the Council cannot punish Sub-Culmit Zexlon, this Council cannot punish you. Your record, along Sub-Culmit Zexlons will be completely purged of this incident . . ."

"I must object to our records being purged, sir," immediately counters Verright. "If our records are expunged, the records of this meeting shall also have to be expunged. Since there is no current precedence for what has taken place, or agreed to, the act must itself become the precedent and therefore must remain as part of the official Council records."

"You want this incident to remain on your permanent record," asks Hops?

"It's not that I want it to remain, sir, but if our personnel files are to be corrected, the entire record of the incident, the verdict and the final revocation of the punishment has to remain in our official personnel files for legal purposes."

"Council General," quietly says Council Member Quince.

Yes, Council Member?"

"I believe Ensign Verright is correct, and she has definitely missed her calling. I believe that she should be transferred to the Judge Advocate Section and become a Citizens Advocate."

"Ensign," says Lamminta as he again looks as the two officers in front of the Council, "Would you accept a transfer to the Judge Advocate Section?"

"I would, sir," answers Verright, "but only after we find a safe place to live. I would like to remain where I am and help Sub-Culmit Zexlon with the hydro-processors. It is what I have been trained for, and at the moment, where I would be more useful."

"Then that is where you shall remain. However, I recommend that a letter from the Council shall be placed in both records, along with a complete transcript of these proceedings, explaining what just took place and that the original incident shall in no way be held against either of you during any future considerations for whatever," says Hops.

"Then it is agreed that your service record, along with that of Sub-Culmit Zexlons, shall reflect everything that has transpired here today," says Lamminta with a slight nod towards the two officers in standing before the Council. "I think we have all learned that since we are together in our search for peace, we also need to come together as one in our search for justice. It appears that we are not as perfect as we think. Thank you for showing us our mistake, Ensign. This meeting is adjourned."

CHAPTER TWENTY-NINE

The Hidlok Group maintains its course towards Tirgonia. Telecoup Veskin, after reviewing all the contact reports between the various Tirgonian Battle Groups and Armadas, activates the intercom from his ready room.

"Communications, inform Sub-Telecoups Envela and Cigaklin that they are to report here in one hour. Insure the message is coded and as short as possible. They do not need to acknowledge the message. I do not want the Guardians to gain any more information than they already have."

"Message sent, sir, but without an acknowledgement I cannot confirm it was received."

"They received the massage," says Veskin as he leaned back in his chair, closing his tired eyes.

Upon the arrival of the two Fighting Stars, the two commanders are quickly ushered to Veskins' ready room.

"Come in," orders Veskin. As the two officers salute their commander, he continues, saying, "I have a plan that will finally trap these figglerites who call themselves Guardians, and at the same time will rid the Empire of the traitor Teka."

"Culmit Cudrosia," calls Sub-Culmit Dramek. "I'm picking up an unusual increase in the ion emission emanating along the course taken by the Hidlok. I'm also getting the same emissions readings from the Quiger and Junnack. The readings are intermittent. I haven't been unable to establish any pattern yet."

"Are the emissions interfering with the concealment device?"

"I don't know, sir. I haven't been able to determine if the concealment image projector is affected. All concealment systems are operating normally," answers Dramek as he continues to enhance the scanner imager.

"Very well, keep monitoring. Inform me immediately of any change or fluctuation in the frequency modulation, and if you can to establish a pattern," orders Cudrosia.

"Aye, sir."

Reaching over the shoulder of the scanner operator, Cudrosia touches the intercom sensor and says, "Telebisque Teka, High Commander, please report to the bridge."

Within a few minutes, both officers enter the bridge and go immediately to the scanner station where Cudrosia is still monitoring the strange emission trail.

"Sir," begins the Palups' executive officer, "several minutes ago the sensors picked up an unusual ion emission trail from the Hidlok, Quiger, and Junnack. There does not seem to be any pattern to the emissions and we do not yet know if these emissions are an attempt to penetrate the concealment frequencies."

"Then what do you think Veskin to attempting to do" asks Teka?

"That I don't know, sir."

"We still have two weeks before we reach Tirgonia," says Hops as he and Teka look at the latest information. "What do you suggest we do if he's found a way to spoil our fun?"

"I do not see how you can refer to this situation as fun," says Teka as he turns his attention towards Hops. "And, as far what I can suggest, I'm not sure. I will remain here while you inform the Council of the situation."

"Sounds like a . . ."

"Sir! The Junnack and Quiger have just reversed course!"

"It appears that Telecoup Veskin has found a way to find us," says Teka as he sees the scanners showing two of the three images reversing course and heading directly towards the Palup. "Enhance the scan. Could these particles may not be simple ions could be masking something different?"

"I don't know," says Hops as he observes the same information. "Under-Culmit Matilosk, inform the fleet to be prepared to deploy in a Diamond Four formation. I want all Division Commanders in my ready room in fifteen minutes. Serligh, it looks like we have some fancy planning to do."

"Culmit Cudrosia, you have the bridge," says Teka as he follows Hops off the bridge and into the ready room.

"Ladies and gentlemen, please be seated," says Hops as the three commanders and Commander Williams enter the ready room. "It appears that Veskin may be trying to play a little cat and mouse game with us again. Telebisque, which Groups are the closest and could get to us the quickest?"

"The last reports indicate the Loksija is within thirty-six hours from our current position. The Costic and Tablor could be here within two days and the others couldn't reach us in less than four days. We do not have any information on any other Groups or Armadas that could possibly get here any sooner than that."

"If this fight does happen, it looks like it will have to be a quick one. I don't think we should wait until we know for sure that Veskin has found us before we deploy. Commander Williams, I want you to position the Hope behind the Palup. Vic, put your division up front. I want the scouts far enough out front to be useful but not so far as to be without protective cover. Triheadly and Cutler put your division on the flanks and just slightly behind the First Division. Scouts will be out first, then the cruisers, and destroyers. Spread out as far as possible but still be close enough to provide cover. The Dragons will fill in the gape. Telebisque, I want the Horses held back in reserve to protect the Palup.

"If Veskin has found a way to detect us he may be trying to divide his forces so as to be able to come at us from three different directions, just like he did before, forcing us to divide what we have to counter. That would spread us out too thin to protect the Palup which I suspect would be a big feather in his cap if he could capture her and Teka in one piece. If we spread out first we just might be able to have a slight advantage. What we don't want to do is to let Veskin penetrate past the destroyers, our last line of defense. Once the Stars get close, the scouts and Dragons will pull back to take up secondary positions with the Horses to help protect the Palup. Any questions?"

"Only one, sir," says Cutler. "If Veskin is successful, and his Horses are able to penetrate and reach the Palup, how do we distinguish our Horses from his?"

"All of our Horses now carry Guardian markings. They all have new transponder and intruder identification codes installed. We also updated all major systems, including the fire control system. If you engage a Horse and it's one of ours, your weapons system won't fire."

"High Commander," says Triheadly, "ever since we've started joint training operations, some of the Tirg pilots have, shall I say, have not been exactly enthused about flying with us. In addition, a number of our pilots don't exactly trust some of the gunners on the Palup. I don't mean any disrespect to Telebisque Teka, but even if one turns against us, the others may follow. It would be impossible to fight off Veskins attack from the front while being hit from the rear. We'd be caught in the middle with nowhere to go."

"Commander Triheadly," begins Teka, "all pilots and defensive battery gunners of the Palup will not attack any Guardian ship. We only wish to survive as you do, and the only way we can do this is to fight beside you, not against you. To do anything else would be foolish, and no one would find peace. The Empire has branded us as traitors. If we were to support Telecoup Veskin in his attack, and if he were to win, he would return us to Tirgonia, charge all aboard with treason, and as I have stated before, condemned to death. Every Tirgonian aboard the Palup understands the only way he, or she, can possible survive is to fight by you side as your ally. On this you have my word."

"I accept your word, Telebisque."

"Now that we have that settled that, I suggest that we all get the fleet deployed," says Hops as he ends the short meeting. "If Veskin turns around and follows the Junnack and Quiger, we won't have much time to get everything ready. Return to your division and prepare to get everything launched. I want to be ready for whatever he has in mind."

The four commanders nod their understanding as they rise and leave the ready room, as Hops and Teka return to the main bridge. In less than an hour, all ships are deployed and waiting for the arrival of the Junnack and Quiger.

"High Commander, Telebisque, Fighting Stars maintaining their intercept course," reports Nuk-Ma as he sits at the scanner station, Sub-Culmit Dramek, his Tirgonian counterpart, nodding in agreement. "Contact with their Hunters in ten minutes. Speed is constant at three-quarters light."

"Serligh, do you think he's found a way to detect us or do you think he may just be playing a hunch," asks Hops?

"I'm not sure," says Teka. "The ion emissions still have me puzzled. Why ion particles? Do you believe that he can detect us with simple ions?"

"I don't know," answers Hops as he activated a communications sensor. "Commander Trilla."

"Trilla here, sir," responds the Guardians head of Research and Development.

"Veskin has the Hidlok, Quiger and Junnack projecting ion streams out in front of them. We're trying to figure out if it's just a simple ion stream or if these ions could be camouflaging something else. Can we be detected if one of these beams hit the concealment shields?"

"I've been working on that theory sir, and the ions they are emitting don't have any charge and should not have any effect of the concealment shields. I don't have any idea why he would be releasing simple ions unless he's found something that I've overlooked."

"If you've overlooked anything I'll have you tarred and feathered as soon as we get out of this mess."

"Acknowledged. Trilla, out."

"Tarred and feathered," questions Teka?

"Just a joke," answers Hops.

"High Commander," reports Nuk-Ma. "Fighting Stars within twenty minutes from our outer defenses. Speed reduced to half-light."

"Half-light," wonders Hops aloud? "Send a static signal to bring the fleet to full stop. Serligh, any theories yet?"

"Nothing that would indicate Veskin is following standard attack doctrine. If he has indeed discovered our presence, he would not have slowed down to attack. I think he may be attempting to make us reveal our position by making the first move."

"Then it might be wise to allow him to make the first move towards an engagement," comes the quiet voice of Lamminta from behind them.

"Council General," says Teka. "As I have stated to the High Commander, I am not quite sure as the exact intentions of Telecoup Veskin. If he has found us, Tirgonian battle doctrine would dictate that he attack at full speed to disrupt any counteroffensive we would employ against his forces. To continue this probing tactic suggests that he has not actually discovered our presence and is only attempting to entice us to attack first, thus revealing our presence. I am in agreement with the High Commander in that we should hold this position and continue to allow him to come to us."

"Then the fleet has already deployed," asks Lamminta?

"Yes, sir," answers Hops. "I would rather be prepared for a fight that doesn't happen than to be caught with my fly down. It's not quite as embarrassing that way."

"What do you plan to do if Veskin has not found us and continues through our defenses" asks Lamminta? "This could be a ploy that would allow him to get inside our formation, acting as if he's not sure we're here, and then suddenly attack."

"We're still protected, sir. All Dragons and Horses are providing close cover for the Palup. As Veskin proceeds, the fleet will move with his Stars and re-deploy into secondary blocking positions to maintain a defensive posture between them and us. I really don't think he knows our exact strength."

"I hope you're right, Hops," says Lamminta. "Three Fighting Stars can produce quite a bit of firepower, and if they do attack from inside our defenses we will end up fighting on three fronts at the same time. It could get congested out there and that would not be a very bright prospect."

"Agreed, sir, and with what we have, and what he has, this would definitely turn into one hell of a fight. However, I think we'll still be able to hold our own and send him packing with a lot more than just a little bloody nose."

"What about reinforcements," asks Lamminta?

"The Landex is about thirty-six hours out. The Costic, Tablor, and Loksija will need about a little longer to reach us. Everyone has already been briefed and understands to make this one a short fight."

"Very well. It appears that you have everything under control. I'll be with the rest of the Council in your ready room."

"No problem with that, sir. Just make sure they stay off the bridge."

"Of course, High Commander" says Lamminta as he leaves to join the rest of the Council.

"Why does he question every decision at a time such as this," asks Teka?

"Don't let that bother you, Serligh, it's just our way of doing things. Besides, you have a few strange customs of your own."

"Yes, I guess we do. I hope we can adjust to your ways without much more difficulties."

"Quit worrying. You will do . . ."

"High Commander," calls Nuk-Ma suddenly! "Two Fighting Stars just came into scanner range! Unable to get any identification signature yet!"

"Now what in the hell is going on," exclaims Hops as he and Teka immediately return their attention the scanner display! "Do you have any idea who they might be?"

"It's Telecoup Mular with the Landex and Napla. He always carries his support Star to starboard. Everyone else carries their support to port."

"I thought you said it would take him at least thirty-six hours to get here?"

"From his last position report it should have taken him at least that long to arrive. His orders must have been changed."

"This just put a cramp in my style. Nuk-Ma! Static signal the fleet to circle the wagons. This is going to get tight, but get them into a Staggered Complete. Scouts first, then the destroyer and cruisers. Dragons in and down. Serligh, get your Horses to mix in with the Dragons."

"Culmit Cudrosia! Deploy First and Second Flights Squadrons to upper cover," immediately orders Teka! "Third and Fourth Squadrons are to assist with lower cover.

All Pilinicuns are to link up with their assigned Probe. Mix in with the Dragons. Their Probe leaders have operational control."

"Understood, Telebisque. Redeployment will be complete within two minutes."

"Hops? How do you propose to fight five Fighting Stars at once," quietly asks Teka? "Would it not be more advantageous to bring the fleet to full power and leave the area?"

"That would be a good idea, except where would we go? If we move, they would detect our distortion trail. I think we just got trapped."

"High Commander, Mular is attempting to contact the Hidlok," reports Lieutenant Germick.

"Relay the message to this station," immediately orders Teka. "I will decode the message as it comes in."

"Message relayed."

"This is not good, my friend," says Teka as he begins deciphering the message.

> *Hidlok Command. Two Guardian ships are two hundred thousand kilometers directly in front of you. Deploy and launch your fighters at twenty thousand. Barrage fire at nine thousand. If you can surprise them before they have a chance to defend themselves, you can severely damage several of their ships. I cannot detect the Palup but she must be close by in support. It will take me at least two more hours before I will be able to be within range to give you support. Signed, Telecoup Mular. End of Transmission.*

"Thanks, Nuk-Ma. Relay all information to the rest of the fleet," orders Hops.

Teka turns and faces Hops saying, "High Commander, I believe you are definitely going to get that fight which you were trying to avoid."

"Bridge to Commander Trilla," calls Hops.

"Trilla, sir."

"Have you been able to get the concealment device on the Hope and Revenge calibrated to the same frequency oscillation pattern yet?"

"Not yet. I don't understand why the Palups' system accepted the frequency change and our systems won't accept theirs."

"Keep working on it. Hops, out."

"Battle Groups," calls out Germick! "Bearing seven six three by four five two! Bearing four three nine by six seven one! Bearing two one two by two six five!

Confirm five more Groups besides the Landex and Loksija. Hidlok, Costic, Tablor. Closing on our position. Weapon systems armed and on line!"

"Okay gang," yells Hops as move he moves and sits in the main command chair. "This is it. Get me an open channel to the fleet and keep it open. They know we're here."

"Channel open."

"All ship, this is Hops. We have five Battle Groups heading this way and they know we're here. Let's spread out and get ready for a fight. Everyone knows where the weak spots are, so don't get stupid on me. Keep track of your wingman. Keep track of . . . aw hell! Just kick ass and take names! Take out as many as you can! Captains acknowledge."

"All ships acknowledge, sir," reports Nuk-Ma. "Eight scouts, six attack destroyers, two light cruisers, one heavy cruiser, two battleships, and one Fighting Star. Telebisque Teka, there's an incoming message from Telecoup Mular for you."

Hops looks at Teka, sitting in the chair normally reserved for the ships executive officer, with an expression upon his face that indicates he is not at all pleased with the idea of him actually answering the signal.

"Do not be alarmed, my friend. It is our custom to address the one you are about to attack. He only wants to wish me luck."

"He wants to do what?"

"As you have said, there are a few of our customs that you do not understand," says Teka as he touches the blinking sensor on the arm console of his chair. "Telecoup Mular, it is good to hear you voice again."

"And it is good to hears your, Telebisque," comes an immediate reply. "There is no need for you to continue this ruse, Serligh. You have captured our enemy and have delivered them to us. We now only wish to join you in your triumph and escort the Palup back to Tirgonia. You will be made a hero of the people."

Grinning, Teka answers, saying, "Telecoup, you know as well as I do, that would not be possible. Both of us are intelligent men. You should not attempt to dishonor your ways with such a transparent attempt. Both of us know why you are here, along with the, Hidlok, Costic, Tablor, and Loksija. We intercepted your communiqué to Telecoup Veskin. Why would you wish to escort the Palup to Tirgonia when you have already given the order to attack at nine thousand meters? Besides, isn't it a little over dramatic to escort the Palup with eleven Fighting Stars?"

"The Empire will never allow you to continue with this foolish attempt," comes a stern warning from Mular. "The Guardians no longer have a homeland to which they can return. They can number no more than a few thousand. You have turned your back on your own people and your heritage, Serligh. I wish you a glorious death!"

"I thank you for your words of kindness, but there are more of us than you think, Apnor. Yes, a few thousand Guardians survived the devastation we inflicted upon them and their homeland. However, you failed to count the additional members of my crew who have willing joined me in our quest for peace. We only wish to live as we have seen others do. We no longer have a desire to continue this needless war, but if that is what you and the others with you desire, then you will not be disappointed."

"I do not believe that your entire crew has chosen to follow a traitor!"

"I offered them the opportunity to leave and join Telecoup Veskin if they wished to continue the fighting. No one wished to return to the oppressive ways of the Empire. If you are certain you still wish to attack the Guardian ships, the Palup will continue to fight by their side. You, along with the others, will make a worthy adversary. You will not however be successful in your attempt. I will remain here so that you do not have to waste time searching for us again."

"You have become impudent during these past several weeks, Serligh. You should accept your fate and die as the coward that you have become. Anyone who wishes to join me and fight on the side of the victors will be permitted to do so!"

"I will ask, but the answer will be the same," calmly answers Teka. "My crew will remain faithful to me and loyal to their ship. I am growing tired of your words that have no substance. Do you have an offer peace that my friends and I could present to the Council of Elders?"

"Since you have joined them, you have already accepted the only peace that can be offered. Have a glorious death my traitorous friend. Mular, out!"

Teka glances back at Hops, grins and says, "Do not worry, my friend, we will be able to engage the three Stars commanded by Veskin long before Mular or the others arrive."

"And what makes you so sure we can pull off this small miracle?"

"We change our tactics and attack first. Mular has found a way to detect us but has not yet passed this information along to the others. If he had, we would have would have intercepted the message and would have encountered the other Battle Groups before now. Therefore, since we still have the advantage, we attack first. I suggest you bring the fleet to full power and attack Veskin with a combined offensive. Strike all three ships at once. This will not allow one Star to give supporting fire to another. Each will have to defend itself independently. It would be the last thing that Veskin would expect."

"I think you just made a lot of sense to me, Serligh," agrees Hops. "Nuk-Ma, notify the fleet to assume attack formation Whisky Seven. First Division has the Quiger, Second gets the Junnack. Third will remain in reserve. Culmit Tomdoc, bring the engines on line. We'll take on the Hidlok. Attack on my command."

"Orders relayed and confirmed."

"Well, Serligh, this is your show and the ship is yours," says Hops as he returns command of the Palup back to the one person who knows the Palup better than any other person.

Teka assumes the familiar captains' chair with a slight bow, accepting the trust and confidence offered by his longtime friend. Hops, after relinquishing command, leaves the bridge and joins the Council in the ready room.

"Lieutenant Commander Nuk-Ma, inform all ships to move into final attack positions."

"Aye, sir," says Nuk-Ma.

"Major Cherrick, move to a position that will put us fifteen thousand behind and slightly to the port side of the Hidlok."

"Eleven thousand and slightly to port," acknowledges Cherrick after the course and designated position is entered into the navigational computer, he says, "Telebisque, may I ask a question?"

"Of course, Major."

"Why this particular position?"

"All energy cannons batteries are calibrated to have a complete crossing pattern with its' neighboring battery at ten thousand. I have had our batteries recalibrated to have a crossing pattern at fifteen thousand. If we are too far out, or too close, we would not be able to place our maximum firepower upon the Hidlok. Fifteen thousand kilometers allows us to be outside the deadliest range of the Hidloks' fire while still allowing us to remain at our optimum range. Being slightly to port, gives us the ability to target three of the four launch ramps. I want to disrupt their launch sequence by destroying their Horses as they launch, or actually damage the ramps beyond use. It will provide Telecoup Veskin with only one ramp for launch and recover operations during the battle. We can then concentrate the remainder of our fire on other targets that will render the Hidlok ineffective, or completely destroyed. The Hidlok is the primary fighting force with the Quiger and Junnack only providing support. They will be separately engaged, and therefore be unable to perform their primary function. We cut off the head and the body must die."

CHAPTER THIRTY

"Sir," repots Nuk-Ma, "the Junnack and Quiger are still moving apart. They have almost twenty thousand meters separation. Thirty thousand meters before we make contact with the Hidlok."

"Continue to scan for their Horses. Helm, slow to three-quarters light. Culmit Tomdoc, primary target will be the launch ramps. Secondary targets will be the engine exhaust ports, then the Primary Command Center and Defensive Battery Control"

"Distance forty thousand," says Nuk-Ma.

"All stations secure for battle," orders Teka.

"Distance twenty thousand. Junnack and Quiger off port and starboard bow. Horses coming out. Hidlok dead ahead at fifteen thousand."

"FIRE!"

The abruptness with which the attack begins evokes a rapid response from the targeted ship.

"Telecoup! We're under . . ."

"Shields and deflectors up," immediately orders Veskin. "Locate the origin and fire along that vector! Barrage fire! Defensive protection! Damage report!"

The three Fighting Stars under the command of Telecoup Veskin retaliate with concentrated, deadly energy blasts.

"All firing is concentrated on Alpha, Charlie, and Delta launch ramps," reports the Damage Control Officer. "They have sustained slight damage but are still operational. No other damage reported."

"They are attempting to disable the ramps. If they succeed we will be limited to using only one," observes Veskin. "Increase shield and deflector strength to the ramps and concealment array. Continue to launch fighters. Do not allow Teka to cause any further damage to the ramps. Concentrate all batteries from port to starboard between nine and ten thousand. The Palup has to be within effective weapons range somewhere."

"The Junnack and Quiger are also being engaged, sir. No visible targets," reports the Scanning and Sensing Officer.

"Inform them to reverse course. Maintain Ecchoich Three formation. We will fight together from here."

"Sir! We have a target," calls out the Weapons Control Officer. "All batteries! Concentrated fire! Three seven eight by four six five! Fire!"

"Telebisque, we've been discovered," says Cudrosia as the Palup shakes violently.

"No need to report the obvious, Culmit," says Teka in his usual calm voice. "I believe we all felt the impact on our shields. Evasive maneuvers. Damage report."

"No damage, sir. Shields still holding. Deflectors remain at full strength."

"Maintain firing on the Hidlok," orders Teka as he activates the ships' intercom. "High Commander, Telecoup Mular will be here in just a little more than an hour and the others shortly thereafter. We must finish this fight before they arrive. Even with our combines strength we will not be able to withstand the force of that many additional Groups. We must find a way to escape at the earliest possible time. Otherwise we face certain destruction."

"Have you been able to significantly damage the launch ramps," asks Hops? "That's the only way we going to be able to punch a hole in Veskins defense."

"We have been able to disrupt the launch and recovery operation of the Junnack and Quiger so far. The Hidlok still has all ramps operational. We have not been able to penetrate the protection around the concealment array."

"Keep up the pressure as long as possible. As long as the ramps remain in operation, we're going to have our hands full. If you can't knock them out, concentrate on the concealment array. What are out losses so far?"

"Surprisingly light."

"Just do what you have to so we can get out of here with a whole skin. Hops, out."

"Telebisque, damage and casualty reports updating now."

"Relay the reports to the High Commander so he may be immediately informed," orders Teka.

"So far we've lost eight Dragons, six Horses. The Allekia, Puzi, and Fetting have severe damage and are withdrawing. Minor damage reported by the Yatdown, Osage, Vinsoke, and Dormet. Ninety-six dead, one hundred and eighty-seven wounded."

"Let's hope we do not lose any more. Inform the Dragons and Pilinicuns to concentrate on the concealment arrays. I want all of our firepower concentrated the launch ramps. If they cannot launch or recover their Horses our fighters will have a better chance of success."

For what seems an eternity for the crews of the Guardian ships the battle rages on with a fierce intensity.

"Telebisque," calls out Sprahvic, "the Hidloks' concealment array has been damaged! Now visible!"

"Inform all fighters, cruisers and destroyers are to concentrate all fire on the upper structure. The Hope and the Revenge are to concentrate on the lower section. What about the Junnack and Quiger?"

"Exterior structural damage to the lateral arms on both Stars," reports Nuk-Ma. "Primary and secondary hulls have been breached at several locations. They are attempting to withdraw closer the Hidlok."

"It appears that Veskin is consolidating his forces. He may have sustained more damage that we know about. Is there enough room for us to move past the Hidlok without suffering any additional damage?"

"We should be able to pass to port with minimal additional damage," reports Cudrosia. "The Junnack and Quiger are still too far out to give any effective support to the Hidlok."

"Plot a course and inform all ships to begin their disengage procedures and to follow us."

Veskin receives the report of the actions taken by Teka.

"What is he trying to do," asks the commander of the damaged Hidlok. "How soon before the other are able to join us?"

"It will be at least another hour before the Landex will be within range to provide any effective support," reports Harlinkin.

"Then Teka is attempting to evade the trap. Maintain only enough fire on the Guardian ships to keep their attention. Focus all other available batteries on the Palup. He will not be as successful in his attempt as he thinks."

"Sir, we do not have sufficient weapons energy available to continue firing on all targets," reports the Weapons Officer. "Weapons energy down to sixty percent. Shield and deflector strength are at twenty-five percent. We cannot maintain shield and deflector integrity with all of the Guardian ships attacking at once."

"That is what Teka is hoping for," answers Veskin! "He wants us to withdraw and allow him an escape route through our defenses. I will not give him that luxury! Maintain all systems! I want the Palup destroyed!"

"Yes sir," acknowledges the weapons Officer.

"The Quiger and Junnack are still attempting to consolidate on our position," reports Harlinkin.

"Understood," acknowledges Veskin as he resumes watching the main view screen in front of him.

The battle between the Guardian fleet and the Battle Group Hidlok continues without any easing of its original intensity.

"Sir," yells Nuk-Ma over the noise of the battle, "the Hidlok is not withdrawing. Veskin is trying to cut us off. The Landex is down to less than an hour out."

"High Commander," calls Teka, "please report to the bridge."

Upon entering the bridge Hops moves with practiced ease to Tekas' command chair.

"I believe I am going to need a little advice," says Teka as he turns the small display screen to allow Hops to see the display of the tactical situation. "The Hidlok is sustaining severe damage but Veskin still refuses to withdraw. The Quiger and Junnack are still attempting to consolidate with the Hidlok and provide support. Mular should arrive in less than an hour. We may not be able to escape. This is our current situation."

"Shit," mumbles Hops as he studies the small screen. "We just can't stay here and wait for Mular and the other to arrive. What we need right now is a hat with a rabbit in it. Otherwise we're going to have to pull this one out of our ass." Suddenly Hops face light up as he activates the intercom. "Council General! I'm going to need the ready room cleared."

"Understood," acknowledges Lamminta.

"Come on, Serligh," says Hops as he rushes for the bridge door. "I think I know what we can do!"

The two military leaders leave the bridge, one with a look of confidence, the other with a look of confusion. As they enter the ready room, Hops begins asking a series of rapid questions.

"Where's the weakest defensive firing pattern from a Star?"

"The lower section just under the crew quarters."

"Then the heaviest firing has to come from the upper section?"

"Yes," agrees Teka.

"Okay, here is what I propose," says Hops as he begins explaining his idea. "I've been working on a new strategy and I hope it works. Computer, begin simulated battle scenario based on recent calculations and battle objectives."

The computer generated holographic scenario begins, continuing until the most likely outcome becomes visible.

"Not much of a chance, but this seems to be our only hope of success," says Hops as the simulation ends. "Options?"

"We will only know for certain once we try," answers Teka.

As they enter the bridge, Hops motions for Teka to give the orders to begin this one last reckless gamble.

As the orders aboard the Palup are given, Mular enters the bridge of the Landex and immediately asks, "What is the current battle situation?"

"The Guardians are unable to break contact with Telecoup Veskin," reports Olderin. "It appears that we will be able to end this fight as it should be."

"It does appear as if we will finally be able to achieve a glorious victory, Culmit, but do not begin your celebration too soon," warns Mular. "How many times did we believe that we had these infidels trapped only to find that they were no longer within our grasp? We should wait until we are certain they have been defeated before beginning our victory celebration. Bring all weapons to full power. Telecoup Zu-Art, prepare all fighters to be launched as soon as we reach maximum support range."

"All squadrons have been . . ."

"Telecoup! The Palup is closing on the Hidlok," suddenly interrupts Sub-Culmit Dramek!

"Increase power," immediately orders Mular! "All batteries! Lock on to the Palup and fire as soon as we are at maximum effective range!"

"Mular is still heading this way," reports Lieutenant Germick calmly. "Energy surge indicates that he powered up his defensive batteries."

"Keep an eye out for his Horses," warns Hops. "He may try the same trick as before and launch them as soon as the Landex reaches maximum support range in an attempt to draw off our protection."

"Commander Nuk-Ma, please inform the remainder of the fleet to follow us," instructs Teka. "Commander Fab, if you will increase the energy level to our defensive batteries by fifteen percent?"

"All ship acknowledge."

"Power increased by fifteen percent" acknowledges Fab as he continues to direct the fire of the Palups energy cannon batteries against the Hidlok.

"Telebisque," replies Under-Culmit Dramek, "the Hidloks' shields are beginning to buckle. Deflector failure should occur in less than fifteen seconds. Shield strength is down to thirty-two percent."

"Sir, the rest of the fleet is disengaging and following," reports Germick.

"Helm, maintain speed and execute," orders Teka with the composure of someone who has just ordered dinner instead of a desperate attack against a Fighting Star.

Cherrick fingers move rapidly over the helm control input panel. The Palup slowly begins a maneuver that places the Fighting Star on its side in relation to the Hidlok. Once the lower energy batteries cease firing, the upper defensive batteries are able to use more energy, concentrating all firepower on a single point. A single target, barely five hundred meters above the lowest tip of the Hidlok, receives the increased energy bursts from the Palups upper batteries. Initially, only the scanners and sensors of the Palup are able to detect the damage inflicted upon the Fighting Star. Slowly, the lower section begins to show signs of complete structural failure. Suddenly, the entire lower section explodes, spewing debris in all directions at an unbelievable speed. In an instant, all that remains of the lower section of the Hidlok is a few hundred meters of torn, twisted, and jagged metal. The upper section of what was once a formidable fighting force, remained intact, but is no longer firing. The Guardian crews feel the secondary explosions as their ships shutter from the violent secondary explosions, flames erupting from the shattered hull.

"All ships follow the Palup. Rendezvous Alpha Nine Two," calmly orders Teka as he witnesses the destruction of the Hidlok. "It appears that we do not have much time to leave this sector. Telecoup Mular will be within weapons range in less the thirty minutes."

"Telecoup! The Hidlok has been severely damaged," reports Culmit Sprahvic. "The Quiger and Junnack are unable to prevent the Guardians from escaping!"

"What is their course and speed," demands Mular as he sees the scanner display and realizes that his prey has once again escaped!

"Course is eight three four by six five two at eight point five."

"Who is this man who has the luck of seven figglerites? I want to know his name," screams Mular as he watches the images of his enemy move steadily towards the edge of the scanner display! "Culmit Olderin! Have you been able to find out who this magician is?"

"Yes, sir. I received the information just before you informed Telecoup Veskin of their position," reports Olderin cautiously.

"All batteries are to stand down," orders Mular hotly! "We must help rescue the survivors of the Hidlok. I want a complete briefing for all senior officers immediately"

"Understood, sir."

The senior members of Mulars' command staff assemble in the main briefing chamber of the Landex. As Mular enters, everyone can see his aggravation at the loss of the enemy. As soon as Mular takes his seat, Olderin begins the briefing.

"Telecoup, the name of this man is Hoppinzorinski. He was one of their long range Probes Leaders assigned to Capricorn Seven and is believed to have been on patrol duty when we attacked."

"The one who joined with the traitor Teka and managed to convince the Supreme Commander to end our last expansion attempt with disgrace and dishonor," mutters Mular. "And who are these other whore dogs," loudly demands Mular! "Now can evade our traps and destroy a Fighting Star! How do they now possess the skills of a veteran warrior?"

"From these unconventional tactics the Guardians have used thus far, this Hoppinzorinski has to be the same man. We have also learned the names of several others who we have not yet been able to account for."

"Continue," angrily orders Mular.

"The outpost commander on Capricorn Seven was a man by the name of Lamminta. He, along with what we now believe to be several hundred others, managed to escape on a newly designed battleship with a concealment device, which we were unable to penetrate until their recent encounter with Teka."

"Lamminta," says Mular as he slowly regains control of his emotions. "The one who would hide behind a Fighting Star during our last war. His trick did not last long. I soon discovered his tactic and turned his strategy into defeat."

"There are only two other officer of consequence at this point who are believed to have survived. We believe that they were the Probe Leaders on patrol duty when we attacked the other two outposts. They are Major Quince from Alpha Cheris and Major Williams from Status Duo. Our intelligence indicates that they are both formidable officers."

"From the current size of their fleet there must be others who will also require our attention," observes Mular.

"Of course, sir," replies Olderin. "Dossiers have been prepared on these four individuals. I have also included dossiers on Teka, his senior staff, and other Guardians who believe may still be alive. All of the information we had access to was accurate until the beginning of our expansion efforts. We do not have any hard evidence that these are actually the ones who managed to survive but as I have indicated, by their actions and unconventional tactics, I believe they are the current Guardian leadership."

"Indeed, they do appear to be the same minds and individuals that we have attempted to extinguish in the past, it must be them," says Mular softly. "If these are the Guardians with whom we are dealing, it will be easier to use their recklessness against them and we can prepare our final blow to complete our domination."

"Telecoup," says Zu-Art?

"Yes?"

"Have you forgotten about Telebisque Teka?"

"Of course not, you fool! He is now only a minor pawn in their game of survival. Since he surrendered the Palup, they have learned her operations and secrets. He no longer serves any useful purpose to them. His actions will be as predictable as before. Only now, we must become the ones who become unpredictable. No, I have not forgotten about Teka, I have only put him aside for the moment. When we rid the Empire of these puny Guardians, we will also rid ourselves of the traitor. Now, Culmit, I want a conference with all Battle Group Commanders in this quadrant in one hour on a secure frequency. They are to have all information they possess concerning their contact with the Guardians ready to present in complete detail"

"Teka will be able to intercept the signal," counters Olderin.

"I know," agrees Mular, "but we must still follow our normal procedures until we can find a better way. Besides, he and his so-called friends will not be learning anything that they do not already know. You will inform the others of the conference."

"Yes, sir."

"That will be all. Be prepared to attack and destroy them as soon as they are found."

Mular dismisses his officers but remains in the solitude of the conference room until the commanders, having returned to the ships as ordered, are prepared for the exchange of information.

Mular, with a grave look on his face, begins the conference with solemn words, "Telecoups, we have lost the Hidlok. The Quiger and Junnack are conducting recovery operations for survivors at this time. It could take several days to complete the operation and complete her destruction. Once the crew of the Hidlok has been accounted for, Telecoups Envela and Cigaklin will be joining us.

"I have the probable names of the ones who are continuing to fight. All information indicates that Telebisque Teka has again found the Guardian called Hoppinzorinski and is once more attempting to dishonor the Empire with his ideas of peace. It appears that Hoppinzorinski, along with the Guardians called Lamminta, Quince and Williams are their primary leaders, tacticians, and strategists. We have seen them use deceit, deception and trickery to elude us at every turn. They now have help from Teka, and the knowledge contained in the computers of the Palup, at their disposal. We must forget every tactic, strategy, doctrine, or principle we have ever learned, or have used against them in the past. We must devise a new plan of attack if we are going to complete their annihilation.

"Everyone here has had contact with them at one time or another, and under a variety of circumstances. I need to know exactly who was engaged, and by what type of ship? How did they attack, or defend, themselves? What damage did you sustain, and what damage did you inflict? You already know how they used the Landex on which to hide and escape, as well as their use of shuttlecraft to avoid the minefield I set for them. These encounters have been well publicized throughout the Empire."

"Telecoup," begins Sub-Telecoup Vandilkor, "there is another commander whose identity is yet unknown, the commander of the Guardian fleet that was attacking us while you were chasing after the original ship."

"Yes," replies Mular, "I understand that there is yet another we have not identified, but we will. Now, if you will begin with your encounters."

The report from the commander of the Battle Group Loksija begins the long conference session. Every commander understands that this was not to be a normal briefing. Mular constantly interrupts them as he requests clarification of a particular point or tactic, as they present their individual reports. The conference lasts several days before all of the intimate details of each encounter are exposed.

"As soon as I have analyzed all of this information, I will inform all of you of the battle plan," concludes Mular. "Return to you assigned sectors and report any contact."

"Well, Telebisque," begins Hops as he begins a similar meeting with his Division Commanders, "what do you think Mular is up to this time? He isn't chasing after us and that's something that he wouldn't normally do."

"From his last communiqué, it would appear that he might be attempting to get as much information about us as possible before he makes his next move. He has apparently learned that he will not be able to trap us by using normal tactics, so I would guess that he is collecting all available information and trying to find a weakness he could exploit and use to defeat us."

"How much time do you think he's going to need before he comes up with another idea for a better mousetrap?"

"That I cannot say, High Commander. It would depend on the amount of information he needs to evaluate. It could be a day, maybe two, or it could be longer. Only he knows the answer to that question."

"Okay, then where do we go from here? This is your backyard and you know the best places to hide."

"First," begins Teka slowly, "I do not think it would be wise to continue on our present course towards Tirgonia. By now, the news of the destruction of the Hidlok has reached the Supreme Commander. He will undoubtedly be prepared to defend Tirgonia without any regard to their losses or any devastation that we might be able to cause. He will only want to finish the carnage he began and will accept nothing less than total victory.

"There are a few smaller planets, considered to be insignificant, on the other side of the Empire. One or two are believed be considering rebelling. Neither the Supreme Senate nor Supreme Commander has ever taken any of these threats seriously. If we are lucky enough to make it that far, we then try to convince the leaders of one of these planets that we only want the same thing that they do. We offer to join with them if they are actually anticipating a rebellion against the Empire."

"Do you think the leaders one of these planets would be receptive to total strangers, holding out an olive branch, and just happen to escorting a Fighting Star, joining their fight?"

"Again, my friend, you ask a question that I cannot answer."

"Telebisque," asks Triheadly?

"Yes, Commander?"

"Two questions, if I may, sir?"

"Of course."

"How far are we going to have to travel and how long would it take us to reach one of these planets?"

"It is a lot farther than you may think," says Teka. "It will require that we remain undetected for almost six months at light seven."

"I don't believe that we have enough fuel or supplies to get there from here," says Commander Cutler.

"I believe we do," counters Teka. "With the current losses we have suffered, there is now enough room aboard the Palup to accommodate the entire fleet. We then use the fuel reserves of the fleet to supplement the current supplies of the Palup. We should have more than enough fuel for such a journey. I estimate that we shall have enough fuel to complete this voyage with enough left over for other uses should we be required to defend ourselves again."

"What do you think our chances are of making it that far without being discovered," asks Hops?

"Right now I would say the odds are slightly in our favor," says Teka. "Mular will be engaged with trying to find a technique he can use to penetrate the concealment frequency of the Palup. That should give Commander Trilla a little more time to reconfigure the frequency modulation of the devices on the Hope and Revenge. If we take the most direct course, it would save time but increase our chances of detection. If we take a more indirect route, we would be safer but expend more fuel and supplies. Both routes have distinct advantages and disadvantages. I can only offer the possibilities available."

After a few moments of quiet thought, Hops announces his decision saying, "Then we try to make it to of these planets following an indirect course. Now, Serligh, which one would be the best option"?

"I would suggest Paporia Two."

"That name has a familiar sound to it," mutters Williams.

"It is the closest planet to the far border but I think we would be safer there than any of the others," says Teka. "If we cannot make peaceful contact, we can continue across the border. It will only take one more day to get there. There is a civilization across the border that might be willing to allow us to settle on one of their smaller, uninhabited planets."

"Then why don't we just go straight across the border and don't worry about stopping at Paporia Two," asks Freslof?

"That would not be as easy as you may think, Commander. There is another Agreed Zone at the border. The only one, who has the authority to grant the Paporians permission to enter the Agreed Zone, or to cross the border, is the Supreme Commander. I do not believe he would be willing to make contact with the Paporians or the Alikiatasians and inform them that a large group of armed traitors, hiding an equally large enemy fleet, which includes a Fighting Star, wishes to enter and cross the Agreed Zone through the Paporian sector. However, there are rumors that the Paporians have established safe corridors through the Zone and may even have established a secret trade pact with the Alikiatasians. Therefore, we must first contact the Paporians in order to gain access to the Alikiatasians. This is the only way we will be able to make safe contact. Even with our concealment device, it would not be wise to cross the border without permission. If this plan fails, then we can attempt to make direct contact, but I do not believe that would be advisable. The Alikiatasians are a fierce warrior people who only wish to live in peace, until they are provoked. It would not be a good idea to provoke them. Even the Supreme Commander understands this and does not desire any contact with them except that which is extremely necessary."

"You certainly don't believe in leaving very many options do you," says Hops with a slight grin.

"If there were another way, I would offer it. I can only offer what I know," says Teka, "and, as you have said, I never promised you a . . . some sort of a garden?"

"It's a 'rose garden' and I know that you can't give what you don't have. I just don't like the idea of running from one fight just to get into another one."

"I agree," says Teka. "I cannot find any other options that we could pursue? Mular is behind us and we do not know how long he will remain there before he comes after us again? We cannot go back the way we came so our only choice is forward. Peace can only be found where we have not yet been, not where we just left."

"Sir," says Cutler, "I agree with Telebisque Teka. We know what lies behind us. We won't know what is in front of us until we get there. Who knows, we might not have to fight at all. We just might be able to find what we are looking for. If it comes to a vote, I am in favor of going ahead until we can find a place where we can return to our ways of peace. Besides, I'd like to find a nice quiet lake so I can go fishing again."

"I also agree with Telebisque Teka and Commander Cutler," says Triheadly. "We can't go back the way we came, so the only thing that we can do is to go forward. I've never been fishing but I think I might like to try it one day."

"Okay," says Hops, as he looks to the next officer. "Vic?"

"Like Cutler said, if you're asking for a vote, I'm in favor of putting out the 'Gone Fishing' sign."

"Make that five in favor of going fishing," says Williams.

"Then I guess we start packing our lunch, beer cooler and head for the fishing hole," says Hops as he looks at the officers seated around the briefing table. "Now we need to get all ships aboard. Vic, I want you to back the Revenge into Delta Bay. Cutler, you take Charlie, Triheadly goes in to Bravo and Orin, back the Hope into Alpha. Serligh, as soon as everyone is aboard, tell Cherrick to plot a roundabout course towards Paporia Two. Let's hope they want to be friendly to a bunch of strangers packing a Fighting Star for protection. If no one has anything else, I suggest we all get all ships aboard and get out of here."

The officers rise and file out of the ready room. Even if they are no longer in any immediate danger, they all feel an urgency to put as much distance as possible between themselves and their enemy. Hops and Teka notify the Council of their decision to continue towards the remote planet of Paporia Two. Cautiously, the Guardians once again begin their journey across the Tirgonian Empire.

Telecoup Mular continues his own search for any information that will lead him to his prey. The meeting with his commanders has lasted almost three days, during which time the Guardians seemed to have once again disappeared. The Supreme Commander, annoyed by the lack of progress in the search for the Guardians, has given Mular only two more weeks in which to complete his assigned mission to find and destroy the elusive enemy. If they cannot be located during that time, they, along with Teka and the crew of the Palup, and be regarded as nothing more than common criminals, charged with crimes against the Tirgonian Empire. The hunt will become the responsibility of the Empire Police, the Tirgonian law enforcement force that has the authority to use any means necessary, to include deadly force, against any escaped criminal, who will hunt the Guardians, and Teka, down. The war, according to the Supreme Commander, is over.

ON THE OTHER HAND, IS IT?

WHAT'S PRISON REFORM?

By Jennifer Lombardo

Published in 2025 by
KidHaven Publishing, an Imprint of Greenhaven Publishing, LLC
2544 Clinton Street
Buffalo, NY 14224

Designer: Deanna Lepovich
Editor: Jennifer Lombardo

Photo credits: Cover (top) FOTOKITA/Shutterstock.com; cover (bottom) Gorodenkoff/Shutterstock.com; p. 7 melissamn/Shutterstock.com; p. 9 JosephRouse/Shutterstock.com; p. 11 Everett Collection/Shutterstock.com; p. 13 Gagarin Iurii/Shutterstock.com; p. 15 Marjorie Kamys Cotera/Bob Daemmrich Photography/Alamy Stock Photo; p. 17 Canna Obscura/Shutterstock.com; p. 19 Motortion Films/Shutterstock.com; p. 21 Tawat Kambum/Shutterstock.com.

Cataloging-in-Publication Data

Names: Lombardo, Jennifer.
Title: What's prison reform? / Jennifer Lombardo.
Description: Buffalo, New York : KidHaven Publishing, 2025. | Series: What's the issue? | Includes glossary and index.
Identifiers: ISBN 9781534547919 (pbk.) | ISBN 9781534547926 (library bound) | ISBN 9781534547933 (ebook)
Subjects: LCSH: Imprisonment–United States–Juvenile literature. | Corrections–United States–Juvenile literature. | Alternatives to imprisonment–United States–Juvenile literature. | Criminal justice, Administration of–United States–Juvenile literature.
Classification: LCC HV8705.L66 2025 | DDC 365'.973–dc23

Printed in the United States of America

Some of the images in this book illustrate individuals who are models. The depictions do not imply actual situations or events.

CPSIA compliance information: Batch #CSKH25: For further information contact Greenhaven Publishing LLC at 1-844-317-7404.

CONTENTS

Living in a Prison

When someone breaks the law, they may be sent to prison as a **punishment**. The punishment is that they lose their freedom. Depending on which law they broke, someone might be in jail or prison for anywhere from a few months to the rest of their life. One word for being sent to prison is "incarcerated."

A loss of freedom is generally supposed to be the only punishment that comes with being incarcerated. However, most prisons have a lot of problems that make this punishment worse. Some people want to reform, or change, prisons to make them less dangerous, or unsafe, to live in.

Facing the Facts

A jail is where people must stay for a short period of time, often while they're waiting for their **trial** to happen. A prison is where they stay for a long period of time.

Number of People in U.S. Jails and Prisons in 2023

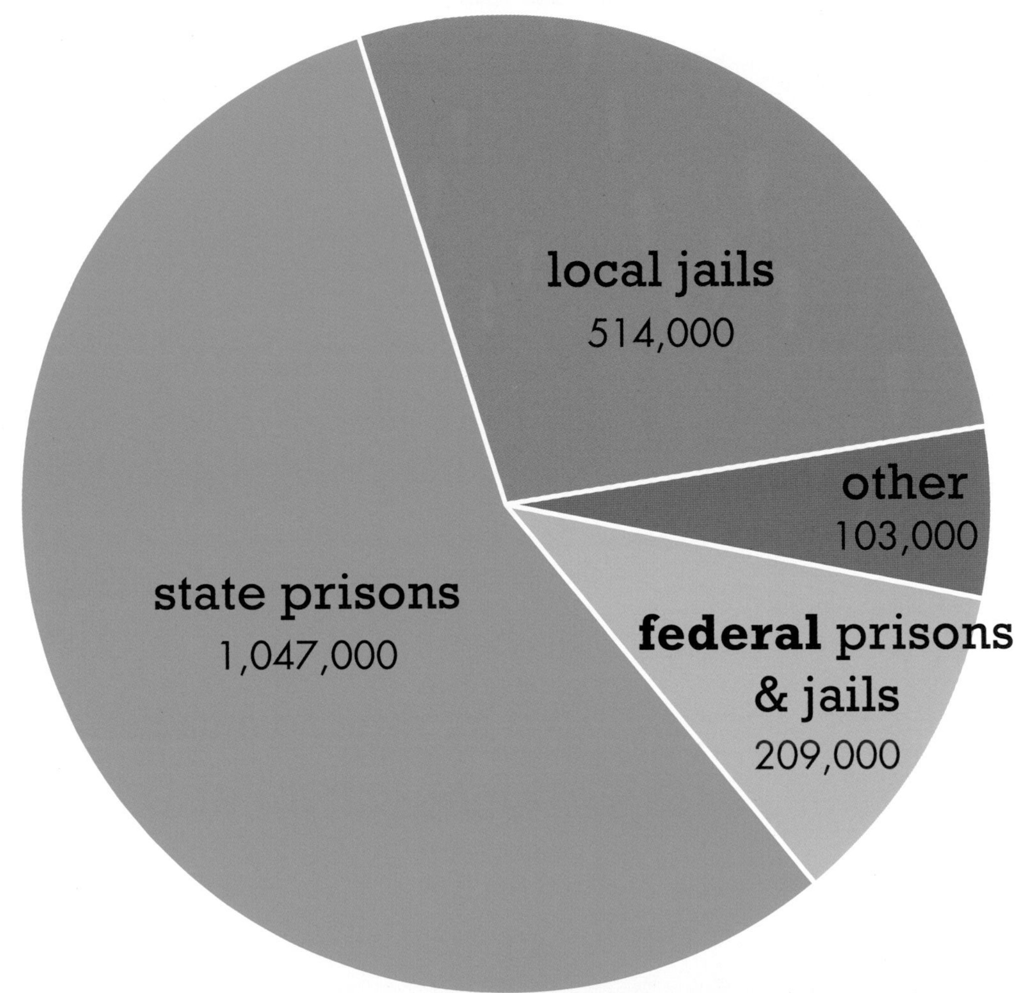

Nearly 2 million people are in prison or jail in the United States. These people are called prisoners or inmates. The "other" piece of this pie chart, based on information from the Prison Policy Initiative, includes youth prisons, prisons for **immigrants**, and military prisons.

Prisoners Are People

It's hard for some people to care about the living conditions in prisons. They think that criminals, or people who break the law, **deserve** to be treated badly and should be very unhappy in prison.

Prison reformers want those in charge of prisons to care more about inmates' **human rights**. Reformers want prisoners to be treated with respect and to have their health and safety cared for. They also want prisoners to be allowed to learn new skills and to have a job that pays them fairly. These two things are an important part of helping people have a normal life after they leave prison.

Facing the Facts

The food in prison is often unhealthy and sometimes not even edible, or able to be eaten. Some prisoners have found bugs in their food. Prison reformers say prisoners deserve fresh, healthy food.

The people in orange are prisoners who have jobs keeping trails clear for hikers, such as the woman in the yellow shirt.

Prison as a Business

Some U.S. prisons are run like businesses. Large companies, or corporations, make deals with the government. A corporation agrees to run a prison, and the government agrees to pay them to do it.

The companies and the government agree to **privatize** these prisons so the government can save money. The companies promise to run prisons for less than what it would cost the government to run them on its own. Prison reformers say this is a problem because it gives the corporations an **incentive** to spend too little money on prisoners' living conditions.

Facing the Facts

Because corporations are paid for each prisoner they have, many private prisons are too crowded. Some corporations illegally pay judges to send more people to prison.

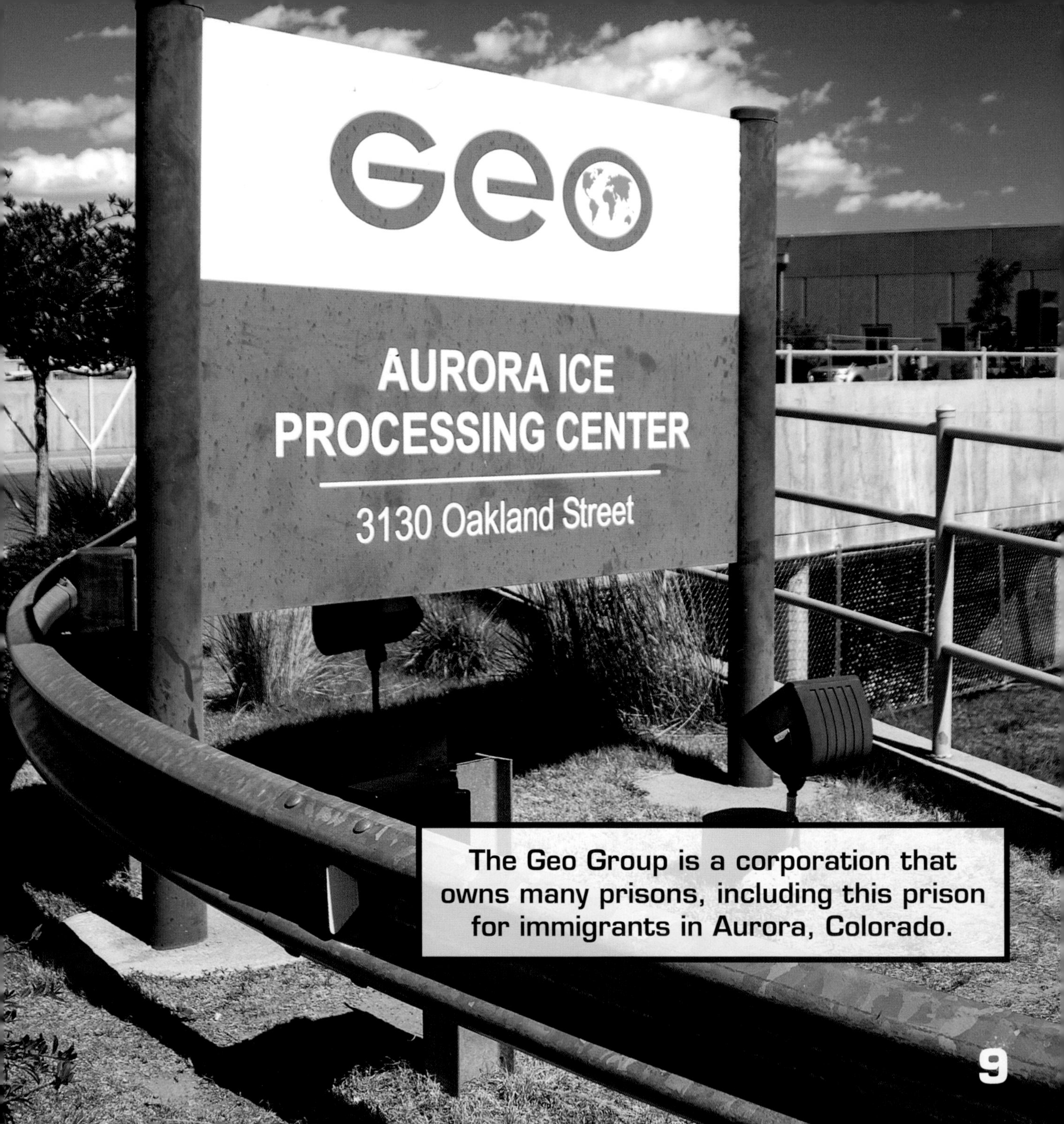

The Geo Group is a corporation that owns many prisons, including this prison for immigrants in Aurora, Colorado.

Slavery in Prison

The 13th Amendment, or change, to the U.S. **Constitution** made slavery, or enslavement, illegal except as a punishment for a crime. Today, many prisoners are forced to do jobs that pay them very little or nothing at all. Some have called this a modern form of enslavement.

In federal prisons, inmates must have a job unless they're too sick to work. They often don't get to choose their job, and they get paid between 12 cents and $2 per hour for their work. Prison reformers want prisoners to be paid much more than that. They also want prisoners to be able to say no to jobs that are very dangerous, such as fighting wildfires.

Facing the Facts

Many prisoners come from poor families. Paying them fairly for their work would let them send money to their families. It would also help them pay for things such as books and visits to a doctor.

Prisoners have been enslaved for much of U.S. history. This picture from 1940 shows incarcerated men breaking up rocks with tools called sledgehammers.

Prison Health Care

Most private prisons hire another company to take care of the prisoners' health. Because corporations want to spend as little money as possible, however, these companies are often not good at the job. Sometimes prison health-care workers don't let sick inmates have medicine or see a doctor because that would cost money.

Prison reformers say health care is a human right. They say prisoners should be able to exercise, see a doctor and a dentist when they need to, and have time off work when they're sick and need to rest.

Facing the Facts

COVID-19 spread very quickly in prisons, and many people died. This is mainly because prisoners live very close together, and they often weren't given the things they needed to keep themselves safe from the disease.

Prison reformers care about prisoners' mental health, or the health of their mind, as well. Living in a cell like this one can make people very **depressed**. Giving prisoners something to read or watch can help their mental health.

Leaving and Returning

Most people aren't in prison for life. When they get out, they need to adjust, or get used, to life outside prison. This can be very hard, especially if the inmate spent many years in prison. People who can't adjust often end up back in prison. When a person commits another crime and goes back to prison, it is called recidivism.

Reforming prisons can help lower recidivism rates. One way to do this is to give prisoners classes so they can get better jobs when they leave prison. A major cause of crime is poverty, or being poor. People with better jobs tend to make more money.

Facing the Facts

The United States has one of the highest recidivism rates in the world. About 44 percent of U.S. criminals return to prison within 1 year of getting out.

Many prisons have computers inmates can use for studying.

Pushing for Reform

There are many ways reformers are trying to change prisons. One thing reformers want is less overcrowding in prisons. A good way to do this is to change the punishments we give people who commit **nonviolent** crimes, such as using illegal drugs.Some people believe they should be sent to a place that helps them stop using drugs instead of being sent to prison.

Another way to make prisons less crowded is to reform the courts. Between 4 and 6 percent of people in prison are innocent, or blameless, and were sent to prison by mistake.

Facing the Facts

Some schools hire police officers to make sure students behave. When a student acts up, they may be arrested or sent to a prison-like school. This is part of the "school-to-prison pipeline."

As of 2023, 23 U.S. states as well as Washington, D.C., and Guam have made growing and using marijuana legal. Prison reformers want people who were arrested when marijuana was illegal to be released from prison early.

Everyone Is Affected

Prison reformers say that changing the way U.S. prisons work has effects that can help everyone. When nonviolent criminals aren't sent to prison, more families can stay together. Studies show that kids who have a parent in prison are more likely to have depression, problems in school, and trouble sleeping.

Recidivism rates show that sending people to prison isn't a good way to stop people from committing crimes. Instead, reformers say we need to address the things that drive people to commit crimes in the first place, especially poverty.

Facing the Facts

In most places in the United States, police are sent to respond to calls about someone having a mental health **crisis**. However, police aren't always trained to deal with mental illness, so they often end up arresting the person, who may end up in prison.

Kids can send letters or make phone calls to a parent in prison, but it isn't the same as having their parent at home with them.

Making a Change

The U.S. government has said it will work on prison reform. It has already made a few small steps in this direction. For example, in 2022, the Federal **Bureau** of Prisons announced that it had ended all contracts, or deals, with private prison corporations. However, prisons for immigrants are still run by corporations.

You can work to change the prison system by writing to government leaders. You can also help by raising money for organizations, or groups, that work to make life better for prisoners.

Facing the Facts

A prison sentence is the amount of time an inmate must stay in prison. Prisoners are supposed to be treated fairly after they finish their sentence. However, people often **discriminate** against former prisoners.

WHAT CAN YOU DO?

If one of your friends has a loved one in prison, ask your friend how you can support them.

If you meet someone who used to be in prison, treat them like you would treat any other person.

Write to government leaders to tell them you want them to support prison reform.

Donate books to prisoners through an organization such as Books Through Bars.

Learn more about what prison reformers want and how they're working to get changes made.

If one of your loved ones is in prison, keep in touch with them through letters, phone calls, or visits.

If this issue matters to you, there are many ways you can help!

GLOSSARY

bureau: A smaller part of a government department.

constitution: The document that lays out the laws of a country.

crisis: An unstable or difficult situation.

depressed: Suffering from depression, a mental illness that causes feelings of sadness and worthlessness.

deserve: To be worthy of something.

discriminate: To treat someone unfairly, often for something they can't control.

federal: Relating to the central government.

human rights: Things that everyone should have just because they are human.

immigrant: A person who comes to a country to live there.

incentive: Something that makes a person work or try harder to achieve a goal.

nonviolent: Not doing anything to hurt another person's body.

privatize: To allow a private company to take over something that the government formerly provided.

punishment: The act of making someone suffer for doing something wrong.

trial: Hearing and judging a criminal case in court.

FOR MORE INFORMATION

WEBSITES

BrainPOP: Trials

www.brainpop.com/socialstudies/usgovernment/trials

Watch a movie, play games, and take quizzes to learn more about what happens at a criminal trial.

Kiddle.com: Prison Facts for Kids

kids.kiddle.co/Prison

Learn more about what prisons are like in the United States and other countries.

BOOKS

Felice, Frank. *What Happens When My Parent Is in Jail?* New York, NY: PowerKids Press, 2019.

MacLeod, Elizabeth, and Frieda Wishinsky. *How to Become an Accidental Activist*. Victoria, British Columbia: Orca Book Publishers, 2021.

Senghor, Shaka. *When You Hear Me (You Hear Us): Voices on Youth Incarceration*. Washington, DC: Shout Mouse Press, 2021.

Publisher's note to educators and parents: Our editors have carefully reviewed these websites to ensure that they are suitable for students. Many websites change frequently, however, and we cannot guarantee that a site's future contents will continue to meet our high standards of quality and educational value. Be advised that students should be closely supervised whenever they access the internet.

INDEX